1992

TO BLIGHT WITH PLAGUE

TO BLIGHT WITH
PLAGUE

Studies in a Literary Theme

BARBARA FASS LEAVY

NEW YORK UNIVERSITY PRESS
NEW YORK AND LONDON

NEW YORK UNIVERSITY PRESS
New York and London

Library of Congress Cataloging-in-Publication Data
Leavy, Barbara Fass, 1936–
    To blight with plague : studies in a literary theme / Barbara Fass
Leavy.
        p. cm.
    Includes bibliographical references and index.
    ISBN 0-8147-5059-1
    1. Communicable diseases in literature.   2. Diseases and
literature.   3. Literature—Social aspects.   4. Literature—
Psychological aspects.   5. AIDS (Disease)   I. Title.
PN3352.S5L4   1992
809'.93356—dc20   91-40135
                                                       CIP

New York University Press books are printed on acid-free paper,
and their binding materials are chosen for strength and durability.

Manufactured in the United States of America

c 10 9 8 7 6 5 4 3 2 1

This book is dedicated to
ANN LEAVY OLSSON
JANUARY 20, 1960–MAY 19, 1991

Contents

Acknowledgments

S ome of the discussions in this book were oral presentations to the Seminars on the History of Psychiatry and Behavioral Sciences, Department of Psychiatry, History Section, The New York Hospital-Cornell Medical Center, where I hold an honorary academic position as adjunct professor. I would like to thank the members of the section and department for help with and interest in my work; particularly Eric T. Carlson, chairman of the section, for always making me feel welcome at the seminars and for sharing his work on dissociation, which influenced my own on the self; Cornelius J. Clark for unhesitatingly scheduling my presentations on plague literature; Jacques M. Quen for being a consistent resource for my research efforts in medicine and psychology, and for pointing my way to the mid-nineteenth century French syphilologists; Lawrence Friedman for help with theory, in general, and, specifically, distinguishing different ideas of narcissism; Nathan M. Kravis for discussions that led to my thinking about the body-mind problem; Leonard C. Groopman for suggesting I consider the theoretical importance of civic duty during plagues; Christopher S. Nelson for making me a gift of an important book from his personal library; Doris Nagel for listening encouragingly to the progress of this book; the late Mary-Louise Schoelly for helpful discussion of Camus; and Samuel Perry for urging me to think about how plagues differ from other catastrophes, and to distinguish among different meanings of the word "self." Both Dr. Perry and Helen E. Daniells provided insight into how plagues affect individuals and families. I would also like to express my appreciation to William A. Frosch, interim chairman of the Department of Psychiatry, for his attendance at my presentations to the section; his interest has helped inspire my efforts. Sander L. Gilman read the first draft of this book: many of what I believe to be improvements in the final version resulted from his helpful criticism.

I owe several debts to the English Department of Queens College, where I am a professor. The first is for a rigorous undergraduate education in literary studies. The influence of my teachers Charles Dahlberg and Robert

P. Miller is reflected in my chapter on the Middle Ages. Second, the department gave me the valuable gift of released time to work on this book: I am particularly grateful to its chairman, Charles H. Molesworth, for his support of my endeavor. David H. Richter read and commented on parts of this study; his own scholarly work is reflected in two of its chapters. William Green gave me the text of his unpublished lecture delivered in Stockholm on theatrical treatments of AIDS. Steven F. Kruger and Gordon E. Whatley served as consultants on Boccaccio and Chaucer; Richard C. McCoy drew my attention to the connection between earthly paradises and sports stadiums; and Barbara E. Bowen shared my interest in the feminist implications of Miranda—Shakespeare's and Porter's. Fred Kaplan helped me think about Henry James and plague, although I decided not to include James's work in this study. In the Rosenthal Library, Suzanne Katz, Shoshana Kaufmann, and Richard L. Wall facilitated my research by seeing to it that I had speedy access to books and essays I needed to consult.

My coauthor on an earlier study of Ibsen, Per Schelde Jacobsen, was very helpful on Ibsen and other dramatists in the present book. I was very pleased to work with him again. A friend as well as director of medicine at a New Jersey hospital, Norman Riegel, read an early draft from a physician's point of view; because of him, I avoided some technical errors. (He does not think one can contract syphilis from smoking one's father's pipe.) Joan Riegel was a veritable research aide in directing me to valuable books and essays. Carol Marie Bensick of the University of California at Riverside was very generous in sharing research on Hawthorne that she had not included in her own book. And my husband Peter provided for the third time editorial assistance as well as patience while I wrote a book. And I thank my editors at New York University Press, Despina Papazoglou Gimbel, Kitty Moore, and Jason Renker, for their help and their confidence in me.

Some years ago the National Endowment for the Humanities awarded me a summer grant to work on the subject of the individual conscience. This study of plague literature has utilized research I did at that time.

I would also like to thank the following for granting me permission to quote from copyrighted material: Penguin Books Ltd for permission to quote from *The Decameron* by Giovanni Boccaccio, translated by G. H. McWilliam (Penguin Classics, 1972), copyright © G. H. McWilliam, 1972; Random House, Inc., and Brandt & Brandt for permission to quote from *Collected Stories of Wallace Stegner* by Wallace Stegner. Copyright 1990 by Wallace Stegner; Alfred A. Knopf, Inc., and Hamish Hamilton, Ltd. for permission to quote from *The Plague* by Albert Camus, translated by Stuart

Gilbert. Copyright 1948 by Stuart Gilbert; Oxford University Press for permission to quote from *The Oxford Ibsen* by Henrik Ibsen, edited by James W. McFarlane, 1970–77; Larry Kramer for permission to quote from *The Normal Heart* by Larry Kramer, New American Library, New York, 1985; International Creative Management, Inc., for permission to quote from *As Is* by William M. Hoffman, Dramatists Play Service, Inc., New York, 1990; and Harcourt Brace Jovanovich, Inc., and Jonathan Cape, Ltd., for permission to quote from *Pale Horse, Pale Rider,* copyright 1937 and renewed 1965 by Katherine Anne Porter.

Finally—in order to write this book, I have for the past year seen less than I would have wished of my four granddaughters: Abby Widom (age three); Jennifer and Jessica Lehman (age two and a half); and Julie Lehman (age one). Shelley Jo Widom, born July 9, 1991, was eagerly awaited as I wrote. May the world they grow up in be free of plagues.

TO BLIGHT WITH PLAGUE

ONE

Introduction

A plague is a formidable enemy, and is armed with terrors that every man is not sufficiently fortified to resist or prepared to stand the shock against.

DANIEL DEFOE

This is a study of literary works whose main themes have to do with some form of contagious or pestilential physical disease, and the social or psychological consequences of the illness. The book will bring together for analysis and comparison several, most of them major, works of western literature that share the subject of plague. The earliest are Giovanni Boccaccio's fourteenth-century *Decameron*, whose framework concerns ten people who flee the city of Florence while it is in the throes of the bubonic plague and who pass their time telling one hundred stories; and Geoffrey Chaucer's "The Pardoner's Tale," which draws on a widely told folktale to which Chaucer adds the setting of plague. The most recent are *As Is* and *The Normal Heart*, dramatic works whose subject is AIDS. Between these are Edgar Allan Poe's "The Masque of the Red Death" and other stories; Daniel Defoe's *A Journal of the Plague Year;* Henrik Ibsen's *Ghosts* and *An Enemy of the People;* Eugene Brieux's play *Damaged Goods*, a dramatization of Jean Alfred Fournier's treatise on *Syphilis and Marriage;* a short story recently argued to be about syphilis, Nathaniel Hawthorne's "Rappaccini's Daughter"; Wallace Stegner's "Chip off the Old Block," and Katherine Anne Porter's *Pale Horse, Pale Rider*, both set in the 1918 Spanish influenza pandemic; and Albert Camus's *The Plague.* To my knowledge, no similar book exists, and there seemed value in bringing together these works on so significant a subject. But—as will be seen—merely putting together discussions of them is not my primary intent.

There was no single criterion that dictated my choice of texts, but neither was the selection random. First, it was necessary to choose, because there will be no attempt made to write a comprehensive history of plague literature. I have, moreover, remained within the Western literary tradition that unifies the works to be discussed. At the same time, the literary texts are sufficiently diverse to allow me variety in my treatment. And, again, several are works of great literature; it would be difficult to imagine a book on this subject that omitted Boccaccio, Defoe, or Camus, for example. In addition, although it was possible for John Duffy to write as recently as 1966 that "in the twentieth century [we have] finally eliminated the great killer diseases which periodically decimated town and countryside," that although "death is still with us," his "gaunt figure no longer stalks openly abroad,"[1] such a statement in 1991 could only make one wince. By including two plays on what some call a modern plague, AIDS, this book looks at a contemporary crisis as well as the historical past. Another basis for choice is that these works have influenced each other, one author sometimes the direct source for another. In contrast to the view that there would be an inherent similarity in narratives that describe a city under the siege of bubonic plague,[2] for example, I have argued that Defoe was drawing on a Renaissance translation of the *Decameron* for his account of London's 1665 plague. But since this is not primarily a study of sources, I have in some instances been content to point out similarities in motifs from work to work without being concerned to establish direct links.

An additional reason for my selection has to do with the extensive critical debates attached to this literature, which are themselves a significant contribution to the plague theme. It is a theme often surprisingly neglected or underemphasized, so that less than ten years ago, for example, it could be maintained that the controversies surrounding the *Decameron* failed to pay sufficient heed to the importance for Boccaccio of the Black Death.[3] The critical disputes that surround some of the literary texts—those by Boccaccio or Ibsen, for instance—will receive more attention than the texts themselves, which, in any event, have not lacked for analyses. In contrast, some works, such as Brieux's *Damaged Goods* and the plays by Hoffman and Kramer, have received scant literary analysis, and I have in such instances provided an interpretive reading of them. Sometimes I have offered a new reading of literary works already widely discussed. And, finally, a few essential motifs will be traced from work to work, critic to critic, and the presence of these motifs in a work of literature supplied additional reasons for my choice. More about these basic themes below.

Again, no attempt is being made to be exhaustive, to track down every use of *plague* and its cognates in the work of important writers. Despite this disclaimer, some literary works may seem noticeable by their absence, such as Thomas Mann's *Death in Venice* and Henry James's *Daisy Miller*. With reluctance, I decided that while these authors were creating significant metaphors out of cholera and malarial fever, such figurative use of plague was quite detached from any treatment of the diseases themselves. As regards tuberculosis, to which Mann gave both literal and symbolic attention in *The Magic Mountain*,[4] the so-called White Plague will only be mentioned in passing from time to time, not because it fails to make an impact on literature—to the contrary, its impact is a major one—but because the peculiarly romantic equation of tuberculosis and genius, an equation that Mann viewed as itself a sign of disease, forms its own subject, one that lies outside the focus of this study.[5] To generalize, and to admit the deficiencies of all generalizations, authors who treat tuberculosis might be thought of as asking, "Do I owe my talent or inspiration to a diseased state?" whereas those who treat plague in works I have chosen wonder, "What can my art hope to achieve in a pestilence-ridden world?"

Not all plagues have inspired literary works. It is one of the memorable features of *Arrowsmith* that its protagonist fights all kinds of plagues, but Sinclair Lewis's book is not *about* pestilence. And those who have studied the influenza pandemic of 1918–19 have noted how sparse was the literature evolving from an illness that killed perhaps more than twenty million people within a year. (The antithetical argument is that the writing that did emerge from the pandemic is neglected because the epidemic itself has made, despite its morbidity and fatality, only a slight mark on world consciousness.) A disease that once inspired literature, leprosy, appears to have receded from the literary imagination as it has receded as a threatening disease.[6] Moreover, characters who suffered from leprosy in medieval literature (for instance, Criseyde in Henryson's continuation of Chaucer's great work) exist more as illustrations of how moral opprobrium gets attached to physical illnesses than as major literary characters in their own right. The interested reader should consult Saul Brody's important work, *The Disease of the Soul.*

The reasons for the inclusion or exclusion of texts having been explained, some discussion is warranted concerning the use of the now-controversial word *plague*—which requires consideration of its metaphoric associations. I have, first of all, taken the authors at their own word when they use the word *plague*. When, for example, the young lovers in *Pale Horse, Pale Rider* first talk about the 1918 influenza pandemic, which one of them calls a "funny new disease" that simply "knocks you into a cocked hat," the other replies, "It seems to be a plague . . . something out of the Middle Ages" (281). For me, the issue is not whether the pandemic can legitimately be called a plague, but why Katherine Anne Porter employs plague as a metaphor that reverberates through her renowned work. I cannot, however, hide behind these authors to avoid explaining how I think about the word *plague*, for how I think certainly affects my reading of the texts and my participation in the critical debates.

The problem is that *plague*, rather than the seemingly neutral *epidemic*, is traditionally associated with such ideas as sin and God's judgment on individuals and whole peoples. Therefore, some consideration has to be given to the three words that are used rather interchangeably in the ensuing chapters, two of them more obviously charged with symbolic meaning than the other: *epidemic*, *plague*, and *pestilence*. None of these words has a simple definition, so that, for example, Geoffrey Marks and William K. Beatty have had to admit that in their book *Epidemics*, they have "chosen a fairly loose" definition of that word as meaning "a communicable disease that affects many persons at one time," making exceptions to cover a noncommunicable disease that many people are exposed to because they live in the same locality (this would cover the polluted baths in *An Enemy of the People*, for example); or as designating a particularly frightening disease that "affects a relatively small number of people" (before a vaccine was discovered, polio would have met this criterion).[7] Now it can be seen that terms such as "frightening" or references to quantity raise as many questions as they answer. If a prevalent and usually fatal form of cancer is related to environmental factors, for instance lung cancer, can it be called an epidemic?[8] I am not going to attempt to respond to the question; my point is only that the word *epidemic*, seemingly the least symbolically charged of the three words, is also problematic and capable of being so charged.

The word *pestilence*, understood as a deadly because usually fatal epidemic disease, is deadly not only because it results in death but also because it is thought of as particularly poisonous or evil—these adjectives needing almost as much explanation as *pestilence*. There would seem to be an almost infinite regression in an attempt to make these terms clear. But it is the word *plague* that, again, has raised specters of a world of sin and damnation, so that the word itself may seem inappropriate today. Susan Sontag, in her book *AIDS and Its Metaphors*, has claimed that for the "moralistic inflation of an epidemic into a 'plague,'" it is necessary that the "epidemic be one whose most common means of transmission is sexual."[9] But her argument against the designation of AIDS as a plague—which she finds dangerous both for the sufferer who then must endure in addition to the illness the burden of extra, unnecessary emotional distress, and for the society that will respond not to a disease but a *plague*—has been challenged. For example, a reviewer quotes from the "eloquent usage" of another writer on AIDS that " 'the plague' conveys not only the physical agony of the disease itself, but the reverberant sense of catastrophe and reasonable despair the epidemic has unleashed."[10] Neither sex nor sin nor punishment for wrong, then, need be associated with a plague. What is necessary is that some sense of a global (in terms of magnitude) catastrophic significance be attached to the disease. Indeed, it was just such an idea of plague that Katherine Anne Porter says she had in mind for *Pale Horse, Pale Rider:*

I think the situation in which my young people found themselves was enough to warrant any emotions they could possibly have been capable of—in fact, my point was, partly, to show rather decent, not extraordinary, young and modest persons, facing a disaster too great for them to grasp. I think they behaved characteristically, holding on to their realities as long as they could, masking as well as they could from themselves the desperate and sinister nature of their predicament.[11]

Four infectious diseases will be represented in this book. The bubonic plague has been treated by Boccaccio, Chaucer, Defoe, and Camus. Poe, who resisted defining his "red death" too precisely, though his reading about cholera is often described as his source, also seems to have drawn on materials related to the Black Death. Its visitation has been described by Hans Zinsser as "one of the major calamities of history, not excluding wars, earthquakes, floods, barbarian invasions, the Crusades, and the last war."[12] He was referring to World War I; since World War II, the Black Death has been demoted to second place in the rank order of worldwide catastrophes.[13] The meaning of the Black Death for Boccaccio is, however, the subject of debate. About his treatment of the fourteenth-century bubonic plague, Giuseppe Mazzotta has said that the "world of the plague is transformed into an ominous text, with its signs proliferating, shifting and only decipherable as presages of death."[14] This is only partially true: divine providence might prove inscrutable, but for centuries authors believed it was nonetheless operative in the world. In a secular world, the question becomes one of the degree of human input in any disease; as Philip Thody has said about Camus's treatment of bubonic plague, the disease cannot be

placed on the same level as syphilis, radiation sickness, AIDS, lung cancer or heart disease. It is not an illness which human beings either cause or make worse by their own unwise or immoral conduct. It can be explained, if at all, only by saying that the universe makes no sense whatsoever if you look at it in terms of human ideas of right and wrong.[15]

Camus's novel treats plague as if it were itself, however, the one simple thing in a complex world: it exists and it must be eradicated. Then the philosophical issues can be addressed. But, of course, *The Plague* itself belies such a view, because *how* it is to be eradicated has to do with human behavior, with *how* individuals choose to interpret the universe, and that is never simple.

Syphilis, a virtual plague until the discovery of accurate tests and effective treatments (in its present status as a contagious disease of growing incidence, it is once again provoking increasing concern), has undoubtedly inspired authors because of the association between venereal disease and sin. And, as Theodor Rosebury has remarked in *Microbes and Morals,* "Sex is now and perhaps has always been the most engrossing of all subjects." He opposes the argument that "sex itself is dirty, and VD is dirty in its own right," with the combination of the two being "just about untouchable," contending instead that sex is good and natural whereas "disease is unnatural and bad."[16] In this confrontation between Roseburys views and what Ibsen would deem ghosts of outmoded and dangerous ideas can be found another reason for writers' interest in syphilis: it readily allows for the portrayal of an individual in conflict with society.

Sander Gilman's essay "Seeing the AIDS Patient" reveals the many connections between AIDS and syphilis, especially the similarities between the way the two diseases were and are represented. There has recently been a conscious attempt to change the initial image of Acquired Immune Deficiency Syndrome from that of a sexually transmitted disease mainly afflicting homosexual men (later, intravenous drug users joined them in the so-called high-risk group) to that of a disease endangering the population at large. The original perceptions have been difficult to eradicate, and, as the play *The Normal Heart* makes clear, so long as a large portion of the public believes, consciously or otherwise, that AIDS operates as a kind of natural selection by which society is rid of its deviants, this perception of the disease will be damaging to the effort to raise the funds necessary for research, treatment, and cure. To change the image of the AIDS patient, it may be necessary to await some powerful fiction and drama about female heterosexual sufferers of the disease. So far, however, no such literature is available for study. But contemporary folklore suggests, ironically, that when such literature appears, it may contribute to another negative stereotype, woman as polluter, the legendary poison damsel against whom man must remain ever on guard.[17]

The appellation of "Spanish Lady" for the 1918 influenza pandemic suggests how pervasive such a stereotype is. But the epidemic seems to have inspired some of the authors who treated it not because of this association but because of the coincidence of its appearance with the last months of World War I. The specific timing of the epidemic virtually literalizes plague as a metaphor for war. It allows an exploration of a world of mutual parasitism: as Zinsser wrote, "a cow eats a plant, man eats both," and "bacteria (or investment bankers) eat the man."[18] Similarly, William Mc-Neill depicts humanity engaged in a struggle to ward off both microparasites and macroparasites, the latter being most deadly when they are other people.[19] The simultaneous existence of the influenza pandemic and World War I may, in short, have made the epidemic a more compelling—even if not often treated—literary subject than it otherwise would have been.

In addition to bringing together literature about these four diseases, the present study has the doubtlessly more ambitious purpose of arguing that plague literature brings into sharp relief the complex issues surrounding that both essential and ephemeral entity known as the "self." Of course, in our postromantic world, what literary subject does not? Moreover, I am not the first to suggest that "plague and the threat of infection force the drama of self and other to be played out at its most intimate and terrifying level."[20] Unfortunately, this drama has recently been rendered almost totally ahistorical. The potentially solipsistic self has become *the* self; for example, a study of Defoe has it that like others of the eighteenth-century novelist's characters, the narrator of *A Journal of the Plague Year* looks "into the abyss, where all that he sees with certainty is himself."[21] The language of modern existentialism is compelling but also capable of limiting a subject. It is one thing to recognize that the *Journal's* narrator is more important than earlier studies of Defoe would suggest and that his perspectives are, as will be later indicated, socially and psychologically constructed, but it is quite another to eliminate London as Defoe's collective protagonist. Much is said in the *Journal* about the quarantining of infected persons, the shutting up of houses—the unbearable alienation, that is, of people isolated from their community. Such alienation, however, had not yet become virtually synonymous with the human condition. Civic duty, a very important concept in the *Journal*, not only supplies a grounds for moral action in 1722 London but also supplies a way out of the shut-up houses of the mind that would become Poe's almost obsessive subject. The view of selfhood that modern criticism takes for granted is the very one that the *Journal* struggles against.

What constitutes the self and how much importance is given to the individual person (as opposed to the "idea" of "man" rejected in Camus's *The Plague*) varies from age to age, writer to writer, but consistent in plague literature is the "I" who strives to survive a deadly danger only to confront questions about what it is *in addition to the body* that is being preserved. Katherine Anne Porter has described her own near-fatal bout with influenza, not only how she emerged from it changed, virtually a different person, but also how she subsequently felt unlike other people, alienated from them. This informs her portrayal of Miranda's illness in *Pale Horse, Pale Rider*, as the afflicted young woman reaches down through delirium to her subjective self. In the state of unconsciousness brought on by infection and high fever, the need to adapt to the external world is suspended,[22] and the self's defenses against such adaptation are revealed.

This experience is not, of course, restricted to pestilential diseases. All potentially fatal illnesses raise questions concerning the body *plus* whatever else it is that makes humans human. But contagion additionally brings into heightened conflict the "I" and the "not-I" who may not survive plague or who may pose a danger to others. In *The Plague* Camus forcefully drives home this separation by describing how, during the pestilence, people had to use buses, public transportation, on which paradoxically they attempted to avoid each other: "A queer thing is how the passengers all try to keep their backs turned to their neighbors, twisting themselves into grotesque attitudes in the attempts—the idea being, of course, to avoid contagion" (110). And it is hardly surprising that the same author who created a literary character who experienced total isolation from other human beings, Robinson Crusoe, should also create a narrator who publishes his account of the London plague of 1665 and celebrates at the very end of it his outliving the hundred thousand souls who perished: "yet I alive!" (248).

The moral implications of personal selfhood asserted in the midst of a plague emerge from the structure of the *Decameron*. Dividing his work into ten sections, Boccaccio assigns his narrators a song with which to end each day's storytelling session. The beginning of Day One is the description of the plague that was decimating Florence, whose citizens completely failed to live according to a Christian ethic that would have commanded charity towards fellow human beings and that required that they give the soul priority over the body. The lyric that concludes Day One celebrates instead self-love:

> In mine own beauty take I such delight
> That to no other love could I
> My fond affections plight.
>
> Since in my looking-glass each hour I spy
> Beauty enough to satisfy the mind,

Why seek out past delights, or new ones try
When all content within my glass I find?

(113)

This coincidence of self-preservation and self-love has supplied one perspective for interpreting *Pale Horse, Pale Rider*. Drawing on Otto Rank's
concept of narcissism, the argument is that Miranda's drive for survival can
be understood in "its broadest sense as self-love, in which is 'rooted the
instinct for self-preservation, and from which emerges the deep and powerful longing to escape death, or the submergence into nothingness, and the
hope of awakening to a new life.' " According to this view, Miranda thus
becomes a case history in narcissism, for when the fear of death becomes
inordinate, and mortality itself is virtually denied in the attempt to evade it,
then a "consuming preoccupation with self"[23] prevents her from loving
another.

But narcissism as a character disorder (some view it as a contemporary
moral pestilence) has become far more subtle than anything the ancient
myth of Narcissus and Echo implies. Narcissism also has to do with an
individual's subjective representation of the world. In the area of psycho-
therapy this subjectivity, rather than an abstract model of human personality, is the starting point for exploring the patient's way of living in the world.
Not surprisingly, any kind of object relations theory will prove useful for the
analysis of literature.

But for some, modern theory—for example that of the self psychologists
—is meaningful because of its ethical implications, and this is what makes
such theories significant for a study of plague literature. To (of necessity)
oversimplify, a psychology that talks in terms of psychic fragmentation or
integration frequently invokes as a precondition for the cohesiveness of the
self the individual's recognition and acceptance of boundaries between self
and other. Others then exist as more than mere extensions of self; they are
respected as separate agents with their own requirements that are to be
honored. According to Stephen Toulmin, such

contemporary developments in the psychology of the self are bringing psychoanalysts
very close to one of Immanuel Kant's central ethical insights. For one of the most
telling formulations of Kant's "categorical imperative" principle is concerned, precisely, with the proper relationship between different co-existing agents in the world
of active, practical affairs: "So act, that you treat all other agents as ends in
themselves, never as means only."[24]

Widespread contagious infection will surely test the individual's capacity to
draw the line between self-interest and ethical behavior toward others. On

the other side, a strong sense of "self" helps ward off various kinds of invasions by others—for example, the ruthless bond salesmen in *Pale Horse, Pale Rider*. In short, plague literature raises ethical issues that become psychological crises during epidemics, for plagues will inevitably strain the tension between total moral relativism and the facile judging of others. When one of the characters in Camus's novel is defensive about his attempts to run away from the plague to rejoin the woman he loves, he admits, "Maybe I'm all wrong in putting love first," to which the narrator of the book responds "vehemently," "No . . . you are *not* wrong" (150), although he himself has placed fighting the pestilence above his own quest for personal happiness.

If the cohesive self develops through relations to other agents, then it would seem to follow that there can exist no cohesive self in isolation, that "some social completion of identity is a necessary part of personhood." [25] Rather than the individual existing in an essential conflict with society, and civilization generating psychic discontents, "human destiny and authenticity are not antagonistic to, but rather *require*, one's embeddedness in the human culture or 'system.' " [26] The conflict between the individual and society thus takes on another layer of complexity. And plague threatens not only the body but also the psychological self that may begin to disintegrate without some firm anchoring in an environment of other persons. Poe's tales of pestilence reveal keen insight into this process of psychic fragmentation.

A telling example of the relation of plague to the cohesive self is provided by AIDS. For many reasons, including the stigma of the disease and the loss by the sufferer of precisely those persons who would provide a stabilizing environment (who have already died of AIDS or who draw away from the sick person due to fear of contagion), AIDS has been called "a crisis of the self." [27] As such, AIDS evokes several concepts of narcissistic disorders. A kind of chicken-or-egg dilemma can be perceived by juxtaposing the conceptions of Sander Gilman and Stanislav Andreski on (implicitly or explicitly) psychological boundaries and the AIDS sufferer. Andreski presents a very bleak outlook concerning the possibility of containing AIDS in any but the most ruthlessly totalitarian state, one that discards reliance on the individual conscience or even on enlightened self-interest. Since, according to Andreski, sexual transmission is one of the major ways the AIDS virus is spread, "the risk increases with the preference for promiscuity which is connected with cold self-centred sensuality or loveless vanity. So people who are most likely to catch AIDS are also least likely to be motivated by concern for others." Such persons are, for example, unlikely to be swayed by educational programs: only self-interest could activate their concern.[28] But, to apply the language of the self psychologists to Andreski's argument, that "self" that is part of their interests is already so fragmented as to render even that appeal problematic.

On the other side, Gilman depicts the widening chasm between the sufferer and "the society in which he or she dwells."

[AIDS patients] respond to the isolation and stigmatization that is the social boundary of their disease, not part of the disease itself. The necessary constraints placed on our dealing with fantasies of disease by our need to create a boundary between ourselves and the afflicted, our image of the patient as the container and transmitter of the disease, and, indeed, our sense of our own selves as mortal beings are all embedded in our need to distance and isolate those we designate as ill.[29]

Gilman's account supplies an additional irony: isolation would result in or accelerate psychic disintegration, bringing on depression or other mental disorders that have their own traditional stigmata, and these get added to the signs of the disease itself. In the wider social arena, the isolated patient is a microcosm for the groups that, alienated from the dominant culture and, at the same time, at greater risk for the disease, must be reached but are unlikely to be if they are defined as essentially "other."

Self psychology is modern, but its almost traditional ethical implications make it an appropriate vehicle for extending the ethical concerns that plague raises in the contemporary world, where the traditional grounds for moral behavior have been significantly weakened. But this is not to say that it will supply the overall perspective in my discussion of literature, for it too has a place in the historical development of ideas of the self. History will supply an important dimension to this book, although chronology will not be followed. What is being argued here, and what will be contended in following chapters, is that despite changing conceptions of the "self," the psychological and moral issues concerning what constitutes human beings as a group and what individuates its members serve to unify works of plague literature written over centuries and within the contexts of vastly different ideas of a human relationship to the universe.

It is this relationship as well as the tenuous connection between physical survival and human morality that supplies the basis for William McNeill's metaphorical construction of a kind of chain of being on which human beings are both victims and generators of plague:

Disease and parasitism play a pervasive role in all life. A successful search for food on the part of one organism becomes for its host a nasty infection or disease. All

animals depend on other living things for food, and human beings are no exception
... [One] can properly think of most human lives as caught in a precarious equilib-
rium between the microparasitism of disease organisms and the macroparasitism of
large-bodied predators, chief among which have been other human beings.[30]

Microparasites in *Plagues and Peoples* are the viruses and bacteria associated
with epidemic diseases. Macroparasites were first the predatory animals that
early human beings had to defend themselves against; but later such predators were conquering tyrants with their armies and, in general, large bureau-
cratic governments. McNeill concentrates on history up to the eighteenth
century. The great English poet of that century, William Blake, extended
the class of macroparasites to large commercial interests that drew their
model from, existed because of, and supported governmental bureacracy.

As Zinsser's witty placing of investment bankers on the universal food
chain suggests, present-day economics leads to McNeill's disease model:
for example, the hostile takeovers of businesses by each other and the
attempts to defend against them. Recently, leveraged buyouts were virtually
epidemic, resulting in a high mortality rate among companies and economic
suffering among individuals. Computer "viruses" supply another example
of how individuals must defend against malicious attacks. And—to extend
this model of a world of interactive micro- and macroparasites—the individual must sustain a delicate psychological ecology as it draws its boundaries between and around self and other.

One way to read the major English romantic writers, for example, is to
recognize their attempts to affirm individuality without surrendering essential ties to others. Coleridge's Ancient Mariner, who willfully kills an alba-
tross, has to endure a living death worse than death itself, his punishment
—to live as a social outcast—an affliction associated with a figure whose
skin "was as white as leprosy." It is not the survival of his body that he
comes to value, but a "soul" that cannot truly be defined outside of that
which, it seems, will be forever denied him—sustained companionship
within a social group:

> O Wedding-Guest! this soul hath been
> Alone on a wide, wide sea:
> So lonely 'twas, that God himself
> Scarce seemèd there to be.
>
> O sweeter than the marriage feast,
> 'Tis sweeter far to me,
> To walk together to the kirk
> With a goodly company!

And yet the isolation that the mariner comes to dread will eventually become the distinguishing sign of an individual brave enough to defy society. This shift supplies a perspective for understanding the complex viewpoint behind William Blake's "London," a poem that has provoked controversy over whether the poet's depiction of plague is to be understood literally or symbolically, and over the role of Blake's speaker as an observer of London's micro- and macroparasites. The poetic voice in the sixteen lines that are "London" is an unidentified "I," wandering through London's "charter'd streets," marking in the faces he sees "marks of weakness, marks of woe." What he hears in the cries of "every Man" and in "every Infant's cry of fear" are the "mind-forg'd manacles" that are both social and psychological. The former suggest the bondage brought about by class distinction, organized religion, and the unholy alliance of both of these with civic government:

> the Chimney-sweeper's cry
> Every blackning church appals;
> And the hapless Soldiers sigh
> Runs in blood down Palace walls.

But even more insidious for Blake are the "plagues" that afflict sufferers caught in a vicious cycle created by a society that both spreads moral disease and ultimately deteriorates under its physical manifestations.

The infection begins with psychological "ban[s]," with the taint of sin being attached to human sexuality so that one of the basic relationships upon which marriage rests is blighted from the start. Blake's reader must supply the social context for the poem, and the poet writes with confidence that this could easily be done. Young men, raised with a double standard that excludes women, satisfy sexual drives by frequenting prostitutes, who are themselves victims both of the way sex is construed by their society and of the poverty that afflicts so large a portion of London's citizens. Infected, then, by so many literal and symbolic diseases, these women in turn infect men with the venereal diseases they then pass on to the socially acceptable women who are their brides:

> But most through midnight streets I hear
> How the youthful harlot's curse
> Blasts the new-born infant's tear,
> And blights with plagues the marriage hearse.

The marriage "ban[n]" announces, then, both the intention to wed and the cultural source of the blight that turns the wedding coach into a conveyance of death. Congenital illness extends from sexually transmitted diseases to what Ibsen would later view as the inherited ghosts of deadly ideas internalized by children who would continue to transmit physical and ideological plagues to countless generations. Wedding and propagation, which had supplied the structural and thematic framework for Coleridge's "Ancient Mariner" as well as the cultural ideal from which the mariner would in a sustained punishment be forever excluded, are represented in Blake's "London" as inherently disease-ridden.

Blake's London is thus the antithesis of the earthly paradise. Images of Eden drawn from Genesis as well as borrowings from the New Testament pervade the *Songs of Innocence*. In "London," one of the *Songs of Experience*, is depicted a "fall" from an earlier, happier, and disease-free state. Such associations between the fall and the plagues that blast human life are traditional: Adam and Eve sinned, and so sickness and mortality entered the world. But Blake repudiates this so-called historical process: sin lies not in the individual rose that is sick but in the socially engendered parasites that infect it. Again, there is some disagreement over whether images of illness, death, and even ecological decay in "London"—the "blackening church," the "blood" running down palace walls, the "plagues" that blight marriage and parenting—are to be understood literally or metaphorically. It is a foolish bit of controversy; the images are to be understood both ways: as one critic notes, "the blood of the soldiers is real, as well as apocalyptic, and so is the venereal disease."[31]

But the complexity of Blake's "London" does not end here. As in others of Blake's *Songs*, the speaker in the poem is a figure whose role as observer is ambiguous:

"London" identifies its speaker as a lonely wanderer, who passes through the streets of a particular city, and sees it from a lamenting distance ... [as] a place of bewildering diversity, changing and growing rapidly, in which a new kind of anonymity and alienation was becoming a remarked-upon fact of life.[32]

Heather Glen defines the literary tradition in which such a poetic voice can be placed. Understanding this background helps illuminate the moral distance between the speaker and the devastation he witnesses. During Blake's time, the terrain of the poetic subject was undergoing a transformation: Oliver Goldsmith's "The Deserted Village" and William Wordsworth's "Tintern Abbey" supply instructive examples. Like Blake, Goldsmith surveys the devastation of a community by its social macroparasites; the village's population is forced by the Enclosure Acts to migrate to cities or foreign lands against whose physically and socially unhealthy environment they had developed no antibodies. Goldsmith's speaker reflects on these changes: "If to the city sped—what waits [them] there?" he asks. His speculations anticipate the romantic meditative lyric, but the subject of his speculations is something other than himself and thus he maintains a public moral stance.

In "Tintern Abbey," Wordsworth, like Goldsmith's speaker, has returned to a locale not visited for a period of time to muse on the changes that have taken place. The alteration, however, is not in the scene but rather in himself, and he ruminates on how "thoughtless" youth had given way to the moral capacity to hear the still, sad music of humanity. As the concrete nouns in the poem give way to the abstract, the spiritual insight that is achieved must yield to the faith that to be in touch with human suffering is to grow in one's capacity for empathy, that to known the *self* is to recognize essentially ethical ties to others. Such confidence in the inherent link between the public and the private was not, however, to be sustained in the nineteenth century. Matthew Arnold, for example, associated the dialogue of the mind with itself with the *disease* of modern life. It is in this context that Blake's "London" raises a central problem in plague literature—the relation between the subject, infectious disease, and the narrative or lyric form of the work.

Glen is correct to perceive in the "lonely wanderer" of "London" an isolated dweller in an alienating city. But the wanderer figure in romantic poetry, as the earlier references to Coleridge's Ancient Mariner suggest, is also the lonely egotist who may experience difficulty balancing the requirements of self and other. The voice in "London" is that of experience, and for Blake experience is a fallen state in part because the perspective of innocence is lacking. The first quatrain of "London" depicts the failure of integration:

> I wander through each charter'd street,
> Near where the chartered Thames does flow,
> And mark on every face I meet
> Marks of weakness, marks of woe.

"Charter'd" is usually interpreted in the context of the corporations that established privileged interests in the city. The river is thus similarly chartered in that commerce is conducted on it. But the repetition of the word "chartered" with respect to the Thames suggests that London is caught in a larger nature-culture dialectic in which the river must give up its natural freedom. In the ensuing struggle, culture itself is an abstract macroparasite; environmentalists will have no difficulty picturing the Thames in as diseased a condition as London itself.[33] Dickens is probably drawing on such pollution in the opening of *Our Mutual Friend*, where the nighttime life of the river involves those whose boats prowl in search of dead bodies to be sold as cadavers to schools of medicine.

But boroughs and other legal-geographical entities, not only business corporations, are chartered, and the word has within it *chart*, which implies the delineation of boundaries—not only to establish private property but also to draw maps, for example. It is striking that Defoe's *Journal of a Plague Year* begins, in effect, with chartered streets.[34] The outbreak in 1665 of plague in London began in one house and then the disease seemed to go away, only to reappear when "another died in another house, but in the same parish" (2). Few cared to walk in Drury Lane "unless they had extraordinary business, that obliged them to it" (2). To delineate boundaries is also to define the difference between those within them and those without, as Gilman's depiction of the AIDS sufferer indicates. It is here that the alienated wanderings of Blake's speaker pick up added significance.

He keeps himself psychologically outside boundaries because of his perception of society's "mind-forged manacles." As observer, he maintains this distance because to do otherwise is to risk his freedom. "Mark" and "marks," the words that express both how and what he observes, acquire an added level of meaning. From a distance he *remarks* on what he sees, which are marks—that is, visible signs, the external symptoms of widespread disease—of the city's pathology. But *mark* contains further associations. There is, for example, the mark of Cain, not only the first man born in sin after the fall, but also, from McNeill's perspective, the first human macroparasite, who killed his brother. Condemned to exile, Cain's mark, placed upon him by God, is ambiguous. As a protective mark, it preserves his life and wanderings and thus, perhaps, his loneliness: Cain is often invoked in studies of "The Ancient Mariner." But the mark also sets Cain apart; it would take the romantic perspective to turn this discriminatory sign from a taint to an emblem of superior nonconformism.

For Blake's speaker to "mark . . . marks" is to suggest that he is both the superior being who actively assigns moral value to what he sees as well as the observer who merely notes it. More than that, marks are also indications of what is to be avoided, and while the speaker of "London" himself probably ought not to be seen as shrinking from some kind of contagion, however symbolic, his concern for his freedom from the bans that govern those who live within the chartered streets may lead to troubling implications. He may have bought his independence at the expense of others. There may, that is, be a parallel between the objective observer who watches a diseased state from a passive distance and one who, in the face of contamination, shrinks from those whom he pities but cannot or will not help.

The Edenic imagery of Blake's *Songs of Innocence* is echoed throughout plague literature, which is replete with bowers of bliss and false paradises. It is hardly surprising that it would be in time of plague—literal or metaphorical—that the human impulse to recreate the earthly paradise would assert itself. As historian Dolores Greenberg has argued, in "the modern period, the active quest for an earthly Eden is a phenomenon unparalleled in other cultures."[35] The new paradise would be a technological rather than a horticultural and zoological marvel. Plague would be atavistic, a reminder of the fall, the pestilence immediately defeated by effective magic bullets.

In Western thought there also exists a belief in a cosmic fall according to which nature—not only man and woman—fell when the fruit of the forbidden tree was tasted. Not only disease but also natural catastrophes such as earthquakes, volcanic eruptions, and tidal waves were punishments for the first human transgression against God's bans. In his introduction to Defoe's *Journal*, Louis Landa quotes from a writer who argues the miasmatic theory of plague origins (that the disease exists in the air breathed) in a language that literally and figuratively connects plagues to other cosmic catastrophes:

"Plagues are often bred in the Bowels of the Earth" where "Reeks and Fumes of various Kinds" are generated and then "burst their Prisons by furious Earthquakes, and break thro' the Chasms and Disruptions of the Ground in violent and contagious Tempests [filling] the Regions of the Air with crude pestilential Seeds."[36]

The question may arise, how do plagues differ from these other catastrophes, so that pestilences can be singled out to be unique in their effect on human life and human interaction—leaving aside the fact that disease often forms the wake of other natural or humanly caused disasters, or even puts an end to them (for example, the speculation that in seventeenth-century London, the great fire brought an outbreak of bubonic plague to an end). The most obvious difference has to do with contagion and the recoil of other people from an infected person. But it would be wrong to argue that plagues alone result in a rapid breakdown of the social contract: lootings that take place after other kinds of disasters only point up the fragility of social organization. Moreover, disasters sometimes forge bonds among those who might otherwise not form them. But the relationship of individual survival to social organization seems to be brought more sharply into question in conditions of plague, nature red in tooth and claw manifesting itself on a basic level of human interaction.

There is, however, more. As Eudora Welty has said about Katherine Anne Porter, there "was an instinct I had, trustworthy or not," that certain qualities in her stories "had something to do with time. Time permeates them. It is a grave and formidable force."[37] Defoe's *Journal of a Plague Year* similarly introduces time as a factor that differentiates plagues from other catastrophes. Perhaps borrowing from Boccaccio, Defoe has his narrator describe the popular belief that before the 1665 plague as well as before the London fire, a blazing star or comet appeared over London, "that the comet before the pestilence was of a faint, dull, languid colour, and its motion very heavy, solemn and slow; but that the comet before the fire was bright and sparkling, or, as others said, flaming, and its motion swift and furious."

One foretold a heavy judgement, slow but severe, terrible, and frightful, as was the plague: but the other foretold a stroak, sudden, swift, and fiery as the conflagration. (20)

It is often, then, the inexorable advance of a plague that helps differentiate it from other catastrophes, for example floods, which, according to Biblical literature, are also punitive visitations from God. But on May 17, 1990, the *New York Times* reported on a flood in Texas, watched by citizens of a town helpless to stay the waters.

[This] flood is unlike other natural disasters, which strike suddenly and are gone, allowing victims to mourn and then rebuild. The flood has been coming for more than two weeks, inch by inch. Once it peaks it will probably remain through the summer. There is a weary frustration being felt by residents here, a feeling that this disaster is endless. Already it is eroding their spirits as it erodes the land around their homes.[38]

There may be an echo from Camus here: as one of the characters in the novel laments, "if only it had been an earthquake! A good bad shock, and there you are! You count the dead and living, and that's an end of it. But this here damned disease—even them who haven't got it can't think of anything else" (105). It is, moreover, often the case that a catastrophe such as an earthquake will foster cooperation, people working together to rebuild their community, whereas communicable diseases intensify the isolation of individuals that eventually affects all social organizations and relations.

Plagues differ with respect to time. Some strike swiftly, killing their victims quickly, although from the sufferer's point of view, the agony may appear endless. As Camus's dying Tarrou complains, "It's a long business" (259). Other plagues stay around for longer, unpredictable lengths of time, sometimes becoming endemic. And some infectious diseases, which advance like the flood in Texas, linger, threatening to erode the spirit as well as the body, which may remain asymptomatic for a period of time. The integration or fragmentation of the self is a process that occurs over time; it is a process that may be catalyzed by the shock and trauma of a sudden cataclysmic event, but sudden and long-term effects are not identical. The passing of time, moreover, contributes to the idea of life as consisting of borrowed time. Human mortality extends this idea to all areas of life, but terminal illnesses and plagues bring with them a particularly keen awareness of time, and in the case of plague, this awareness can extend to the entire pestilence-ridden society.

One can conceivably live an entire lifetime without directly experiencing war, natural disaster, or serious accident. In an absurd universe, happenstance may point up the meaninglessness of human existence, but only one particularly despairing or especially convinced of the meaninglessness of existence finds in every disaster a microcosm for life itself. Illness, however, constitutes the common experience of human life: the person who survives another day of the plague that kills another human being has won but another, uncertain period of time. In that sense, all living people are experiencing a symbolic period of remission from disease. It is this element of time that contributes to plagues standing as special signs of the human condition itself. And what plague literature consistently asks is what it means to be human and just what that condition is.

The *timeliness* of this book is obvious as the world faces one of the deadliest communicable illnesses ever known. Whatever advantage is gained from the subject commanding especial relevance to contemporary reality, however, is had at the expense of a formidable question. What can a book on plague literature expect to accomplish? It certainly cannot cure, but can it even hope, for example, to change public policy or the actions or consciousness of a single human being? Defoe's narrator expected that the publishing of his *Journal* could provide a guide to anyone who had to decide, as he did, how to act should such a "distemper" fall upon the world, whether or not to save one's own life by running away from the pestilence. To this end, he withheld purely private meditation from public view. Defoe's contemporary, Jonathan Swift, was less optimistic about literature's effect on the reader. One project of his fiction is to call fiction itself into question. Gulliver prefaces his *Travels* by asking the one who had urged him to publish them whether his doing so had resulted in any improvement in society, starting with "party and faction" and finishing his series of offenders with "all disgracers of the press in prose and verse, condemned to eat nothing but their own cotton [paper], and quench their thirst with their own ink." Party and faction are among the macroparasites that supply plague literature with some of its themes. But the writer's "thirst" for ink suggests that problems of the individual *self* have acquired an added layer of significance, the artist needing to define the role *of artist* in a pestilential world.

Swift's challenge is rhetorical, but it does put the author's (and the scholar's) ego on the line. Keats experienced the conflict between the indulgences of art and the aims of medicine when he wondered in a late poem whether the poet could be physician to humanity. The Keatsian metaphor that links writer to doctor makes the problem especially applicable to plague literature. One way to write the history of literary criticism is in terms of the breakdown of the Horatian ideal according to which literature is a superior teacher because it has pleasure as its means, the spoonful of sugar that makes the moral medicine go down. As the medicine threatened to become mere candy, the writer's identity was transformed. Ironically, both Boccaccio, who starts from the premise of the writer as moral instructor, and Poe, who denounces that premise, use the plague motif to call into question the significance of art in a mortal world. A reading of their works reveals something paradoxical, even self-canceling, in the whole idea of plague literature, which strains to a breaking point the tension between the instructive and the self-expressive in art. How can the subject of pestilence be consistent with the pleasure principle that separates literary art from rhetoric? Is plague itself—as subject—a bridge between the artist's moral and creative self? As Marshall W. Mason, the director of William Hoffman's drama *As Is* writes in an endnote to the published text, it was crucial that the audience never be distanced enough from the action to feel safe, for "entertaining as the play may be, the subject is deadly."[39]

TWO

The Historical and Ethical Significance of Daniel Defoe's *A Journal of the Plague Year*

A prolific eighteenth-century author best known for his novel *Robinson Crusoe*, Daniel Defoe is now receiving increasing attention for *A Journal of the Plague Year*. It is an important literary work in its own right, one particularly significant for an age confronting a new and deadly plague, and also noteworthy because it was a source and model for one of the twentieth century's masterpieces, *The Plague*. In the epigraph for his novel, Camus quotes from Defoe and obvious similarities exist between the two works, one of which is the critical uncertainty about how to identify the works' genre. There is some disagreement about what kind of a narrative Defoe wrote, and Louis Landa has surveyed the long-standing scholarly argument: "[The *Journal*] has been called history, a historical novel, historical fiction, fictional history, a true narrative, a false narrative. Defoe was content to call it a journal."[1] Of course, this recourse to "journal" does not obviate the problem of classification: the journal and the private diary that H. F. admitted he sometimes allowed his journal to become have their own generic development and special relationship to fictional forms. But certainly Defoe assumed readers who would understand the historical importance of his *Journal* as well as the eternal human dilemmas portrayed in it. The following discussion will not take up the challenge as to the accuracy of Defoe's treatment of the impact of the bubonic plague that had swept London more than fifty years before he wrote his work: there is abundant critical material on how close to or remote from actuality the *Journal* is. Nor will it pursue the contemporary theoretical argument that "the writing of history is not only an ambition of the *Journal* but one of its themes."[2] Instead, this study of plague literature will begin with the *Journal* because of its particular chronology among the works to be discussed. The 1722 account of bubonic plague that ravaged London in 1665 supplies a significant perspective from which to look back at plague-ravaged Florence in the fourteenth century and forward to New York in the twentieth.

The seventeenth century has been portrayed as a Janus-faced period that harkened back to a time of strong and relatively secure religious beliefs, scholasticism, deductive reason, and reliance on authority in most areas of life; and forward to an increasingly secular age influenced by induction, the growth of empirical science, and a shift from the general to the particular, with a concomitant emphasis on the individual. In his classic study of the background to the age, Basil Willey characterized it as a time when there was "a general transference of interest from metaphysics to physics, from the contemplating of Being to the observation of Becoming."[3] As a result, the seventeenth was perhaps the last century about which one could attempt to create a cohesive background. John Donne's claim that the "new philosophy calls all in doubt" anticipates William Butler Yeats's depiction of a modern world in which the center no longer holds and "mere anarchy is loosed upon the world." Part of the historical significance of *A Journal of the Plague Year* is that it can be located at the end of that crucial period of transition, and as a result, it depicts the collision of old and new. Defoe's narrator, powerfully influenced by the disparate ideas of his time, often fascinated by the tensions they created, appears at times, however, unwilling to follow where the new was leading. As Laura Curtis argues (if to a somewhat different point), Defoe's writing reveals a division between "an ideal world of order and rational control and a real world of disorder and impulse."[4] In the eighteenth century, Yeats's anarchy was represented by a reversion to chaos, an apocalyptic vision that rivaled plague itself in the horror it could evoke.

A significant area of change had to do with grounds for ethical behavior, a matter inseparable from the treatment of plague. Thus the historical place of Defoe's *Journal* leads to its ethical significance. To explain, it will be useful to move quickly forward in time to Robert Bolt's contemporary play, *A Man for all Seasons*, to which Bolt added a preface in which he explains his anachronistic effort to create a modern hero out of the Catholic martyr and saint, Thomas More. The playwright says of More's decision to defy Henry VIII and thereby risk his life that More's choice was, if not an easy one, at least a simple one.[5] That is of course the problem with his play, for by Bolt's own admission, ethical decisions are no longer either easy or simple. Historians of Western thought trace some of the difficulty to the Protestant Reformation and the replacement by private conscience of external authority. Defoe's *Journal* reflects that loss of at least the theoretical simplicity attached to important moral decisions.

As Defoe's narrator—who signs himself "H. F." at the end of his account—says about the point of personal "choice" (8) concerning whether to flee or stay in London during the plague, if a person "be one that makes conscience of his duty, and would be directed what to do in it," then "he should keep his eye upon the particular providences which occur at that time, and look upon them *complexly*" (10; emphasis added). Providence, unfortunately, supplied no clear guidelines for behavior; individuals who sought to obey their consciences had to make their way through a wilderness of ambiguous signs. H. F. chooses to remain in London, as he of course must if there is to be a *Journal*. But his account of the plague reveals a tension between the pragmatic conclusions he comes to through observation of the pestilence, its spread, its demographics, on one side, and a still-operative Christian ethic, on the other. He decides, and the emphasis is his, "I must leave it as a prescription" that *the best physick against the plague is to run away from it* (197–98). But as has been noted, when the brother of H. F. proclaims, "Master, save thyself," H. F. adds that these words were "the same that was given in another case quite different" (8–9), spoken to Christ, "who had chosen to obey God and to die."[6] Nor had the point of Matthew's gospel been entirely lost in Defoe's time: he who would win his life might have to lose it.

H. F.'s motives for staying in London prove ambiguous, and he comes to doubt his own wisdom when later he shares London's growing desperation as the rate of deaths from plague climbs, the pessimistic expectation being that the plague would spare no one. Not a potential martyr about to sacrifice himself for his fellow, H. F. is an unmarried businessman, a maker of saddles he exports all over the world—in short, he is a successful manufacturer. It is in part to protect his business that he remains in the city instead of joining the exodus from it. The relevance of his commercial prosperity, as well as of his membership in a prosperous middle class, to his decision to remain in London will be taken up again shortly.

H. F.'s brother, also a successful merchant, leaves London with his wife and children at the first signs of the plague. Assigning to brothers different ways of life and values is, of course, commonplace in literature. Ibsen employs this structure in *The Enemy of the People*, as does Larry Kramer in *The Normal Heart*. But no social or political activism attaches to H. F.'s decision to remain in London, although civic duty plays an important part in his account. Rather, H. F.'s concern for others is limited to his own household and thus he supplies no clear contrast to his brother, who withdraws from the city and its plight. Leaving aside for the moment the recent critical controversy over H. F. as a relatively passive observer,[7] who more out of curiosity than anything else roams the city, the *Journal* is, as

Landa says, "perhaps first and foremost a story of London."[8] Only occasionally does H. F. take part in the book's action (if it is possible to refer to plotted events in the *Journal*). But one striking instance is a tavern scene in which a man who has lost his entire family is being goaded into suicide by a group of blasphemous scoffers, and H. F.'s sympathy for the sufferer turns the small mob on himself. But even here, what H. F. sees and how he later obsesses over the event counts for more than what actually happened. What in general H. F. *feels*, that is, beyond the terror and pity inspired by the plague that one would expect from a decent human being and professed Christian, belongs to his private, inner world, and he makes it clear that this he will not make public. This differentiation of public and private belongs to the evolving concept of the individual self in Defoe's time, a subject to be discussed later. In the meantime, the overall structure of the book is simple, although, as one editor reminds his readers, Defoe adheres to the unities demanded by the literary theory of his time by bringing the plague to a miraculous close much sooner than was actually the case.[9] London's miseries lasted months longer and were increased by the great fire that some (although not H. F.) believed brought the pestilence to an end. If divine wrath was operative in 1665–66, God was really angry with London.

It is worth noting, from the outset, that from the perspective of today's scientific knowledge, the medical premise of Defoe's *Journal* is incorrect.[10] It proceeds from H. F.'s adherence to a contagion theory in which the disease was thought to be communicated directly from person to person (without the mediation of rats and fleas, which are now understood to spread bubonic plague). At the time there was, as Landa notes, a "hotly debated controversy" over two theories of transmission, miasma and contagion:

The miasmatic view held that plagues resulted from corrupted or putrid air, chiefly the poisonous exhalations of the earth, with these intensified by foul emanations from rotten vegetable matter, human corpses, mines, pools, streams, dunghills, and filth of various kinds. The air thus becomes laden with pestilential particles.[11]

Both theories are morally charged. Miasma has to do with a world of widespread material corruption, and as such it is easily translatable into a metaphor for the antithesis of civic virtue, which assumes the possibility for society to be organized for the well-being of its citizens. Moreover, as Curtis has argued, accepting "the miasmatic over the contagion theory of infection means accepting the notion that individual effort to avoid the plague makes no difference at all."[12] This view, of course, attaches to the contagion theory the positive associations of public health measures. It thus may tend to deemphasize the psychological, social, and ethical problems surrounding plague. Still, much of what H. F. observes about the plague and how London reacted to it would have lost its point if the miasmatic theory had been advanced by Defoe.

Defoe's choice between two available theories raises the whole question of medical accuracy in a work of literature, a matter that was later to dog *Ghosts,* and this may be the place to address the issue. Lack of precise knowledge about a disease may sometimes prove a boon rather than a hindrance to an author. Defoe's concern is—again—with how society can act to protect itself in times of plague and also with the choices individual citizens must make. The idea of direct contagion serves his purpose better than miasma. This is not to say that Defoe necessarily chose his theory on this basis, although which of rival theories a person decides to adopt often has to do as much with that person as with the objective basis for the chosen idea. To return to Ibsen, *Ghosts* seems rooted not so much in misconceptions concerning syphilis as in the unresolved controversies that existed in the nineteenth century. These allowed the playwright to imbue his play with thematic ambiguities that might have been lost if what is known today had then been definitively known. It is thus a questionable endeavor to consult modern medicine about such matters as whether one could contract the disease by smoking one's infected father's pipe. At least two of the major French syphilologists in Ibsen's time thought one could.[13] And, coming up to the present, one reviewer of *As Is* and *The Normal Heart* has claimed that because more has been learned about how AIDS is communicated since 1985, when these plays appeared, they are already dated.[14] But a close reading of them suggests that it was the the paucity of knowledge that strained the relationships between the main characters and created the ethical dilemmas that keep the plays very much alive. This is not to say that medical accuracy or inaccuracy is not worth considering, only that faulting an author for errors may be not only to expect the writer to know what was not known but also to mistake the nature of the literary endeavor.

On the subject of the medical profession, physicians if not nurses are portrayed favorably in Defoe's *Journal*—although, again, this may be another example of a class perspective. H. F.'s approval excludes, of course, the charlatans who exploited the panic of London's population, as well as legitimate physicians who quickly fled London and, returning after the disease had abated, found themselves received much as collaborators were

145947

after World War II. Some doctors at first made sincere and laborious attempts to treat the ill but then followed the general population into panic and despair toward the end of the pestilential siege, but the narrator withholds moral judgment. Without actually saying so, he appears to ask who could throw the first stone. The dedicated physicians who remained— according to the *Journal* many of them died—endeavored to the extent that medical science made possible to alleviate the misery of the afflicted and save their lives. But unhappily the procedures by which buboes were lanced and burned resemble medieval tortures, and the *Journal* describes their horrors as well as the excruciating pain suffered by the plague's victims. It is also noteworthy that pamphlets instructing people on what to do and not do to protect themselves were supplied to the people. The information, of course, was rather useless, but certainly well intended. And, finally, H. F. speaks fondly of one Doctor Heath, not only an excellent physician but also a principled one, supplying in addition to medical advice the comfort of a friend. He plays only a minor role as the ideal doctor, but is nonetheless a fitting literary antecedent of Camus's persona, Doctor Rieux.

Other matters concerning medicine and science warrant more attention than this discussion can give them. Briefly, however, the plague was attributed by H. F. to God's judgment, but while exhorting his reader to prayers, fasts, and other Christian devotions if faced with such a calamity, and lamenting that when God miraculously put an end to the disease, people did not express enough gratitude to Him, H. F. does not find a sufficient explanation for the pestilence in divine providence, denying that God operated "without the agency of means" (75). He keeps a close eye on statistics and demographic patterns, analyzes which remedies work and which do not, and concludes that while the "visitation it self is a stroke from Heaven upon a city," a "messenger of [God's] vengence," it is not "less a judgment for its being under the conduct of human causes and effects" (193–94). H. F. equally rejects what he takes to be many of the wrong-headed naturalistic theories of his time (including miasma), believing some of them to be hardly distinguishable from those fantasies to which the poor in particular were susceptible. The *Journal* is thus a source for popular superstitions surrounding plague. But reiterating his acceptance of the contagion theory, H. F. insists, "I say, I must be allowed to believe, that no one in the whole nation ever receiv'd the sickness or infection, but who receiv'd it in the ordinary way of infection from some body, or the cloaths, or touch, or stench of some body that was infected before" (194). The spelling of the pronoun *somebody* in some modern editions of the *Journal* obscures Defoe's emphasis on the material, on the *body* that is infected with plague, the *body* that, as will be seen, is by no means identical to the entire person.

Strikingly, late into the book emerges a realization that shocks and worries H. F., something bound to reverberate in the contemporary consciousness. Physicians and careful observers had discovered that asymptomatic persons could be harboring the disease, dying even before its visible signs appeared. At a time when medical opinion and practice was dependent on symptoms, and public policy as well as individual reaction were dependent on medical opinion, it was particularly frightening to learn that it was "impossible to know the infected people from the sound; or that the infected people should perfectly know themselves" (191). But it only served to increase public panic to think that "those people who thought themselves entirely free, were oftentimes the most fatal" (209). A large portion of the population, already fearful of contagion but not yet inclined entirely to shun others, "locked themselves up, so as not to come abroad into any company at all" (209). It is striking to contemplate what the *Journal* does not dwell on as thoroughly as Camus does in *The Plague:* the growing alienation of people,[15] who longed for human companionship as comfort during the pestilence but feared each other. To fully understand the implications of what H. F. describes, it is only necessary to envision the extent to which self-preservation would drive people if the AIDS virus were to mutate so that even casual contact with contagious but asymptomatic persons could result in a person's becoming infected with HIV. The entire world would then be constituted of *others*, the gap between them and the *self* transformed into a virtually unbridgeable chasm. Indeed, merely to contemplate such a situation is to recognize how relatively muted are both Defoe's and Camus's accounts of how the people, in Defoe's words, "grew more cautious" (85) as a result of their fear of contagion.

From H. F.'s awareness of persons both asymptomatic but contagious emerge the questions of, first, where the "seeds of the infection" (204) hid during this short latency period, and, more important, how one *might* distinguish the infected from the uninfected. Among the debated theories is a striking, even charming, example of the Janus-faced century—provided that it is possible to put aside the potential dangers posed by a belief in evil as a tangible entity. H. F. reports the notion that one could breathe upon a glass that would then be examined by microscope. What would be found in the event of infection? "Strange monstrous and frightful shapes, such as dragons, snakes, serpents, and devils, horrible to behold." Traditional symbols, that is, of evil. But, H. F. goes on pragmatically to note, "we had no microscopes at that time, as I remember, to make the experiment with" (203).

By invoking the changes that were occurring in the seventeenth century, and distinguishing popular superstition from the then-current scientific theory with which the more educated segments of London would be acquainted, and by attributing H. F.'s perspective to his class status, this discussion has in effect tried to describe how plague was socially constructed by Defoe. In his work on syphilis in the United States, Allan Brandt explains,

Fundamental to the notion that disease is socially constructed is the premise that it is profoundly shaped by both biological and cultural variables. Attitudes and values concerning disease affect the perception of its pattern of transmission, its epidemiological nature. Only if we understand the way disease is influenced by social and cultural forces—issues of class, race, ethnicity, and gender—can we effectively address its biological dimension. A "social construction" reveals tacit values, it becomes a symbol for ordering and explaining aspects of the human experience. In this light, medicine is not just affected by social, economic, and political variables—it is embedded in them.[16]

H. F. supplies an example of how diseases can be socially constructed. His position in society somewhat resembles the significant but problematic situation of human beings on the universal great chain of being—an important model for eighteenth-century writers. H. F. looks up at the nobility and down at the masses of poor who were quantitatively and qualitatively most devastated by the plague. About the royal court, which had fled London for Oxford, H. F., without denying the charity it dispensed, suggests that its vices may have invoked God's judgment on London. More pragmatically, he adds that the "joy of the Restoration" (18) had brought more people to London, thus increasing the population afflicted by the disease.

About the lower classes, he has much more to say. The plague of course threatened a complete breakdown in civic virtue, and the shadow of a Hobbesian reversion to nature and state of war of all against all loomed over the city, as threatening as the plague itself. That London's grade for how it comported itself during the plague was, as has been claimed, at least passing,[17] H. F. attributes to various factors. Among these is the good sense and benevolence of the magistrates who had to administer law as well as dispense charity during the crisis. Like the doctors who have H. F.'s general approval, these governing officials belong to the same class as Defoe's narrator. This is not so much to say that Defoe's depiction is faulty—although it has been argued that no magistrates died during the 1665 plague, which mainly afflicted London's poor, as, it is argued, Defoe well knew[18]—as it is to examine the social construction of his depiction. The story might indeed be told differently by one of London's masses of poor citizens, or even by a member of the nobility.

Defoe's narrator provides an almost perfect example of the person R. H. Tawney depicted in his renowned study, *Religion and the Rise of Capitalism.* Strikingly, H. F.'s decision to remain in London rather than flee to a place hopefully free of plague parallels the situation described by Tawney, who relates how from the "reiterated insistence on secular obligations as imposed by the divine will, it follows that, not withdrawal from the world, but the conscientious discharge of the duties of business, is among the loftiest of religious and moral virtues."[19] But as conscience replaced the authority of the church, it became increasingly difficult to recognize visible signs of God's grace, the indications of which had to be sought both within the individual and in the equally difficult to decipher external signs of his spiritual condition. In this context, it is immediately clear why, when H. F. describes his dilemma concerning whether to flee or remain in London, he links personal to economic survival. Although his very success in business and prosperity supply positive signs of God's favor, so that he is from the outset inclined to trust providence, he cannot, of course, be sure that he is reading such signs correctly:

I had two important things before me; the one was the carrying on my business and shop; which was considerable, and in which was embark'd all my effects in the world; and the other was the preservation of my life in so dismal a calamity, as I saw apparently was coming upon the whole city. (8)

His brother points out the logic of his position as well as his predicament. Is it not as reasonable, he asks H. F., "that you should trust God with the chance or risque of losing your trade, as that you should stay in so imminent a point of danger, and trust him with your life?" (9).

Many of the legal or civil rights issues raised by the *Journal* rest on what has been called the divine right of property.[20] It is, in part, the absence of property that makes the masses of poor appear so threatening to H. F., since in lacking an economic stake in society, they remain unaffected by the essential grounds for the social contract as it was generally understood at the time. Significantly, then, although H. F. is on the whole sympathetic concerning the plight of the poor, despite their susceptibility to wild fancies and to medical quacks, he at one point raises a rather chilling instance of natural selection. Again, the poor were at a great disadvantage in the plague.

The more affluent could retire to second homes outside London, whereas the poor who fled often starved to death before the pestilence overtook them. The well off could also lay in large stores of provisions and wait out the disease, which measure H. F. asserts was quite effective against the plague. Also, the rich could go into what was called the pest houses, hospitals that H. F. claims offered a degree of success in treating the disease but that demanded payment or guarantee of payment. It is difficult to imagine what could be done against the plague in hospitals, H. F. admitting that the "plague defied all medicine" (35); perhaps H. F.'s view is an extension of a generalized recognition that the rich were generally privileged over the poor.

That the poor, even more desperate among a population portrayed as growing increasingly despairing, did not rise up in general revolt is attributed by H. F. to two factors: first, again, the good sense and benevolence of those who gave and those who dispensed charity; and second, the fact that the plague struck hardest at the lower classes. Effectively, it was the plague itself that helped preserve the public peace. As H. F. notes, it "rag'd so violently, and fell in upon [the poor] so furiously, that they rather went to the grave by thousands than into the fields in mobs by thousands" (129). In addition, H. F. realizes that "had the plague, which raged in a dreadful manner from the middle of August to the middle of October" not "carried off in that time thirty or forty thousand of these very people, which had they been left, would certainly have been an insufferable burden, by their poverty," the city would probably have had to abandon them, in which case they would have risen up and "put the whole nation, as well as the city, into the utmost terror and confusion" (98). This image of a plague-ridden city unable to cope with a disease and its outcome undoubtedly provides the *Journal* with much of its contemporary significance.

Why people do or do not help maintain law and order[21] always has to do with some spoken or implied ideas about human nature. To confront this issue is to consider some of the most difficult philosophical dilemmas raised by the *Journal,* it being important to remember that much of what Defoe expresses through H. F. has to do not only with his defense of civic virtue as a positive ethical ideal but also with his desire "to encourage Englishmen to behave in sober, orderly ways should plague break out."[22] Whatever serves to further this end will claim priority over pure ideas. It was not, that is, expedient for Defoe to argue the case for original sin, even if, as Maximilian Novak has argued, it still dominated his view of humanity.[23]

Again, Defoe's *Journal* occupies a point of transition during which original sin (so closely tied to the concept of plague) was as a doctrine losing ground, beginning to compete with romantic ideas concerning innate innocence. In the *Journal*, the drive toward individual survival is derived from natural law, and if Defoe is eventually going to persuade his reader that in general, "solutions to the problem of self interest" lay "in the power of the state to make laws which would work for the common good" as well as "in the spiritual power of religion,"[24] he would have to take an ameliorative position with regard to self-preservation. But plague itself challenges such a generality; moreover, the ethical implications of self-preservation are harder to evade in times of plague than they might be under other conditions. Alas, writes H. F., "this was a time when every one's private safety lay so near them, that they had no room to pity the distress of others." He continues, "This, I say took away all compassion; self preservation indeed appear'd to be the first law." The "danger of immediate death to ourselves took away all bowels of love, all concern for one another" (115).

From H. F.'s point of view, London *did* on the whole behave well during the crisis, it being only "self-preservation [that] oblig'd the people to those severities, which they wou'd not otherwise have been concern'd in." But when "there was room for charity and assistance to the people, without apparent danger to themselves, they were willing enough to help and relieve them" (152–53). But as the plague raged on, self-preservation became easier to make a first priority, since people were forced to steel themselves against painful emotions:

Tears and lamentations were seen almost in every house, especially in the first part of the visitation; for towards the latter end, mens hearts were hardned, and death was so always before their eyes, that they did not so much concern themselves for loss of their friends, expecting, that themselves should be summoned the next hour. (16)

One way that H. F. softens this judgment is to extend self-preservation from the physical to the psychological realm. Those who took the most drastic means to conceal from their neighbor that they were stricken by plague did so not only to avoid being shut up in their houses, a prospect that terrified them on many grounds, but also "to prevent their neighbours shunning and refusing to converse with them" (6). Human interaction is thus acknowledged by Defoe to fulfill a basic human need, and it was not merely the moral but also the psychological distance that plague situates between persons that H. F. recognizes as one of its severest effects.

Second, a touchstone for the narrator's ambiguous position on human nature is his skepticism, sometimes outright denial, of the belief that a large number of infected people deliberately and out of malice "did not take the least care, or make any scruple of infecting others." He does not deny that there might be some instances of this, but maintains that such behavior was not "so general as was reported" (54). There exists a similar perception of the AIDS sufferer, and Hoffman treats with irony in *As Is* what H. F. calls "a seeming propensity, or a wicked inclination among those that were infected to infect others" (153).

H. F.'s phraseology on this point makes it clear that it is human nature, not just human behavior, that is at stake: it was probably the aimlessly wandering homeless who, he believes, helped "give birth to report that it was natural to the infected people to desire to infect others" (70). Denying this, H. F. searches for other explanations, noting that the point was one of debate among physicians. He himself is inclined to disbelieve that the afflicted are "seized" with a "kind of a rage, and a hatred against their own kind—as if there was a malignity, not only in the very distemper to communicate it self, but in the very nature of man, prompting him with evil will, or an evil eye," turning him into a mad dog (154). He is more inclined to see the suffering of the disease as maddening, and the sufferer who inflicted injury on others as the victim, not the perpetrator, of evil.

Such a liberal view is antithetical to a Hobbesian vision of the collapse of society into a state of nature—and the *Journal*, while expressing fears of such a collapse, does not depict it. First, it apparently did not happen. But, second—and again—H. F. does not begin from the premise of innate human depravity. If, for example, he denies that female nurses, as was generally reputed, murdered their patients in order to steal from them, he denies this not only because he reasonably concludes that it is hardly necessary to murder those who are overwhelmingly likely to die, and soon, but also because he just does not think so little of people.

Because H. F. has a more benign view of humanity than would be likely to emerge from ideas of original sin, and because the plague itself supplied a kind of ironic system of checks and balances, Defoe's *Journal* suggests that the social contract is viable without the kinds of governmental coercion that a Hobbesian view would require. Indeed, the book portrays the creation of such a contract in an extended anecdote concerning three men who left the city together, pooled their talents, and worked together to escape the plague and survive other dangers in the effort.[25] This trio illustrates how mutual need can lead to mutual benefit, since one of them, who had the most money, was lame and thus most unfit to fare well on the journey, so that "he was content that what money they had should all go into one public stock, on condition, that whatever any one of them could gain more than another, it should, without any grudging be all added to the public stock" (126).

Given such a comfortable approach to the social contract,[26] it is hardly surprising that H. F. proves an advocate of civil rights. But the matter is not so simple, since Defoe's narrator stops short of advocating personal liberty for its own sake. It should be recalled that the Restoration followed twelve years of a republic in England, which followed the execution of Charles I. During this time, the poet John Milton had written his tract defending the regicide as well as his famous essay against censorship. Defoe's *Journal* upholds these liberal principles. H. F. remarks on the government's probably well-intentioned but failed attempt to maintain order by suppressing "the printing of such books as terrify'd the people, and to frighten the dispersers of them, some of whom were taken up, but nothing was done in it, as I am inform'd, the government being unwilling to exasperate the people, who were, as I may say, out of their wits already" (25). In this way, Defoe himself was apparently spared censorship, since according to his critics his obsessive concern over plague was forever breaking into print and he was deemed to have been spreading unnecessary alarm among London's reading population.[27]

But it is out of pragmatism rather than idealism that H. F. comes out against one of the most critical ethical and social issues raised by the *Journal* —the shutting up of houses. He understands that he faces a conflict between individual rights, on one side, and the public good on the other, admitting that quarantining the sick was "authorized by a law, [having] the public good in view, as the end chiefly aim'd at, and all the private injuries that were done by the putting it in execution, must be put to the account of the public benefit" (158). H. F.'s reference to the danger of contagious people at "liberty" indicates his understanding of what is at stake in the public policy, but insists nonetheless that it was "a public good that justified the private mischief" (48)—that is, mischief consisting of acts against individuals who were unwillingly shut up in their houses when they or any members of their household, family or servants, were known to be infected. But mischief was also the crimes committed by those, for example, hired to watch the houses, who were bribed to look the other way when their inhabitants escaped, suffering punishments that H. F. portrays as in excess of the crime—for example, being whipped through the streets. That he views their offenses as relatively petty is not due to his defense of individual liberty, which he is not ready to put on equal or superior grounds with public good, but to his perception of the inefficacy of quarantining people in their houses.

If H. F. opposes this quarantine, it is because he does not believe it works, for several reasons. First, people shut in went to extraordinary lengths to escape, and many did. Instead of dying in the at-least emotional comfort of their own surroundings, many died miserably in the streets, obeying an instinct for freedom but also contributing to the disease's spread to a wider geographical area. Second, shutting up the well with the sick— which H. F. takes to be medically outrageous—only killed those who might otherwise have survived and, moreover, prompted them to extreme measures to escape their doom. And, finally, since the asymptomatic but still contagious walked the streets freely, what good did it do to shut up the visibly ill?

Despite his opposition to the obligatory shutting up houses, H. F. advocates the voluntary seclusion of people anxious to protect themselves. The difference has been well explained: "to lay in provisions in advance, to choose one's own quarantine, is to construct a fortress or a citadel: to have quarantine imposed by others is to allow oneself to be imprisoned." [28] But the knotty matter of private property complicates such a neat view because, as already has been noted, the poor were deprived of such measures against the plague. Moreover, the *Journal* reflects rather than resolves a philosophical tension that was extreme in Defoe's time. As Pocock has described the problem,

In the territorial and jurisdictional monarchy, the individual took on positive being primarily as the possessor of rights—rights to land, and to justice affecting his tenure of land—and a structure of "ascending authority" existed mainly as a structure of customs, jurisdictions, and liberties, in which such rights were embodied and preserved and which rose to meet the descending structure of authority that existed to command its continuance and enforcement.... [The] individual possessed rights and property ... that which rightfully pertained to him and was subject to authority which, since it descended from God, was never the mere reflection of his rights; and the central debate was, and has remained, how far the two conceptual schemes, ascending and descending powers ... rights and duties, were integrated with one another. [29]

Plague heightens this debate as individuals confront the different laws by which they are governed: divine law, natural law, and civic laws—all of which combine in historically generated theories and pressures on the individual that not only collide with each other but also, in the last instance, run counter to a basic drive towards self-preservation. If part of Defoe's praise of London's magistrates is aimed at constructing a positive model of civic polity during times of crisis, it is because — as Boccaccio's depiction of Florence during the Black Death makes clear — the total breakdown of civic order results in a stark confrontation between natural law (defined here as self-preservation) and divine law, no other frames of reference existing to mediate between them.

H. F. thus applauds the vigilance of city government for the respect showed to shut-up or temporarily deserted houses (Boccaccio describes just the opposite: during the plague, privately owned houses became common property). But, again, H. F. does *not* take the final step from private property to the inviolable rights of all individuals, resisting the kind of deadlock described by Andreski concerning mandatory testing for AIDS: "Why should [the AIDS carrier's] right to peace of mind through ignorance be rated as more important than the right of others not to be exposed to a deadly infection? . . . Nobody (as far as I know) has explicitly asserted that the right of a carrier to enjoyment through ignorance is more important than the safety of others." [30]

The pragmatism by which H. F. sidesteps the contradictions resulting from the antithetical ideas of the eighteenth century does not mean that the *Journal* avoids them altogether. That a deadlock between conflicting self-interests might occur is raised in the account of the three journeymen who flee London, needing passage through towns intent on keeping out them and the plague they might be carrying. The three are inclined to respect private property: they were "obliged to keep the road, or else they must commit spoil, and do the country a great deal of damage in breaking down fences and gates to go over enclosed fields, which they were loth to do if they could help it" (134). This respect for boundaries puts them at a seeming disadvantage when a constable denies them access to a town where they wish to buy provisions. The problem is complicated because the official is also a person of good will, equally concerned with self-preservation. Even one of the three travelers admits that the people of that village "have a good reason to keep any body off, that they are not satisfied are sound" (123). This ethical dilemma is inevitably expressed through the legal: does the king's highway belong to the whole country or could it be controlled by individual communities through which it ran — a kind of federal versus states' rights issue. The constable points out that the tolls his village is entitled to collect suggest a wider provenance; but the men insist on right of passage. If the people are afraid of them, let them shut themselves in their homes while the three men travel through (which is also to acknowledge that self-preservation cannot rest fully on civic law), but to "deny [them] leave to pass thro' the town in the open high-way, and deny [them] provisions for [their] money, is to say the town has a right to starve [them] to death, which cannot be true" (123). Moreover, if self-preservation be granted to be a right, is not "flying to save [their] lives, a lawful occasion?" (124).

By 1722 the rights of the individual were gaining ground and self-preservation occupied an important place in moral philosophy. Both Defoe's journeymen and Boccaccio's brigada make a similar appeal to natural law in their flight from plague, but the status of such law had changed from the fourteenth to the seventeenth century as views of nature themselves had altered. Novak quotes from a poem on this point:

> The Laws of God, as I can understand
> Do never Laws of Nature countermand;
> Nature Commands, and 'tis Prescrib'd to Sense,
> For all Men to adhere to Self defence.[31]

But what Defoe's *Journal* avoids confronting—at least until its last four lines—is some definition of what that *self* is that is implicated in self-preservation.

Defoe's contemporary critics depart from Landa's claim that H. F. "lacks the dimensions" of other Defoe characters.[32] They seem to take it as a given that "H. F.'s spiritual crisis is central to the book,"[33] and that with his fellows in Defoe's literary canon, H. F.'s self is not only the object of human thought but also autoreferential. As a forerunner of individuals who confront the absurd, H. F. becomes a "narrator who is what he saw all men as being: a solitary soul—a lonely individual in a hostile world in which he inevitably finds himself the prey."[34] It is arguable, however, that whereas Defoe could conceive of such a world and of the literature that would emerge from it, the *Journal* indicates that Defoe was actively resisting such a reading of this work.

A Journal of the Plague Year has a rather cumbersome but significant subtitle: "being Observations or Memorials of the most Remarkable Occurrences, as well Publick as Private, which happened in London during the last great visitation in 1665. Written by a Citizen who continued all the while in London. Never made public before." Now this distinction between public and private has many reverberations. On one level, it is only necessary to differentiate H. F.'s general observations from the specific anecdotes he supplies about individuals suffering the plague, anecdotes that are supposed to be diverting in this treatise that—drawing on the prevalent literary theory of the time—aims to instruct but can only please in the most precarious way. But even with regard to these human interest stories in the *Journal*, Defoe has not gone too far in numbering the streaks of the tulip. A grief-stricken husband and father still remains a generalized grief-stricken husband and father, not a unique instance of one.

It is noteworthy in this regard that the reader learns relatively little about H. F. beside the meager biographical facts he supplies. He is, for example, a bachelor, but has he no one left in the city whom he loves, no friend or mistress whose death would result in personal devastation? Again, even the feelings he describes as he witnesses the plague's ravaging of London are sentiments one would expect as well as emotions he could admit. To use the words and metaphor of Defoe's contemporary, Alexander Pope, H. F. is not about to put on public view "this long disease my life." Nonetheless, H. F.'s inner world makes itself felt in the *Journal*. At one point he admits that when death seemed unlikely to spare anyone in London, he shut himself up in his house in a desperate effort to survive, occupying himself with his journal. Most of this work, "as it relates to my observations," he made public. But, he adds emphatically, some of what he put on paper was very personal: "What I wrote of my private meditations I reserve for private use, and desire it may not be made publick on any account whatever" (76–77). About a century later, Shelley would define the poet as a nightingale who sang to himself in darkness to ease his own solitude, and in H. F.'s cryptic comment can be found this entirely different view of literature, the writer writing for the writer's, not the audience's sake.

Moreover, H. F.'s individualism asserts itself in his role as observer. Again, he must remain in London and he must not shut himself up in his house—even though it is medically sound—if he is to provide Defoe's narrative perspective. But he concedes that what drove him to put himself in danger was his curiosity, thus revealing that speculative intellect that was distrusted in his time but that was to prevail and contribute to the growth of scientific and other knowledge. In addition, H. F.'s aimless wandering of London's streets and fields foreshadows the speaker in Blake's "London," who observes, also from a distance, the plague that blights human hopes.

Perhaps even more important is the self-*consciousness* that H. F. reveals at critical times in his *Journal*. He not only makes practical and ethical decisions but also seems to stand aside and watch himself doing so. As he writes at one point, "I now began to consider seriously with my Self, concerning my own case, and how I should dispose of my self" (8).[35] Even when he turns to his Bible for a sign from God about whether or not he should remain in London, and finds the passage that appears to be a positive directive to stay, he is aware that he is engaged in a very personal dialogue with God. Also, in the scene earlier referred to, in which he comes to the defense of a miserable man tormented by a small mob in a tavern, only to put himself in jeopardy, he contemplates his own sense of outrage, relating, "I was doubtful in my thoughts, whether the resentment I retain'd was not all upon my own private account." He is not sure how he—or anyone— could "distinguish between zeal for the honour of God, and the effects of their private passions and resentment" (69).

His individualism asserts itself most strongly in the last four lines of the *Journal*, a short ballad stanza in which H. F.'s survival of the plague is celebrated:

> A dreadful plague in London was,
> In the year sixty-five,
> Which swept an hundred thousand souls
> Away; yet I alive!

(248)

Defoe's formal construction of this verse is noteworthy. The traditional ballad stanza is usually made up of four end-stopped lines, the second and fourth of which rhyme, in this case connecting London's history with H. F.'s personal fate. Defoe's third line is enjambed, form paralleling meaning: a hundred thousand souls are quite swept away to the following line, where they contrast with the speaker, who remains triumphantly alive. But an additional feature of the enjambment is that "souls" as a word is highlighted, standing alone in a line whose number of characters lengthens its appearance on the printed page.

Very shortly before writing the *Journal*, Defoe had written another treatise entitled (without its subtitle) *Due Preparations for the Plague, as well for Soul as Body*. It has been argued that in the *Journal*, Defoe drew his most important images from the body ravaged by plague. Such corporeal imagery is supposedly symbolic and actually conveys the didactic, spiritual content of his work, the "brunt of his religious intentions."[36] Defoe might have been surprised at such a facile assurance that this could be done. In the verse with which he concluded the *Journal* can be found the individuated "I,"[37] as well as a gap between self and other, survivor and nonsurvivor. But here the "soul" receives the specific attention it does not command anywhere else in the *Journal* despite H. F.'s sincere evocations and professions of religious faith. By the eighteenth century the word had lost its specifically religious denotation; atheists would be and are quite capable of referring to "good souls" or "poor souls." But it is arguable that when he came to the end of *A Journal of the Plague Year*, Defoe finally confronted the implications of an ethic based mainly on self-preservation and contemplated that self that was to be preserved. Citing the hundred thousand *souls* that perished in the 1665 plague is a way of acknowledging that however high a priority self-preservation may claim, it is also true that the body is a necessary but not sufficient criterion for selfhood.

THREE

The Diseased Soul in Chaucer, Boccaccio, and Poe

When Defoe wrote his advice about surviving pestilence—"I must leave it as a prescription, viz., that *the best physic against the plague is to run away from it*"—his choice of words suggests an indebtedness to a Renaissance translation (1620) of Giovanni Boccaccio's collection of stories, the *Decameron*. In describing the various ways in which the citizens of Florence coped with the Black Death, Boccaccio differentiates among different groups, one of which advocated what Defoe would later agree was sensible:

Some other there were also of more inhumane minde . . . saying, that there was no better physicke against the pestilence, nor yet so good, as to flie away from it.[1]

However much self-preservation may have conflicted with Christian doctrine, Defoe's judgment, influenced by his observations of how the plague spread in London, led him to this pragmatic solution. Boccaccio, on the other hand, distances himself from such a prescription in order to condemn it. Although both *A Journal of the Plague Year* and the *Decameron* make significant use of people's drive toward self-preservation, their treatment of self-interest as a basis for human action proceeds from different assumptions.

To move from Defoe's seventeenth-century to Geoffrey Chaucer's fourteenth-century London and to Giovanni Boccaccio's fourteenth-century Florence is to locate the earlier authors' treatment of bubonic plague in a context where it could be agreed that it was natural to make self-preservation a first law of existence, the sticking point being that it was not always good to be natural. In a world conceptually divided between the City of God and the City of Man—that is, the unearthly paradise of eternal truths, timelessness, and salvation as opposed to the temporal realm of history—absurdity emerges not from some void discovered in the quest for values beyond the mundane but from a reliance on a mutable, unstable world in which fortune appears to hold sway over those foolish enough to trust her.[2]

The image of fortune's wheel forms a major trope in medieval literature, its circularity implied when at the beginning of the First Day of the *Decameron* Boccaccio embroiders on a Biblical proverb: "And just as the end of mirth is heaviness, so sorrows are dispersed by the advent of joy." Neither the author nor his readers were likely to be fooled by the order in which these supposedly balanced opposites are presented (Chaucer's Pandarus slyly persuades Troilus that there is no better guarantee that he is about to climb back on fortune's wheel than that he has just been thrown off it). Since death was the end of everyone's personal history, to give the body priority over the soul was the height of folly. To ignore the soul altogether was even worse. And if even to describe this fourteenth-century view of things is to appear to preach a sermon much like that of Father Paneloux in Camus's *The Plague,* to ignore this view in any consideration of Boccaccio and Chaucer is to distort the contexts in which they wrote their works. One such context is the meaning and importance attributed to the human propensity to be seduced by fortune.[3]

Plagues that visit suddenly and rapidly kill their victims illustrate the swiftness with which good fortune may reverse itself. For Boccaccio, then, it is the most highly placed citizens of Florence who experience the greatest and hence most paradigmatic fall. Boccaccio elegiacally reminisces,

Ah, how great a number of splendid palaces, fine homes, and noble dwellings, once filled with retainers, with lords and with ladies, were bereft of all who had lived there, down to the tiniest child! How numerous were the famous families, the vast estates, the notable fortunes, that were seen to be left without a rightful successor! How many gallant gentlemen, fair ladies, and sprightly youths, who would have been judged hale and hearty by Galen, Hippocrates and Aesculapius (to say nothing of others), having breakfasted in the morning with their kinsfolk, acquaintances and friends, supped that same evening with their ancestors in the next world! (58)

Like Defoe, Boccaccio is looking up at a class to which he does not belong and describing what therefore is in part illusion, not reality. There is, however, in this description of an earlier bliss also a seemingly deliberate construction of a literary figure, an evocation of a paradisial existence and hence another expulsion from Eden.

Pestilence, traditionally conceived of as the result of the first fall and also the cause of subsequent symbolic falls, strains the tension between worldly and spiritual values, between civic duty and self-preservation. Such conflicts govern the two greatest of the medieval frame narratives, the *Decameron* and *The Canterbury Tales.* But whereas Boccaccio's vivid portrayal of disease-besieged Florence has made it an historical as well as literary text for studying the Black Death,[4] Chaucer appears to have restricted his treatment of the plague to a seemingly minor element in "The Pardoner's Tale."

Scholars have observed the disparity between the importance each author assigned to the plague; there is, however, something ingenuous about the critic who remarked that in the *Canterbury Tales*, "Chaucer uses the word *pestilence* nine times, but on three occasions it merely [!] means 'the highest degree of some moral evil.' "[5] A detailed argument that the plague is structurally intrinsic to "The Pardoner's Tale" was not made until 1982, when it was noted that among the many versions of a story told throughout the world, Chaucer's alone takes place during the plague.[6] Moreover, disease of both body and soul is as central to Chaucer's pilgrimage motif in *The Canterbury Tales* as bubonic plague is to Boccaccio's *Decameron*. In one collection, storytellers gather from every "shires ende" (l. 15) to begin a communal journal to a cathedral; in the other, storytellers begin in a church their flight to the countryside. Without depicting the plague in the same detail as Boccaccio, Chaucer supplies a meaningful context for considering the Black Death as a frame for the *Decameron* tales.

Chaucer's incomplete *Canterbury Tales* are arranged in groups of stories (with their prologues, epilogues, and links) called fragments. The sixth of these includes only two tales, the Physician's and the Pardoner's, very little in the voluminous Chaucer criticism being made of a conjunction that is, however, noteworthy.[7] The stories and their narrators are closely related, especially through the themes and images of disease, the tales acquiring significance from each other. The Physician relates how the daughter of Virginius, a young woman of beauty surpassed only by her virtue, is lusted after by a corrupt judge. The magistrate concocts a scheme to charge Virginius with having stolen a young maidservant from her master's home to pass her off subsequently as his daughter, and thus the father is brought to court and ordered to surrender his child. When Virginius realizes that his daughter's virginity will be forfeited, he tells her she must die rather than be dishonored—to which she acquiesces with sorrow but no hesitation. Death itself holds no horror for Virginia, although the story's subject, a father ready to execute his own daughter to preserve her virtue, may have contributed to the tale's reputation as one of Chaucer's least praiseworthy stories.[8]

In contrast, "The Pardoner's Tale" has been called one of "Chaucer's most remarkable productions,"[9] its source being the widely told folktale of the treasure finders who slay each other,[10] the "best short story in existence" according to F. N. Robinson.[11] In Chaucer's version, three men carousing in a tavern during the plague agree to set out to find death. Discovering a pile of gold under a tree, they ironically achieve their initial goal by greedily killing each other off for the the deadly loot. Chaucer's use of the plague as setting and metaphor—the equation of sin and pestilence—may have impressed itself on Defoe. Several years before composing his *Journal*, Defoe wrote a defense of literature in which he praised Chaucer's poetry. Significantly, in the same paragraph he pressed to doctors in his own time the value of the early writings of Aristotle, Galen, and other ancient writers on medicine[12]—a passage, in short, reminiscent of Chaucer's portrait of his "Doctour of Phisik":

> Wel knew he the olde Esculapius,
> And Deyscorides, and eek Rufus,
> Old Ypocras, Haly, and Galyen.

(ll. 629–31)

Given Defoe's high opinion of Chaucer, expressed in the context of a passage that echoes Chaucer's "General Prologue" to the *Canterbury Tales*, it is arguable that "The Pardoner's Tale" supplies a source for two major episodes in *A Journal of the Plague Year*. Chaucer's drunken blasphemers rioting in a tavern resemble the abusive revelers H. F. encounters in the same kind of place. And the three journeymen whose flight from London is detailed by H. F. embark on what is in effect an inversion of the trip depicted by Chaucer. Whereas Chaucer's three arrogantly seek death, Defoe's are attempting to escape it; Chaucer's are lawless by inclination, Defoe's law-abiding if they can be; Chaucer's are greedily self-interested, Defoe's willing to pool skills, wit, and financial resources for the good of the group; Chaucer's trio form a paradigm for the breakdown of an agreement, Defoe's provide an example of how the social contract can work. Chaucer illustrates people at their worst during a plague, whereas Defoe supplies a more optimistic depiction of human behavior under the same conditions.

Defoe's possible drawing on both the "Pardoner's Tale" and the portrait of the Physician highlights the thematic connection between the two stories in fragment 6 of the *Canterbury Tales*. At first look, the tales appear to have little in common. Nor do their narrators invite obvious comparison. The Pardoner, whose portrait is the last one painted in the "General Prologue," is repellent on every score, whereas Chaucer's doctor is probably no worse than the average in his profession for having benefited "in pestilence,"

> For gold in phisik is a cordial
> Therefore he lovede gold in special.

(ll. 442–44)

There was, as McNeill describes it, no particular remedy possessed by physicians to use against plagues, it not being until after about 1850 that science made real inroads in treatment and survival rates. Before that the "practical basis of the medical profession rested on psychology. Everyone felt better when self-confident, and expensive experts could be called in to handle a vital emergency."[13]

It might be necessary to draw a very discrete scale of values to differentiate the Physician from the Pardoner, who, in selling papal indulgences and fraudulent holy relics, profits from people's spiritual ills as the doctor does from their physical ones. But given the medieval priority of soul over body, the Pardoner's exploitation appears the worse. Moreover, his prologue proves to be a sales pitch as he encourages the other pilgrims to buy his indulgences, fear of plague making them even more valuable and hence more profitable.[14] The opposite would seem to be the case in linking the Physician to his tale. The story itself deemphasizes the survival of the body, and if the tale's moral implications are taken to their final point, then physicians themselves are rendered relatively unimportant. To invoke as an example of this logic Camus's Father Paneloux, the priest in *The Plague* eschews all medical care when he is stricken with the pestilence.

Given Chaucer's consistent subtlety, he is likely to have deliberately structured this inverse relationship between his two tellers and their tales precisely to focus on what are, nonetheless, striking similarities. Plague supplies the Physician with his gold, and gold in turn proves deadly when, in "The Pardoner's Tale," the three seekers after death find it and fall upon each other for its possession. And if the gold itself is the potential carrier of infection, as Peter Beidler hypothesizes as an explanation for why it just happened to be lying under the tree, then there is an additional connection between the Physician and the Pardoner's story. On the other hand, the moral diseases that the Pardoner both is prey to and exploits for his own gain links him to the the corrupt judge in "The Physician's Tale":

Of alle tresons sovereyn *pestilence*
Is whan a wight bitrayseth innocence.

(ll. 91–92; italics added)

It is, of course, fitting that the Physician tells a tale replete with images of disease. He describes Envye, which makes people sorry when others are fortunate, and "glad" of others' "sorwe" (sorrow) and "unheele" (bad health) (ll. 114–16). And when he portrays Nature, God's deputy, empowered to create a woman as beautiful as Virginia, he allows Nature to assert that those things that exist under the moon—that is, in the mutable physical world—are under her "cure" (l. 22), implying that he too possesses the remedy for earthly ills. Both Physician and Pardoner offer material solutions to a spiritually diseased world, but whereas the former is unabashedly worldly, the latter pretends he ministers to the soul.

A seemingly noteworthy contrast between the Physician and the Pardoner only serves ironically to point to an essential similarity between them. In the "General Prologue," Chaucer describes the eating habits of the doctor, whose concern for his body's well-being suggests that

> Of his diete mesurable was he,
> For it was of no superfluitee,
> But of greet norissyng and digestible.
>
> (ll. 435–37)

This is immediately followed by the seemingly irrelevant "His studie was but litel on the Bible." But the addition is far from a non sequitur. Despite the Physician's disdain for rich food and his repudiation of the gluttony that virtually defines the Pardoner, it is clear that both are *worldly* men. Both are concerned with food, even if one eats little and the other gorges himself. It is Shakespeare who supplies the best gloss on the Physician and Pardoner when he writes a sonnet to this point:

> Shall worms, inheritors of this excess,
> Eat up thy charge? Is this thy body's end?
> Then, soul, live thou upon thy servant's loss,
> And let [the body] pine to aggravate thy store,
> Buy terms divine in selling hours of dross;
> Within be fed, without be rich no more.

Despite the Pardoner's railing against gluttony and drunkenness, his tale reveals his obsession with the pleasures of food and drink. His imagined earthly paradise would be a three-star gourmet restaurant. With his inimitible wit, Chaucer even allows the Pardoner to reinterpret the fall: the sin that motivates the eating of the forbidden fruit is no longer pride:

> For whil that Adam fasted, as I rede,
> He was in Paradys; and whan that he
> Eet of the fruyt deffended on the tree,
> Anon he was out cast to wo and peyne.
> O glotonye, on thee wel oughte us pleyne!
>
> (ll. 508–12)

At the same time, the Pardoner disclaims his own sin by turning Christian doctrine against the pilgrims he hopes to frighten into buying his indulgences and relics. He compares the corrupt human body to that of soulless beasts. In a Swiftian image of the cycle of eating and excreting, he describes —in a line whose own extra syllables suggest excess—the chefs who prepare earthly delights in terms reminiscent of the Physician's disdain of "superfluitee":

> Thise cookes, how they stampe, and streyne, and grynde,
> And turnen substaunce into accident,
> To fulfille all thy [lecherous] talent!

(ll. 538–40)

To turn substance into accident is to give external form to what previously was unformed, to transform spirit into matter, to reduce eternal truths to their ephemeral physical manifestations. As Robert P. Miller has written of the "Pardoner's Tale," what "we now call realism was of itself only a point of departure in a world where man's sensible experience consistently reflected the presence and nature of his Creator—whose reality itself lay beneath the sign." [15] Many of the pilgrims fall short of recognizing this principle, but the Pardoner is truly obscene in his concentration on the physical.

For in every move he makes, every doctrine he preaches, every sin he admits to, the Pardoner turns "substaunce into accident," spiritual reality into *only* and thus *merely* its physical manifestations. From his worldliness follows a monistic depiction of human beings as nothing more than their bodies, although, paradoxically, he cynically exploits for material gain the terrors of those who, despite their own physical excesses, fear for their souls:

> For myn entente is nat but for to wynne,
> And nothyng for correccioun of synne.
> I rekke nevere, whan that they been beryed,
> Though that hir soules goon a-blakeberyed!

(ll. 403–6)

Even his disdain for the spiritual destinies of those he hoodwinks is expressed in an image of food.

Only the demise of the body would frighten the Pardoner, and it is fitting that he tells of three men whose quest it is to search out and destroy death itself. And here it is, once again, that—as Gordon Whatley has pointed out —the "Physician's Tale" proves a fitting companion for the Pardoner's. Virginia's willing submission to her father's decree reveals that she knows, as the Pardoner's three searchers do not, how to defeat death. The traditional solution that she would take for granted appears in the concluding paradox of the Shakespearean sonnet quoted above:

> So shalt [the soul] feed on death, that feeds on men,
> And death once dead, there's no more dying then.

In the very depiction of the beauty that eventually leads to Virginia's martyrdom is the reminder of how physical decay and death eventually overtake even the most beautiful example of the human body. Nature tells how God

> Hath maked me his vicaire general,
> To forme and peynten erthely creaturis
> Right as me list, and ech thyng in my cure is
> Under the moone, that may wane and waxe.
>
> (ll. 20–23)

But like the Physician's, Nature's power to "cure" is limited. The "Physician's Tale" parallels Virginia's creation with the story of Pygmalion and Galatea, the analogy serving as a further illustration of how the body is no more—at best—than an empty doll unless completed by the soul, whose survival is the point of the Canterbury pilgrimage.

There is in Chaucer criticism an ongoing debate about whether his pilgrim narrators are typical or individual, whether he had particular persons in mind or was creating fictional representatives of their class and profession. Claims on behalf of the pilgrims as individualized portraits constitute an argument that *The Canterbury Tales* is a landmark in a growing awareness of a self that can claim uniqueness. This may be partially true: Chaucer's tales and their relationship to their narrators seem to yield to an inexhaustible analysis that stands up under any number of modern psychological approaches. But it is also true that the Christian doctrines that inform these tales require a modification of such psychological studies. The motifs of pestilence, which join a tale told by one of the most morally diseased narrators on the pilgrimage to that told by a worldly doctor, draw attention to the distinction between body and soul and reaffirm the priority of spirit over flesh.

To move backward from the tales to Chaucer's "General Prologue" is to recognize that physical and moral disease is a given that informs the Canterbury pilgrimage as well as the role of storytelling in a pestilential world. The essentially fallen state of his pilgrims is intrinsic to Chaucer's description of how they gathered from all over England to begin their journey to the shrine of Becket:

[Pilgrims] from every shires ende
Of Engelond to Caunterbury they wende,
The hooly blisful martir for to seke,
That hem hath holpen whan that they were seeke.

(ll. 15–18)

This juxtaposition of "seke" (seek) and "seeke" (sick)—pronounced almost alike—reinforces the associations between the diseases of the soul and the body, the pilgrimage as both a spiritual quest and a striving for physical health. What McNeill has said of pilgrimages and epidemics provides an additional context for reading Chaucer's work:

More generally, religious pilgrimages rivaled warfare in provoking epidemic infection. . . . Part of the meaning of pilgrimage was the taking of risks in pursuit of holiness. To die en route was, for the pious, an act of God whereby He deliberately translated the pilgrim from the hardships of life on earth into His presence. Disease and pilgrimage were thus psychologically as well as epidemiologically complementary.[16]

However, as individuals, they view their own motives for undertaking the trip to Canterbury, Chaucer's pilgrims agree to amuse themselves on the road to the cathedral and back by telling stories. When they return, the host of the inn at which they stay will judge the tales and award a prize to the best. It is important to understand, first, that the storytelling itself is placed squarely within a framework of their diseased condition:

Ye goon to Caunterbury—God yow speede,
The blisful martir quite yow youre meede!
And well I woot, as ye goon by the weye,
Ye shapen yow to talen and to pleye.

(ll. 769–72)

(You go to Canterbury—God speed you, and may the heavenly martyr reward you. And I know that as you go along the way, you intend to converse and amuse yourself.)

It is moreover implicit in the critical standards by which the host is bound that the curative potential of the narratives must influence his judgment:

And which of yow that bereth hym best of alle,
That is to seyn, that telleth in this caas
Tales of best sentence and most solaas,
Shall have a soper at oure aller cost.

(ll. 796–99)

(And the one of you that conducts himself best, that is to say, who tells a story that best combines meaning [moral content] and solace [enjoyment] will have supper as guest of the rest of us.)

At the end of the *Canterbury Tales* the pilgrims would have gathered for the last time to partake of a dinner that represents their shared plight as mortals in a world that necessitates pilgrimages, their mutual experiences on the journey, their shared pleasure in story itself, and their common enlightenment. This conclusion is foreshadowed in the ending of the "Pardoner's Tale" in which the Host, despite his revulsion and fury towards the Pardoner, nonetheless agrees to bestow a kiss of reconciliation and friendship, an image of charity.

The Host's charity as well as the figure of the communal dinner can also serve as a reminder that the Canterbury pilgrims worshipped in the same church. Despite any theological debates that might have been ongoing, God was essentially present in a unified Catholic world. In contrast, Defoe's Protestantism forced H. F. to turn inward to discover God's mandate concerning whether or not he should stay in London despite the plague or leave the city in the hope of saving his life. How comfortable H. F. is with the grounds for his own decision and his later uncertainty continue to occupy Defoe critics. The existentialist themes modern scholars find in Defoe's *Journal,* the alienation among the plague-besieged citizens of London described by H. F., are traceable to factors brought about by the Reformation, with its deemphasis on church authority and stress on the individual conscience that had as a result the isolation of worshippers from each other. It is noteworthy that this existential loneliness and its particular manifestation in a plague setting should supply the grounds for a comparison of Defoe and Camus. The two writers share the modern theme of the alienated individual, an antithesis of which is the common religious bonds that would unite — despite class and professional differences — Chaucer's medieval Catholic pilgrims.

Yet, the pilgrims' proposed regathering at the tavern from which they began their pilgrimage also creates a strong secular image in which those forces that separate self from other are diminished. At the end of *The Plague,* Camus describes the relief of a pestilence-besieged town when the disease has abated and a quarantine has been lifted. Many surviving citizens congregate in a cafe, fear of contagion gone. "Tomorrow," notes Camus's physician-narrator, "real life would begin again, with its restrictions. But for the moment people in very different walks of life were rubbing shoulders, fraternizing" (267). Here is another example of the importance of others in the world of the self. The scene with which Chaucer apparently intended to close his *Canterbury Tales* and that Camus includes in the ending of his novel, is precisely the one missing from the "Conclusion" of Boccaccio's

Decameron. Storytelling over, his ten narrators *separate* as they prepare to face once again the Black Death from which they fled. The "three young men went off in search of other diversions; and in due course the ladies returned to their homes" (827).[17]

Like Chaucer, Boccaccio wrote within a tradition in which storytelling should serve as a tool in the quest for salvation, should provide both "sentence" and "solaas." As he states in his *Genealogy*, which contains his aesthetics, "such then is the power of fiction that it pleases the unlearned by its external appearance, and exercises the minds of the learned with its hidden truth; and thus both are edified and delighted with one and the same perusal." In the earthly city, poetry can promote civic virtue, "can arm kings, marshal them for war, launch whole fleets from their docks, nay, counterfeit sky, land, sea, adorn young maidens with flowery garlands, portray human character in its various phases, awake the idle, stimulate the dull, restrain the rash, subdue the criminal, and distinguish excellent men with their proper meed of praise." But in contrast to literature that "has to do with many high and noble matters," there is a kind that "contains no truth at all, either superficial or hidden, since it consists only of old wives' tales."[18] That is, literature of "solaas" without any accompanying "sentence."

Because so many of the stories in the *Decameron* appear to fit this latter category, pleasing, often pleasing a great deal, but hardly enlightening the audience on specific doctrine, and because, in any event, there is no obvious fit between the stories and the Black Death that Boccaccio insists is a necessary frame for his work, as there is between Chaucer's pilgrimage and the Physician's and Pardoner's tales, the connection of the plague to Boccaccio's narratives is difficult to define. Considerable controversy exists concerning Boccaccio's intentions with regard to the *Decameron.*[19] Even if the work illustrates the "marginality" of literature in a plague-stricken world,[20] pleasure expanding to fill the space created when "sentence" retreats from "solaas," this very illustration sustains the presence of moral concern on the part of the author who contemplates the role of literature in human affairs. But if there is such a marked "discontinuity between art and life"[21] as to reduce literature to entertainment alone, then it would be true, as some scholars argue and some just imply, that the frame of the *Decameron* is a mere narrative device to explain how seven noble women and three noble men of Florence (referred to as Boccaccio's brigada) happened to leave the plague-besieged city and amuse themselves by telling the hundred stories that make up the collection.

There has been an attempt to displace the Black Death as the frame for the *Decameron*. Completely aestheticizing Boccaccio's work, the argument is that the pestilence exists *outside* the frame, which is constituted instead of the brigada and their beautiful, idyllic world of country villas and gardens, an appropriate setting for storytelling.[22] Boccaccio, however, does not make it easy completely to ignore the shadow of the plague that he depicts in such careful detail, although many try. As recently as 1982 it was possible for Aldo Bernardo to write,

No one can doubt the central importance of the so-called frame story in defining the basic structure of Boccaccio's masterpiece. Yet, while admitting such importance few critics have done more than consider these portions embarrassing but necessary intrusions that constitute one of the work's imperfections. The stories, for such critics, are all that really matter.[23]

Only a decade earlier Giuseppe Mazzotta had made the point that there had been "no sustained examination of Boccaccio's reflections on the meaning of literature in the *Decameron*."[24] Both Bernardo and Mazzotta offer an important alternative to a critical approach that takes the *Decameron* to be a collection whose stories exist only to provide pleasure during leisure time, a respite from reality. What is still needed is a reading that reconciles Boccaccio's use of the Black Death as his frame for the *Decameron* with the ethical component in his literary theories, and both of these with the collection of tales.[25] Such an endeavor would necessitate more than this chapter can devote to Boccaccio, but the following discussion will take as a presupposition that the author of the *Decameron* was working with the same assumptions about literature as Chaucer—they were assumptions that were to prevail until the romantic period—and that Boccaccio too would consider moral pestilence the hidden (perhaps not so hidden) trope behind the Black Death.

If there is a disjunction between Boccaccio's frame and his tales, it is not because he propounds an art whose sole raison d'être is pleasure, but because he may have been skeptical about the positive force literature can hope to exercise in the face of calamity. Moreover, there is no inherent contradiction between such skepticism and the pleasure Boccaccio might have taken in writing his witty, sometimes frolicking, often bawdy stories, or in his identifying himself as author with the brigada that escaped from the Black Death into the luscious gardens where artifice seems to triumph over nature, one aspect of which is plagues. That Boccaccio made no denial of his own pleasure seeking, his own participation in what Mazzotta calls a world at play, does not mean he failed to accept the priority of the soul over the body. Boccaccio never exempted himself from the condition of fallen humanity. As any artist might, he may have experienced *more* than the usual conflict between flesh and spirit.

But Boccaccio was also writing about the city that in his time was almost synonymous with the idea of civic virtue—as Pocock has so persuasively argued. Boccaccio's concern for how Florence as a whole behaved during the plague may illuminate the first and last lines of the *Decameron*—effectively, its dedication:

Here begins the book called *Decameron*, otherwise known as Prince Galahalt, wherein are contained a hundred stories, told in ten days by seven ladies and three young men. (45)

Here ends the Tenth and last Day of the book called *Decameron*, otherwise known as Prince Galahalt. (833)

Boccaccio's allusion is, as his critics point out, to the author of a book read by Paolo and Francesca, the lovers immortalized in literature when Dante placed them in the first circle of his inferno. It was in this book that they read the tale of Lancelot and Guinevere, inspired by it to begin their own adulterous love affair, the author Prince Galahalt thus effectively playing Pandarus to the couple. Just as Chaucer eventually retracted his secular works of literature, all of those writings whose pleasing aspect may have overshadowed their doctrinal intent, so may Boccaccio have invoked Prince Galahalt as moral commentary on the stories of the *Decameron*.[26]

For the importance of Florence itself, the dedication to Prince Galahalt may have further implications. There are in the medieval Arthurian tales two renowned pairs of adulterous lovers, Tristram and Isolde, and Lancelot and Guinevere, both pairs supplying art with subject matter persistent over centuries. But it is arguable that there is a significant difference between the famous couples. One of them illustrates the gratification of self to the final end of self-destruction. Tristram's and Isolde's was a personal sin, however much it embroiled other members of their society and wronged their spouses. Mark may have been king, but Cornwall's survival is not predicated on Isolde's fidelity to her husband. But Arthur was virtually synonymous with Camelot, and for some writers, Guinevere's adulterous love for Lancelot brought down an entire city, which itself then became a major character in the drama. A similar contrast between the private and public may be implied in Boccaccio's allusion to the pairing of Paolo and Francesca with Lancelot and Guinevere. For as London is the protagonist of Defoe's *Journal of the Plague Year*, so is plague-beleaguered Florence in

Day One of the *Decameron,* until its ten citizens leave it to create their fictive enclave outside the city.

The structure of the *Decameron* is almost as complex as that of *The Canterbury Tales,* consisting as it does of a dedication, preface, thematic frame, daily discussions among the brigada, songs that end each day's activities, a conclusion, and, of course, the one hundred stories. The opening words, however, create an ethical rather than aesthetic context for what follows:

To take pity on people in distress is a human quality which every man and woman should possess, but it is especially requisite in those who have once needed comfort, and found it in others. (45)

This somber beginning appears mitigated by what follows, Boccaccio's applying of these words to the lovesick young women for whose supposed benefit the stories to follow are being related. In reading the stories, the

ladies will be able to derive, not only pleasure from the entertaining matters therein set forth, but also some useful advice. For they will learn to recognize what should be avoided and likewise what should be pursued, and these things can only lead, in my opinion, to the removal of their affliction. (47)

There appears to be some tongue-in-cheek irony in Boccaccio's presentation of his literary endeavor; but this does not obviate some weighty issues behind his partially facetious words, a virtually satiric version of Chaucer's "sentence and sólaas." Critics have tended to be content that Boccaccio equates the affliction of his female readers to their lovesickness, that is, the failures of their erotic life. But—as will be seen—love as an idea could not so easily be confined to Eros. Why would it be essential that romantic love be almost immediately placed in the context of the Black Death and the behavior of Florence's citizens toward each other, their decided lack of love as they abandoned each other to the plague?

For taking pity on another's distress is the one thing Florence's citizens did not do:

Almost without exception, they took a single and very inhuman precaution, namely to avoid or run away from the sick and their belongings, by which means they all thought that their own health would be preserved. (52)

If so, then Boccaccio's distinction between the positive *human* quality he extolls in virtually the opening words of the *Decameron,* and the *inhuman* behavior of those whose precautions against the plague involved fleeing other human beings, establishes a moral framework for the *Decameron* that cannot be overlooked. For whereas Defoe, for example, is virtually forced to invoke the "soul" at the end of the *Journal* in order to avoid reducing persons to their bodies, Boccaccio would take for granted that self-preservation must extend to spiritual salvation. It has already been suggested that a source for Defoe's description of London during the plague was a translation of the *Decameron*. That is, similarities between Defoe and Boccaccio go beyond a shared subject matter likely to result in comparable narratives. But even without this direct connection, the two writers warrant more specific comparison than they have received.

Both Boccaccio and Defoe describe the bubonic form of the plague and each author supplies a detailed description of the swellings and dark blotches that became the visible signs of impending death. Neither author can draw on a germ theory of disease, but for each, person-to-person transmission is both a literal and thus a potentially morally charged fact. Boccaccio's image of how quickly the disease spread—"what made this pestilence even more severe was that whenever those suffering from it mixed with people who were still unaffected, it would rush upon these with the speed of a fire racing through dry or oily substances that happened to be placed within its reach" (51)—may have particularly impressed itself on Defoe. The great London fire only added to the city's misery, even if, as some although not Defoe thought, it put an end to the pestilence. Defoe, too, compares the spread of the 1665 plague at its height to raging, spreading flames.

Both authors speculate about the cause of the plague; Boccaccio contrasts his version of Defoe's "means," that is, astrological influences, with God's anger:

Some say that it descended upon the human race through the influence of the heavenly bodies, others that it was a punishment signifying God's righteous anger at our iniquitous way of life. But whatever its cause, it had originated some years earlier in the East, where it had claimed countless lives before it unhappily spread westward, growing in strength as it swept relentlessly on from one place to the next. (50)

Boccaccio is rather offhanded about the distinction between the "influence of heavenly bodies" and "God's righteous anger," probably because he felt less pressure than Defoe to weigh the rival claims of science or naturalistic agencies and religion. For Boccaccio, the issue is not what brought the plague but how the citizens of Florence responded to it. And if, as has been argued, Florence launched a more organized and charitable drive against the plague than Boccaccio's account would indicate,[27] then this claim should only heighten a realization that Boccaccio may have painted the worst possible picture to punish those citizens who fell short of an ethical ideal, to increase the tension in the *Decameron* between play and that which is deadly serious.

Like Defoe after him, Boccaccio surveys the various methods people used to counter the pestilence. There were those who shut themselves up:

They formed themselves into groups and lived in isolation from everyone else. Having withdrawn to a comfortable abode where there were no sick persons, they locked themselves in and settled down to a peaceable existence, consuming modest quantities of delicate foods and precious wines and avoiding all excesses. They refrained from speaking to outsiders, refused to receive news of the dead or the sick, and entertained themselves with music or whatever other amusements they were able to devise. (52)

Others were more hedonistic in their desperation, believing that "an infallible way of warding off this appalling evil was to drink heavily, enjoy life to the full, go round singing and merrymaking, gratify all of one's cravings whenever the opportunity offered, and shrug the whole thing off as one enormous joke" (52). In their "riotous manner of living," such revelers prefigure the tavern brawlers in Chaucer's "Pardoner's Tale" and Defoe's *Journal.* But a large part of Florence's population "steered a middle course between the two already mentioned," and adopted folk remedies, such as walking about with spices or fragrant herbs, not only to protect themselves but also to drive away the "stench of dead bodies" (53).

No remedies were effective, not even "the countless petitions humbly directed to God by the pious." But whereas Defoe indicates that medical knowledge and techniques (such as the lancing of buboes) were minimally effective, in Boccaccio's fourteenth-century Florence, "all the advice of physicians and all the power of medicine were profitless and unavailing." Boccaccio, too, seeks naturalistic explanations for the failure of human endeavor against the plague:

Perhaps the nature of the illness was such that it allowed no remedy: or perhaps those people who were treating the illness (whose numbers had increased enormously because the ranks of the qualified were invaded by people, both men and women, who had never received any training in medicine), being ignorant of its causes, were not prescribing the appropriate cure. (51)

Whatever the case, "few of those who caught [the disease] ever recovered."

Like Defoe, Boccaccio constructs a powerful account of a city seized by desperation, unable to cope with what was happening. He tells of people whose families cannot and will not help them and who are thus left to the greed of servants and nurses, who were in any event in short supply and who, when they did accept the high wages offered, could do little. Boccaccio's depiction is strikingly like Defoe's as he turns to the largest sectors of the afflicted population:

As for the common people and a large proportion of the bourgeoisie, they presented a much more pathetic spectacle, for the majority of them were constrained, either by their poverty or the hope of survival, to remain in their houses. Being confined to their own parts of the city, they fell ill daily in the thousands, and since they had no one to assist them or attend to their needs, they inevitably perished almost without exception. Many dropped dead in the open streets, both by day and by night, whilst a great many others, though dying in their own houses, drew their neighbours' attention to the fact more by the smell of their rotting corpses than by any other means. And what with these, and the others who were dying all over the city, bodies were here, there and everywhere. (55–56)

The ambiguity in this description concerns the disparity between the effectiveness of human intervention against the disease and the horror of people left without assistance as they died. Human bonding is elevated to a principle that transcends pragmatic effectiveness.

Defoe critics frequently point to London's burial pits as among the most horrifying of Defoe's descriptions. It is his burning curiosity about this dread sight that virtually drives H. F. to witness the mass burials. Boccaccio is much briefer and more restrained, but no less horrific on this point:

Such was the multitude of corpses (of which further consignments were arriving every day and almost by the hour at each of the churches), that there was not sufficient consecrated ground for them to be buried in, especially if each was to have its own plot in accordance with long-established custom. So when all the graves were full, huge trenches were excavated in the churchyards, into which new arrivals were placed in their hundreds, stowed tier upon tier like ships' cargo, each layer of corpses being covered over with a thin layer of soil till the trench was filled to the top. (56–57)

It is, however, from these very comparisons that contrasts between Defoe and Boccaccio emerge. There is, for example, a difference in the way the disease is socially constructed in the *Decameron*, as well as a difference in the tone of the narrator. Having defined the "inhumanity" of Florence's citizens, Boccaccio is less concerned to differentiate the classes—all people behaved much the same, badly. And, again, the upper classes served better than the poor or bourgeoisie to illustrate the capricious workings of fortune, their fall being so precipitous. Moreover, the organization of Florence society into classes would have been different from any comparable organization of London. In medieval Florence, the middle class was rising in number and power, but not to the point it had reached in London by 1722, when Defoe published his *Journal*. Nor did Boccaccio explicitly identify himself with a particular class, as does Defoe's persona, H. F. Boccaccio reports neutrally, for example, on a point that must have resonated strongly in Defoe's property-conscious point of view: describing the revelers in Florence, Boccaccio notes that they had to find places for their pursuits of pleasure and that "most houses had become common property, and any passing stranger could make himself at home as naturally as though he were the rightful owner" (52).

In general, Boccaccio remains aloof in his description of the plague, in part, of course, because he is not keeping a private journal but is instead writing a history of events already past. Not that he lacks sympathy for Florence's sufferers: he writes, "The more I reflect upon all this misery, the deeper my sense of personal sorrow" (58). But he is not being called upon to act, to decide himself whether to stay in Florence or leave. A good example of the difference between Boccaccio as his own narrator and H. F. concerns the latter's prescription that running away from the plague was the best medicine against it, a remedy that Boccaccio—again—deems inhuman.

Because Defoe gives more weight than Boccaccio to self-preservation, that is, the survival of the body; because his aim in the *Journal* is in fact prescriptive, since he worries that in his own time (more than fifty years after the 1665 plague) London might import the plague from Marseilles; and because he believes London would be better served by his emphasizing the benevolence of its citizens, he illustrates the efficacy of a social contract adhered to because the good of the individual resides in the welfare of the group. Moreover, the *Journal* derives much of its pathos from Defoe's vignettes of family members tenderly ministering to each other, or sacrificing themselves for or being driven frantic by fear for each other. In contrast, Boccaccio is punitive rather than ameliorative in his condemnation of the city, portraying a wholesale breakdown of both social and familial relations:

It was not merely a question of one citizen avoiding another, and of people almost invariably neglecting their neighbours and rarely or never visiting their relatives, addressing them only from a distance; this scourge had implanted so great a terror in the hearts of men and women that brothers abandoned brothers, uncles their nephews, sisters their brothers, and in many cases wives deserted their husbands. But even worse, and almost incredible, was the fact that fathers and mothers refused to nurse and assist their own children, as though they did not belong to them. (53–54)

It is not, however, until seven of Boccaccio's storytellers, the women, meet in the church of Santa Maria Novella that the principle that operates among the citizens of Florence is enunciated as a doctrine, self-preservation.

Before continuing this discussion of self-preservation in the *Decameron*, it will be useful quickly to survey the related controversies that surround Boccaccio's work, arguments that show no sign of abating in the future. Such an overview is almost required of any analysis of the *Decameron*, because no approach to Boccaccio's work is likely to satisfy any critic save one who is predisposed to follow that critical path. But the arguments are themselves illuminating insofar as they form the dialectic that actually emerges from plague literature, the debaters serving as projections of the tension between ethics and aesthetics.

Critiques of the *Decameron* are likely to proceed—directly or indirectly —from the question of whether Boccaccio is to be placed unequivocally among medieval writers or (even allowing for qualifications) among Renaissance humanists—whether, in short, the City of Man is believed to have overshadowed the City of God by the time he wrote. Those who view the *Decameron* as a secular work will contrast the pastoral idyll Boccaccio creates for his storytellers with the "austere, world denying teachings of the medieval church."[28] It can also be argued that the brigada is guilty of no moral lapses during their stay away from Florence (that is, no sexual indiscretions), something in itself remarkable given the general licentiousness loosed by the plague: "cut off from the general deterioration in civil and moral codes of conduct which had attended the spread of the disease," they "move in a serene and peaceful aristocratic ambience."[29] In contrast, the critical opposition contends that in asking "what distinguishes the behavior of Boccaccio's *brigata* from the general run of the phantom-like figures that remained to face the horrors of the plague, the answer must be the ingenuity of the young people not only in avoiding contact with the pestilence but in enjoying themselves thoroughly during those terrible days." Their immorality thus has deeper roots in the "exemplification of the false good whose self-centredness is the exact opposite of the Christian doctrine and life."[30]

Some conception of the presence or absence in the *Decameron* of an essentially fallen world in which self-preservation marks the alienation of the individual soul from God will determine how one interprets the garden settings for Boccaccio's storytellers. There are many pastoral places in the work, but it is in the introduction to the third day's storytelling that the most paradisial of them is described. But much of its significance comes from the conclusion of Day Two, when one of the brigada suggests in effect that they duplicate their initial flight from Florence:

It will then be four days since we came to stay here, and in order to avoid being joined by others, I think it advisable for us to move elsewhere. I have already thought of a place for us to go, and made the necessary arrangements. (229)

The place to which she refers is a splendid villa with a walled garden so beautiful that the brigada believes "that if Paradise were constructed on earth, it was inconceivable that it could take any other form, nor could they imagine any way in which the garden's beauty could possibly be enhanced" (233).

Boccaccio's description of this bower of bliss is extensively detailed. All the senses are appealed to: the sight of unspoiled nature; the scent of herbs and flowers such as roses and jasmine; the promised taste of wine derived from the abundant crop of grapes yielded by vines already in flower; the sound of twenty varieties of birds, singing as if in a contest; and, implicitly, the touch of water that gushes from a jet of water "before cascading downwards and falling with a delectable splash into the crystal-clear pool below" (232). In addition to this sensuous delight is God's plenitude, for apart from "perfectly charming animals" the brigada witnesses "numerous harmless creatures of many other kinds, roaming about at leisure as though they were quite tame" (233; quasi dimestichi andarsi a sollazzo). This qualification—"as though they were"—is puzzling. Is this Boccaccio's reminder, to use the words of A. Bartlett Giamatti, that "the earthly paradise is absolutely unobtainable, that it is irrevocably lost,"[31] that however beautiful the literary garden of the Renaissance, it is in fact a false paradise?

As symbol and setting, the false paradise embodies the split between what seems and what is; it looks like the true earthly paradise, but in the end it is not. It looks like the image of all a man thinks he has sought in his spiritual wanderings, but in the end it is the scene in which he learns he was wrong; where he learns that his inner wishes were only the illusions a man creates for himself, and through which he must pass in his quest for true inner harmony, for a true earthly paradise existence.[32]

Behind such an earthly paradise tradition, writes Giamatti, stands its essential source, Genesis.[33] Thus it is difficult to substitute a purely psychological account of the fall, one "into fear and loneliness, and man's sense of distance from the place of that Fall,"[34] for an historical or spiritually understood fall into sin, of which plague constitutes both a punishment and reminder. For the fall to be understood in Christian terms means that Christian ethics must be invoked as a guide to human interaction. To return to the "crystal-clear pool" of Boccaccio's garden, Charles Dahlberg has described another source for gardens in medieval and Renaissance literature, the *Roman de la Rose*. In the midst of a garden that makes a similarly sensuous appeal, the *Roman* places "the mirroring fountain of Narcissus, wherein lie the 'two crystal stones' which suggest the eyes of the flesh."[35] It has already been noted that the song with which the first day of storytelling ends in the *Decameron* is one in which self-love is celebrated and the lyric voice of the song looks in her glass to celebrate her own beauty: "To no other love could I / My fond affections plight" (113). If the myth of Narcissus is implied by the image of the mirrorlike pool of Boccaccio's garden, then the figure of the garden itself is a fitting symbol for the brigada's second retreat from human concerns. What had begun as an attempt to save their own lives has become a more aggressive disavowal of a need to be concerned for others. The tame animals that roam the garden as their companions may thus be a disquieting image of the brigada itself, especially given that Boccaccio had already equated being human (that is, not animal) with taking pity on others in distress.

There are more ameliorative views of the various garden settings in the *Decameron*. R. Hastings points out that the plague took a psychological as well as physical toll on the inhabitants of the city, and that many medieval physicians advocated pleasure for medical reasons:

In fleeing from Florence to the country so as to escape from the plague and to recover emotionally from its horrors through the salutary effect of storytelling in congenial company and of other similarly enjoyable cultural pursuits . . . the narrators are taking part in the sorts of activity specifically recommended in medical treatises of the time for the dispelling of anxiety and depression . . . particularly beneficial for those seeking to recover from the traumas of the plague.[36]

Implied here is a belief that mental states affect the body and hence its susceptibility to the plague. And still another argument has it that the gardens in Boccaccio's frames are not false paradises and that they differ from each other as they lead the brigada away from the "sufferings and horrors" of the city to a "traditional garden of love," and from there to a "more remote, more sensuous earthly paradise," and finally to the "nearly perfect Sanctuary of Venus Genetrix" in which are proclaimed the "laws of Love and Nature."[37] How these laws of generation relate to the inexorable advance of the plague is, however, not part of this account, perhaps another instance in which, as Bernardo points out, the plague itself becomes a critical inconvenience. Conceivably, one *could* argue that Boccaccio is depicting a cycle of life and death in treating the gardens as an antithesis to plague-stricken Florence. But this would not obviate the ethical questions that adhere to a tension between earthly and unearthly paradises.

There are, then, two ways in which the garden settings of the *Decameron* can be and have been interpreted. According to one view, the gardens provide a model for the ideal earthly state, a reminder in times of plague of how life might be. The retreat from Florence can be conceived of as a movement towards a "healthy environment," a "passage from corruption and chaos to social order and civilized living."[38] But according to the contrasting view, the gardens are, at best, external projections of human desires whose chief harm is psychological, reinforcing a tragic awareness of what has been irrevocably lost and is forever unreachable; or, at worst, they are misleadingly illusory and hence spiritually pernicious places in which the fall is reenacted over and over. From this point of view, as Bernardo has argued, the brigada's

carefully-organized miniature society, with its air of aristocratic sophistication, is interested only in a reality created exclusively for its personal gratification. But since the roots of such a reality were firmly anchored in the horrors of the plague, the group's hedonism had to reflect a moral and spiritual truancy that was readily recognizable by any reader aware of the Christian ethic.[39]

It is a testament to Boccaccio's subtlety that scholarly arguments parallel the tensions in his own aesthetic theories and in the seemingly uneasy relationship of his frame to the stories of the *Decameron*. Any consideration of the ethic of self-preservation that stands behind the brigada's exodus from Florence will inevitably be extensions of stands taken in addressing such conflicts.

It is probably not insignificant that the member of the brigada who advocates a plan of action already deemed inhuman is a woman. Despite Boccaccio's tenderness for or ministering to what was traditionally viewed as the weaker sex, a strong antifeminist tradition would contend that women were weaker-willed than men, less ready to make moral considerations rather than self-interest the basis for action. That a woman could make the logical case for self-preservation in an argument whose intellectual strength is impressive is no disqualification of such an antifeminist view. Eve, it will be remembered, disobeyed God to eat from the tree of knowledge.

When Pampinea addresses the other six young women who, with her, will make up the female members of the brigada, she begins straightforwardly by evoking their shared self-interest in surviving the plague. Significantly, she adopts a masculine point of view in her argument, eschewing woman's supposedly civilizing role as tamer of the human animal.

Dear ladies, you will often have heard it affirmed, as I have, that no man does injury to another in exercising his lawful rights. Every person born into this world has a natural right to sustain, preserve, and defend his own life to the best of his ability— a right so freely acknowledged that men have sometimes killed others in self-defence, and no blame whatever has attached to their actions. Now, if this is permitted by the laws, upon whose prompt application all moral creatures depend for their well-being, how can it possibly be wrong, seeing that it harms no one, for us or anyone else to do all in our power to preserve our lives? (59)

There is an initial irony in her immediately following this plea by reminding the others that they have just attended morning services at church.

Perhaps a useful gloss for this irony is the early part of a work written about the same time as the *Decameron, Sir Gawain and the Green Knight,* in which the knights of Camelot attend religious services, and—"the chanting in chapel" perfunctorily "achieved and ended"—hurry on to a Christmas party whose essence is play. Gawain's journey away from Camelot to almost certain death can be read as an inverted version of the brigada's retreat from Florence, for what Gawain learns about himself in a resplendent castle comparable to the villas of the *Decameron* is that he has overvalued his life. In a desperate effort to prolong his earthly existence, he had accepted the gift of a green belt magically supposed to safeguard anyone who wears it, hiding it from the person to whom he is honor-bound to hand it over. His subsequent shame is ameliorated by the soothing assurance that his motive, self-preservation, warrants only minimal condemnation:

But the cause was not cunning, nor courtship either,
But that you loved your own life; the less, then, to blame.

But Gawain knows better, and he returns to Camelot, the belt, the sign of his shame, appropriately to be worn on the *body* whose priority he had placed above honor—that is, his soul. That the court turns Gawain's profound self-awareness into but another game, just as it had gotten divine services out of the way in order to enjoy a party, may be the Gawain-poet's expression of skepticism concerning whether his poem will be read for its doctrine as well as its fun. For if there was ever a medieval work in which games formed a major theme as well as structural device, or one in which the sheer delight of the narrative would appeal to the play instincts of the reader, threatening to obliterate what is doctrinally significant in its meaning, it is this contemporary of the *Decameron*. If at one point in the *Canterbury Tales* Chaucer tells his readers not to make "ernest of game," *Sir Gawain*, so full of games itself, warns against making play of that which is serious. To study *homo ludens* in the *Decameron* requires consideration of both possibilities.

In appealing to the other women's concern with surviving the Black Death, Pampinea makes a speech that is a piece of rhetoric intended to persuade her listeners that their first priority is to save their lives. And from a worldly perspective, her argument is persuasive. All they can do in Florence, she tells them, is witness the ravages of the plague or experience the threat of the lawless who roam the city, unrestrained by any criminal justice system, because those who would administer it are dead. Their homes, like hers, are empty, and there remains not only the grief over the departed but also the terrors of solitude: "Wherever I go in the house, wherever I pause to rest, I seem to be haunted by the shades of the departed, whose faces no longer appear as I remember them but with strange and horribly twisted expressions that frighten me out of my senses" (60). All about her is in ruins, including distinctions among the classes and between lay people and clerics; all have succumbed to their appetites: "They will do whatever affords them the greatest pleasure, whether by day or by night, alone or in company" (60). In short, not only the plague but also the dissolution of society threatens the seven women, who, as women, appear especially vulnerable:

If this be so (and we plainly perceive that it is), what are we doing here? What are we waiting for? What are we dreaming about? Why do we lag so far behind all the rest of the citizens in providing for our safety? Do we rate ourselves lower than all other women? Or do we suppose that our own lives, unlike those of others, are bound to our bodies by such strong chains that we may ignore all those things which have the power to harm them? In that case we are deluded and mistaken. (60–61)

Like all rhetoric, Pampinea's arguments hinge on her basic premise, and —again—she derives her most salient points from natural law. But in doing so, what she has created for Boccaccio's readers (and later critics) is more perplexity than enlightenment. First of all, natural law, the appeal to something "wider or more general or more enduring than the mere practical needs of men,"[40] varies according to the interpretations and values applied to nature. And in Boccaccio's time, nature itself still bore the stigma associated with the fall. But even if this were not so, nature is never so clear a guide to ethical behavior as those grounded in natural law theory sometimes appear to maintain: it is one thing to say "follow nature" and another to define just what that nature is that is to be followed. Moreover, whereas "inanimate things and brutes invariably obey these laws, the first out of necessity, the second out of instinct," human beings are distinguished by a capacity to choose, and may exercise choice by *choosing to disregard the laws of nature*. A telling example is implied by Pampinea: she invokes as an instance of natural law the killing of another in self-defense, an instance of murder that even the civil laws condone. First of all, she could not have found a better contrast to the Christian ideal of charity. Second, one is not compelled to defend or protect oneself; one can turn the other cheek or stand on principle. The history and literature of the world are full of persons who had to make that choice. Bolt's dramatic portrait of Thomas More is but one example.

Natural law doctrine, however, is not antithetical to Christian doctrine. Influenced by Aristotle, the teachings of St. Thomas Aquinas advocate natural law, and this itself may appear to validate Pampinea's argument. A summary of Aquinas's position is that "each natural kind is distinguished by the possession of an essence, that the essence stipulates an end, that virtue and goodness are necessarily linked with the fulfillment of these ends."[41] But even if natural law involves the obedience of a being to its essence, in the case of human beings natural law alone cannot define that essence. For assuming that reason distinguishes humans from beasts, it does not follow that reason dictates self-preservation as the highest good—especially not if the *self* in self-preservation is confined to the body at a time when the immortal soul states its prior claim.

Thus an appeal to nature in the attempt to decide just what it is to be human would seem to lead to several problematic conclusions. One is to deny any real difference between humans and animals, the response to which is perhaps typified by the Victorian poet Tennyson's denial that he is wholly brain, a "cunning model cast in clay." Again, the almost tame animals in the *Decameron* garden suggest the ironic equation of man and beast. Another conclusion is the Sartrean position that humans differ from other species, but that the essential difference is that humans have no predefined essence, persons defining themselves by their actions. This covers Bolt's admission that to say that one is human in response to the question "What am I?" is to provide a silly answer, since all that is entailed in the question and the answer is a meaningless circularity.[42] The question that might be asked of the *Decameron* is whether Boccaccio would follow Bolt in his argument that for More the saving of his soul by the devaluation of his body was a simple if not easy matter. Mazzotta's chapter on ethics in the *Decameron* argues that such choices were never easy, and never simple.

What is certain is that in the *Decameron* Boccaccio emphasizes the question of what it means to be human. Indeed, the first word in the work is "Umana." And to be human is to have compassion for the afflicted, the opposite of which is the inhuman behavior of those who, frightened by the pestilence, "took a single" and very "inhuman" (crudele) precaution to avoid the sick and their belongings (52). *Crudele,* meaning both cruel and inhuman, links the two in such a way that a failure to offer aid during the plague is as blameworthy as are aggressive and unlawful acts. Such an equation prepares the way for Boccaccio's description of those who fled the city:

Some people, pursuing what was possibly the safer alternative, callously maintained that there was no better or more efficacious remedy against a plague than to run away from it. Swayed by this argument, and sparing no thought for anyone but themselves, large numbers of men and women abandoned their city, their homes, their relatives, their estates and their belongings, and headed for the countryside, either in Florentine territory or, better still, abroad. It was as though they imagined that the wrath of God would not unleash this plague against men for their iniquities irrespective of where they happened to be, but would only be aroused against those who found themselves within the city walls; or possibly they assumed that the whole of the population would be exterminated and that the city's last hour had come. (53)

It is curious that this passage—virtually describing the brigada—is not routinely invoked in the debate over Boccaccio's attitude towards his storytellers.

Without specifically defining the essence of humanity in terms of the soul (only in a secular age would such a definition need to be specific), Boccaccio invokes the ideal of Christian love in his preface as a basis for a moral stance. To quote the passage once again, "To take pity on people in distress is a human quality which every man and woman should possess, but it is especially requisite in those who have once needed comfort, and found it in others." Suddenly, however, Boccaccio shifts his frame of reference from charity towards fellow humans in distress to erotic love. He alludes to his own past lovesickness, the biographical details of which have occupied many of his critics, in order to offer solace to the ladies who constitute the audience for the *Decameron,* that is, those who are suffering from love and need both diversion and instruction, which he will supply in his many tales of love, bitter and pleasing. Ironically, he ends by thanking Eros, who has freed him from love's bonds and has thus given him power to write his stories, and paradoxically calls upon God that his efforts be successful:

Il che se avviene, che voglia Iddio che cosa sia, ad Amore ne rendano grazie, il quale liberandomi da'suoi legami m'ha conceduto di potere attendere a loro piaceri.

In this passage (paraphrased prior to the quotation) Amore (the pagan god of Love) and Iddio (the Lord) are distinguished. At one and the same time, Boccaccio appears to have swept Christian morality away from his stories while at the same time invoking God and hence a spiritual ideal that seems inseparable from the rest of his work.

Eros and Charity dimmed as theological and ideological opposites in an increasingly secular world.[43] But the essential premise expressed in their opposition has maintained its power in subsequent attempts to formulate an ethic that might prevail in times of literal and symbolic plague. Moving ahead momentarily to the writer who made plague a subject for the twentieth century, Camus, love provides *The Plague* with a dominant theme and in the broadest sense with its ethic. Among the characters who join to fight the plague, one, Rambert, is at first driven by romantic love, all of his efforts being expended in an attempt to escape the quarantined city and rejoin his mistress in Paris. But then he changes his mind and stays to fight the pestilence, his decision consistent with Camus's ethics, which one of his critics metaphorically depicts in terms very significant for the *Decameron*: according to Camus, "once the plague has come [one] must re-enter the city."[44] Rambert can therefore stand symbolically as a direct contrast to Boccaccio's brigada.

Camus's narrator has no moral system by which to sanction Rambert's decision, nor does he commend it unequivocally as a model: "For nothing in the world is it worth turning one's back on what one loves," he says (188–89). Nor does Camus distinguish between Eros and some other, ethically "higher" form of love. But at the end of the novel, as the narrator, bereft of his own wife, who has died of tuberculosis, witnesses the reunions of those who were separated during the plague, it is clear that it is more than the *pleasures* of love that are celebrated as their reward for battling the pestilence:

Those who, clinging to their little own, had set their hearts solely on returning to the home of their love had sometimes their reward—though some of them were still walking the streets alone, without the one they had awaited. Then, again, those were happy who had not suffered a two-fold separation, like some of us who, in the days before the epidemic, had failed to build their love on a solid basis at the outset, and had spent years blindly groping for the pact, so slow and hard to come by, that in the long run binds together ill-assorted lovers. Such people had had . . . the rashness of counting overmuch on time; and now they were parted forever. But others . . .

had, without faltering, welcomed back the loved one who they thought was lost to them. And for some time, anyhow, they would be happy. They knew now that if there is one thing one can always yearn for and sometimes attain, it is human love. (270–71)

Whether or not the *Decameron* was a direct influence on Edgar Allan Poe's tales of pestilence, "Shadow—A Parable," "King Pest," and "The Masque of the Red Death,"[45] it is no exaggeration to say that the way the medieval Italian writer is read today has much to do with the legacy of Poe's literary theory and his "heresy of *The Didactic*" (75). In his essay on "The Poetic Principle," Poe defines "the poetry of words as *The Rhythmical Creation of Beauty*," and his contention that with the "Intellect or with the Conscience, it has only collateral relations," that unless "incidentally, it has no concern whatever either with Duty or with Truth" (78), extends in his aesthetics to prose tales as well as poems. Were he to have critically analyzed the *Decameron*'s use of the plague as a frame for his collection of stories, Poe might very well have uttered these words, written by a Boccaccio critic almost a century after Poe so definitively separated ethics from aesthetics:

The framework of the *Decameron* is the effort to justify and protect a new art, an art which simply in order to be, to exist, required the moment free of all other cares, the willingness to stop *going anywhere* (either toward God or toward philosophical truth) . . . . We have long since ceased to demand justification for the moment of art. We have for so long and so completely accepted an art devoid of the intent to instruct or to further along one's way to God, that it even seems strange when art attempts this thing.[46]

The real question, however, is whether the purely aesthetic approach is adequate even to Poe's own stories, whether his plague tales do not intentionally and effectively subvert his own literary theories.[47]

Boccaccio is not ordinarily cited as an influence on Poe,[48] although one of the suggested sources for the "Masque" is a nineteenth-century biography of Petrarch with its description of the Black Death and the revels believed to be efficacious against it.[49] Nor is the Red Death equated by Poe with bubonic plague. Still, it is possible to read the "Masque" as a grotesque parody of the brigada's retreat from Florence to the remote villas and gardens in which they entertain themselves while death ravages the city. In Poe's tale, Prince Prospero "summoned to his presence a thousand hale and light-hearted friends from among the knights and dames of his court, and with these retired to the deep seclusion of one of his castellated abbeys," leaving the "external world" to "take care of itself" during the

Red Death (670–71). After a few months, Prospero arranges a masquerade, and it is during these revels that death overtakes Prospero and the company:

And now was acknowledged the presence of the Red Death. He had come like a thief in the night. And one by one dropped the revellers in the blood-bedewed halls of their revel, and died each in the despairing posture of his *fall*. . . . And Darkness and Decay and the Red Death held illimitable dominion over all. (676–77; emphasis added)

In "The Poetic Principle," the *soul* is an important and recurrent image, but consistent with Poe's transposition of heresy from the religious to the aesthetic, the soul ceases to be the immortal essence of the human being, but rather is another potentially mutable human faculty, one by which a person apprehends the beautiful:

It has been my purpose to suggest that, while this [poetic] Principle is, strictly and simply, the Human Aspiration for Supernal Beauty, the manifestation of the Principle is always found in *an elevating excitement of the Soul*—quite independent of that passion which is the intoxication of the Heart—or of that Truth which is the satisfaction of the Reason. (92–93)

Like Coleridge, Poe believes that the artistic imagination is capable of recreating the world, achieving the lost unity that was a feature of God's original creation. But like other romantic writers, Poe also appears to have recognized that the centrality of the poetic imagination created a double-edged sword.

In the descent into his mind, Poe could escape the mundane world to become "monarch of the domain of his own visions,"[50] but then he might find himself imprisoned in his own solipsistic universe. Moreover, unity of consciousness, even if achieved, cannot promise the same immortality as does the Christian soul. Personal identity thus not only becomes difficult to achieve and sustain but also belongs to the realm of time. As Joseph DeFalco has said of "Shadow," it "presents a vivid portrait of the shock to human sensibilities that results in the awareness of the loss of individual identity after death."[51] And according to Joan Dayan, Poe's *soul* also represents the understanding, some of his tales to be "read as natural histories of the thinking mind."[52] If so, Poe's ideas can never be detached from the intellect that ponders them. If his writing depicts a "deliberate retreat from the temporal, rational, physical world into his own visionary depths,"[53] then his work will also reflect the social and philosophical implications of that retreat. His own artistic works, that is, can never exist solely as *the beautiful*.

If it is ironically the case that the "Masque" possesses—despite Poe's theory—a "clear moral," and if that moral is as simple as the interpretation "that one cannot run away from responsibility," [54] then it is possible to read "The Masque of the Red Death" as Poe's calling into question his own aesthetics. Its didactic intent then would be that there must be a moral, in which case, of course, the moral is hardly simple. Seen this way, the story is an expression of a romantic dilemma, of the tensions between reality, of which plague is a most dire sign, and art. The nineteenth century helped develop the concept of a "self" who not only creates the world, but also, as concomitant self-consciousness, knows that this world consists largely of self-representations. Coleridge was in English literature the major theorist and poet on this subject, and, as will be seen, had a major impact on Poe. But Coleridge had never sundered aesthetics and ethics as definitively as Poe did in "The Poetic Principle." In the "Masque," Prospero's palace can be read not only as the "prison house of his mind," [55] but also as the realm of the artist similarly entrapped by an art that is extensionless, referring only to itself. During a time of plague, Prospero and his followers flee the pestilence to experience a sustained period of what Poe in "The Poetic Principle" calls the "excitement of the Soul," and each would die, again, in the "despairing posture of his *fall* (677; emphasis added).

Although there appears to be no immortal soul to endanger or preserve in Poe's work, this image of the "fall" is pervasive in his tales, bearing important meaning for his treatment of pestilence and death. Instead of the fall resulting in death's entrance into an earlier immutable world, it seems more often the case that death precedes the fall, being itself the cause of paradise's ruin. The disjunction between art and morality thus becomes implicated in Poe's vision of a return to a prelapsarian perfection in which the moral sense is rendered superfluous. At about the same time that Poe wrote "The Masque of the Red Death," he composed another story, "Eleanora," which begins with an epigraph that in effect makes the soul dependent upon a coherent self: "Sub conservatione formae specificae salva anima" (638; "under the protection of a specific form, the soul is safe," 645). Poe's fallen soul, his version of Chaucer's and Boccaccio's diseased soul, is a figure for the opposite of a coherent form; it becomes the fragmented self.

It is in such terms that Poe bears comparison to Boccaccio, both of them extending the concept of narcissism to the art of storytelling. Boccaccio remains very close to the ancient myth of self-love, using plague to explore the problems surrounding morality and art. In contrast, Poe seems more contemporary: his treatment of narcissism has to do with the individual whose subjectivity threatens to obliterate the outside world, and who disintegrates without a stable anchoring in a world of others. The equivalent of Boccaccio's song of self-love that closes the first day of the *Decameron* can be found in Poe's tale, "A Shadow," written more than a decade before the "Masque," and anticipating the better-known work. It takes place in ancient times during a "year of terror" in which the "black wings of the Pestilence were spread abroad" (189). There is an historical setting for this short narrative that Poe is claimed to have been faithful to, and Poe's complicated cosmology can undoubtedly be invoked to explain the story.[56] On a simpler level, however, the city of Ptolemais invokes the Ptolemaic theory of the universe, which places the earth at its center. As a parallel, the personal unconscious of the individual self endows a person with the same centrality, while at the same time—or so the story indicates—depriving the self of whatever stability it needs if identity is to survive.

Indeed, the room in which a company of seven is encapsulated to enjoy its nocturnal revelries/reveries belies the reality of time and history.

Black draperies . . . in the gloomy room, shut out from our view the moon, the lurid stars, and the peopleless streets—but the boding and the memory of Evil, they would not be so excluded. There were things around us and about of which I can render no distinct account—things material and spiritual—heaviness in the atmosphere—a sense of suffocation—anxiety—and, above all, that terrible state of existence which the nervous experience when the senses are keenly living and awake, and meanwhile the powers of thought lie dormant. A dead weight hung upon us. (189)

Despite the drinking of wine, the laughter and merriment described as "hysterical" (190), the seven are not interacting. In the candlelit dark room illuminated only by lamps, a round ebony table where the company sits forms a mirror in which they "sat each of [them] there assembled [beholding] the pallor of his own countenance, and the unquiet glare in the downcast eyes of his companions" (190).

Horribly, there is another besides the seven in the room, the corpse of one whose "countenance [is] distorted with the plague," whose "eyes in which Death had but half extinguished the fire of the pestilence" (190) seem to take interest in the revels. The narrator, who had begun his story as one now long dead addressing a living audience, describes how he felt the "eyes of the departed" upon him. Forcing himself

not to perceive the bitterness of their expression, and, gazing down steadily into the depths of the ebony mirror, [he] sang with a loud and sonorous voice the songs of the son of Teios. (190)

When the shadow, death, enters this private chamber, only the narrator asks its identity, his words seeming to be the first spoken in this both noisy but essentially silent place, where songs are alluded to but each singer is self-preoccupied. For as has been said of Poe and language, words "create what words are, a demand addressed to an other entailing the necessity of self-narration and the irregularity of transference between selves."[57]

The intruder's reply, in itself cryptic, is not so important as the tone of voice in which it is uttered, which,

not the tones of any one being, but a multitude of beings, and, varying in their cadences from syllable to syllable, fell duskily upon our ears in the well remembered and familiar accents of many thousand departed friends. (191)

The image reflects not only DeFalco's argument for loss of personal identity after death but also a split between incoherence and communication; between what the plural pronoun "our" suggests is community, and individuals, each intent on his mirrored self-image; between songs sung in the darkened room and the world outside—a world of time but also of the "familiar accents" of real human discourse.

Poe's treatment of language in "Shadow" renders particularly significant his borrowing in the "Masque" from Shakespeare's *The Tempest.* The connections are reciprocal. A recent critique of the play has argued that Shakespeare's central theme is symbolically plague related, Prospero's effort being to "tame" the "pest," that is, Caliban.[58] That Poe long ago perceived such a meaning is strongly suggested in his own short story, "King Pest," in which he plays with Shakespeare's title. Among the several characters that in one way or another signify "pest," Poe has created "His Grace the Duke Tem-Pest" (250), perhaps the Prospero of the "Masque" in an earlier guise. One of the Duke's companions, interpreted as a figure of the failed poet, is the "Arch Duchess Ana-Pest" (250).[59] In humorously playing with words, Poe has nonetheless signified the split between poetic language and the familiar accents of usual communication. If iambs are close to normal English speech, anapests are in this respect their antithesis. But the rhythms of human discourse have to do with culture, and from Caliban's point of view, to become tame is to experience a fall from nature. Thus his curse on Prospero—the first part of which has been picked up by Poe critics, the second of which has been neglected—is "the red plague rid ye for learning me your language."[60]

But if Shakespeare's Prospero uses language as a defense of culture against nature, Poe's Prospero has gone one step further by substituting an artificial culture for reality itself. His pleasure palace is intended to keep out the pestilence, his isolated society one from which most remnants of nature are eliminated. Having taken artistic taste to its extreme point, he has become in that sense un*natural*. His taste and his revels are described as bizarre, attended not by people so much as a "multitude of dreams" (673) emanating from another world. As in "A Shadow," there are many noises in Prospero's abbey, laughter and the music of an orchestra, as well as a clock whose chimes disturb the revelers as reminders of time and mutability. There are also pronounced silences during the masquerade, and people do not appear generally to talk to each other, although they at one point make "whispering vows" (673) that they will not be made uneasy by these sounds of time invading their artificial paradise. Significantly, at that moment when Prince Prospero explicitly "uttered . . . words" (675) to demand that the masked figure who dares intrude upon the revels disclose its identity, Prospero's words "*rang* throughout the seven rooms loudly and clearly" — that is, like the clock (675; emphasis added). Whispers are thus associated with timelessness, words with time and act. At first, "as [Prospero] spoke," he seemed to rouse the crowd about him to move against the trespasser: "There was a slight rushing movement of this group in the direction of the intruder" (676). But then they stopped and did nothing. The mysterious intruder is described as a "mummer" (676), a player in a masque but also one who is "mum," without speech. And so it is in this cut-off place of sound but almost no language that death overtakes Prospero and his follow- ers. In his borrowing from Shakespeare, Poe has reinterpreted the dialectic that exists in the two characters of Prospero and Caliban. In the end, Poe's superrefined Prince Prospero is like Caliban the beast man,[61] for both inhabit worlds that eschew what "Shadow" calls the "familiar accents" of ordinary human communication. If Prince Prospero's masque is a metaphor for what Poe calls the poetry of words from which all moral connotations are purged, then such poetry is appropriately described by the music and laughter of the revelries with which Prospero's company hopes to hold the Red Death at bay.

In these Poe stories, language itself appears to presuppose a fall from perfection. The art of the didactic is, again, tied by morality to worldly imperfection. In Prospero's false paradise, there is an illusion of a return to a disease-free and ethic-free prelapsarian state[62] in which there would exist no call to action for which words must be invoked. This is perhaps why the revelers begin to move against the figure of pestilence upon hearing Pros- pero speak, but then stop, it not being clear what the object of words can achieve. These related themes are made more explicit in another story Poe wrote at about the same time as "The Masque of the Red Death." In "Eleanora" can be read a complete "fall" story in which is reinterpreted its prototype, and in which the traditional Christian view that after death the immortal soul will be released to dwell in the heavenly paradise is inverted. It is "Eleanora" that helps link Poe's tales of pestilence to his well-discussed figure of the landscape gardener as artist capable of recreating Eden, and it is therefore worth a digression to consider Poe's treatment of the earthly paradise motif.

The story's narrator and his cousin Eleanora dwell almost like Adam and Eve in a secluded garden. For fifteen years the innocent pair luxuriate in the "exceeding Beauty" of the place that "spoke to [their] hearts, in loud tones, of the love and the glory of God" (640). In their paradise there runs a waterway they call the "River of Silence" (639), for even later, during their passage from innocence to sexuality, they "spoke no words" (640). But time already exists in this garden, as do signs of an eventual fall, trees whose "tall slender stems stood not upright," whose "speckled" bark is reminiscent of "giant serpents" (640). The tradition that links the serpent to sexuality and the fall is emphasized by Poe through the phallic significance of his image, which is sustained when immediately thereafter the couple are drawn to each other by physical love, "locked in each other's embrace, beneath the serpent-like trees" (640). Now the garden changes before their eyes, still beautiful, but transformed by their transformation, the colors of nature heightened by the "passions which had for centuries distinguished [their] race" (640).

Awakening sexuality leads to self-consciousness: they look into the River of Silence at their "images therein" (640), it not being yet clear if the plurality of "images" will yield to the unity evoked by self-love and isolation. But a separation takes place, preceded by their changing perception of the garden, no longer a paradise, but a place "shutting [them] up, as if for ever, within a magic prison-house of grandeur and of glory" (641). But even this inversion of paradise into a Dantean inferno of eternal togetherness would imply immutability. For Eleanora, however, change presages death, whose finger she senses upon her. Having "*spoken* one day" of the "last sad change which must befall Humanity" (641; emphasis added), she uses words to extract from her lover a fidelity that will outlive her and through which her identity may then survive in him. But for him, her death marks the beginning of a descent into himself. He enters what he calls the "second era of my existence" (643), which he admits was the period others would call madness. As a "shadow gathers over [his] brain" (643) the garden reflects this crossing of another "barrier in Time's path" (642) and mental degeneration begins. In desperation to avoid the disintegration of self that is experienced by other Poe protagonists, for example Roderick Usher in the renowned story significantly entitled "The *Fall* of the House of Usher" (emphasis added), the narrator of "Eleanora" leaves the garden of his imagination in a self-imposed expulsion from Eden into the social realm of other human beings: "I left it forever for the vanities and the turbulent triumphs of the world" (644).

If "Eleanora" is a tale about a fall and (self-) expulsion from the garden, "The Domain of Arnheim" depicts the wanderings of the equally self-exiled Ellison in search of the perfect place to build the new paradise.[63] The "august purposes for which the Deity had implanted the poetic sentiment in man" (1272) is interpreted by him as fulfilling not only his own destiny but also God's intentions. Fortunate enough to have inherited an extraordinary fortune, he is free to pursue his dream of reversing the effects of the fall. But there is a contradiction in Ellison that may from the outset thwart his attempt. Like Eleanora and her lover, he is essentially innocent of sin: the narrator says that in Ellison's brief existence, "I fancy that I have seen refuted the dogma, that in man's very nature lies some hidden principle, the antagonist of bliss" (1267). But Ellison is also one of "pre-eminent endowments" (1268) and what he seeks to evade is the "common vortex of unhappiness which yawns" for such as he. Unlike Prince Prospero, Ellison flees not pestilence and death but that other pole of human misery, what Wordsworth called the dreary intercourse of daily life, the ordinary life Ellison might have immersed himself in had he not committed himself to the "spirituality of his object" (1269), to the creation of that garden that would display the best of nature and of artifice. Yet it is his short life that renders his garden what Dayan calls a "fool's paradise,"[64] which may be to say that Poe, a romantic, constantly builds and rebuilds the palace of art, only to depict its collapse. It is telling that when Poe's narrator describes the various supernatural beings and nature spirits that helped construct Ellison's miraculous gardens, the last of these are the "gnomes" (1283), the word itself the last one of the tale, evoking the image of Caliban and gross nature instead of Ariel, a creature of the air. Ellison's paradise, so full of contraries, provides important clues to Poe's plague tales.

In "The Poetic Principle," Poe had designated the landscape gardener to be an unrecognized artist; in "The Domain of Arnheim" it is said of Ellison that in the "widest and noblest sense he was a poet" (1271), although he eschews the more conventional expressions of his genius. "But Ellison maintained that the richest, the truest and most natural, if not altogether the most extensive province, had been unaccountably neglected. No definition had spoken of the landscape-gardener as of the poet" (1272). Which means that he must seek not only the perfect site for his creation but also the poetic principle that will govern it. And thus Ellison studies theories of gardens, rejecting as sufficient either the theory derived from the superiority of nature over art or the one extolling art over nature. On one side, no human creation does more than come near the "living and breathing beauty" of nature (1273); moreover, in the wildest and most savage scenes in nature there is apparent the "*art* of a creator," although apparent only on "reflection" (1276). Moreover, nature is flawed by "known geological disturbances" (1273) that are presages of death. On the other side, "no paradises are to be found in reality as have glowed on the canvass of Claude" (1272). In artifice can be found a nature purged of all its defects, and, in addition, the "show of order and design" is not only pleasing but "partly moral" (1275).

Consistently, Ellison draws analogies between the landscape artist and a divine Creator, free—as Boccaccio's brigada can never be—of the moral significance of the heavenly paradise that calls into question any attempt to recreate the earthly Eden. Ellison's failure will thus have to be understood in psychological rather than theological terms. Ellison's improvements on nature are what Dayan calls "steps back to God's original design."[65] The landscape gardener mediates between the Almighty and fallen creation, to reconstitute "harmony" and "consistency" (1276)—and, like Prince Prospero, the illusion of immutability:

Admit the earthly immortality of man to have been the first intention. We have then the primitive arrangement of the earth's surface adapted to his blissful estate, as not existent but designed. The disturbances were the preparations for his subsequent conceived deathful condition. (1274)

Ironically, it is soon after finding his ideal spot that Ellison dies, his garden thrown open to visitors who must journey to it via a symbolic replication of Ellison's own quest. Theirs becomes a phantasmagoric journey not entirely unlike Poe's horrific description of the descent into the maelstrom. It is as if Prospero's abbey, after the Red Death gains on him and his followers, were thrown open to gaping tourists.

In his quest to recreate the earthly paradise and inhabit it with the "loveliness and love" (1277) of a woman in whom "Ellison thought to find, *and found,* exemption from the ordinary cares of humanity" (1277), from, again, the "common vortex of unhappiness" (1268). But he experiences an obvious discomfort that makes it difficult for him to locate the perfect spot in which the self need not acknowledge its own apartness. He voices a concern, for example, that on a mountain top, "Grandeur in any of its moods, but especially in that of extent, startles, excites—and then fatigues, depresses." His fear appears to be that in any place too remote from the ordinary world, the "sense" of seclusion should prove the real thing (1268). He wants the "composure but not the depression of solitude" (1277), and proclaims that in "looking from the summit of a mountain, he cannot help feeling *abroad* in the world. The heart-sick avoid distant prospects as a *pestilence*" (1278; emphasis added). In Ellison's musing, Poe provides a clear and significant clue to the way in which he has interiorized plague in his works.

A link between the sunny gardens of "Eleanora" and "The Domain of Arnheim" on one side, and the dark interiors of "A Shadow" and "The Masque of the Red Death" on the other, can be found in what has long been recognized to be a source for Poe, Coleridge's "Kubla Khan."[66] Coleridge had written an incomplete, fragmented work (whose form significantly mirrors Poe's themes), a poem that nonetheless achieves unity because of its coherent patterns of imagery and integrated series of antitheses: external and internal space, nature and mind, narrative and lyric poetry— or, to put this last in another context, audience and poetic self. As a narrative, the poem begins by relating how Kubla Khan decrees the construction of a pleasure dome in a beautiful natural spot, and later hears prophesies of war that could threaten his creation. Other characters appear in a phantasmagoria of images appropriate to a vision in a dream: a woman wailing for her demon lover in a "savage" place that is also "holy and enchanted"; an Abyssinian maid whose composition of songs upon her dulcimer is a a trope for poetic creation; and the awe-inspiring figure of a person who seems to encompass the powers of magician, seer, and poet, capable of reproducing the Khan's act of creating a "miracle of rare device, / A sunny pleasure dome with caves of ice." The poet-magician might achieve the same miracle and with his imagination similarly "build that dome in air." The final scene in Poe's "Domain of Arnheim" echoes Coleridge's poem in both language and concept: it describes the visitor's arrival at the now-dead Ellison's dreamlike garden, from which upsprang as if a phantom work a mass of semi-Gothic, semi-Saracenic architecture, "sustaining itself as if by miracle in mid air" (1283).

But if Poe's works create fables of the mind, as Dayan convincingly argues, then the most important lines in Coleridge's poems are not those that Poe drew on for his own landscapes of the mind, but rather the *destination* of Coleridge's waterway:

> the sacred river, ran
> Through caverns measureless to man
> Down to a sunless sea.
> So twice five miles of fertile ground
> With walls and towers were girdled round:
> And here were gardens bright with sinuous rills,
> Where blossomed many an incense-bearing tree,
> And here were forests ancient as the hills,
> Enfolding sunny spots of greenery.
> . . . .
> Five miles meandering with a mazy motion
> Through wood and dale the sacred river ran,
> Then reached the caverns measureless to man,
> And sank in tumult to a lifeless ocean.

Poe's river journey in the "Domain" virtually duplicates Coleridge's, and the mazy motion of meandering Alph to the caverns measureless to man is reflected in the "Domain" as well as in "The Masque of the Red Death," where the masquerade is held in apartments that "were so irregularly disposed that the vision embraced but little more than one at a time. There was a sharp turn at every twenty or thirty yards, and at each turn a novel effect" (671). It is the seventh apartment, shrouded in black with "blood-tinted panes," that "produced so wild a look upon the countenances of those who entered, that there were few of the company bold enough to set foot within its precincts at all" (672). It is this room that—to sustain the comparison with Coleridge—suggests Prospero's descent into the disordered caverns of the mind. And again, in the corresponding realm of nature, the traditional beings who inhabit the dark areas beneath the surface of the earth are the gnomes.

In the "Domain of Arnheim" the visitor's boat retreats from nature, at first passing cultivated shores with grazing sheep, then going on to places where the "idea of cultivation subsided into that of merely pastoral care" (1279). But then the banks become more precipitous and at "every instant the vessel seemed imprisoned within an enchanted circle" (1279) reminiscent of that drawn three times around the mysterious figure at the end of "Kubla Khan." Similar to Prospero's recreation of this landscape scene in the interior of the abbey, Arnheim's stream "took a thousand turns, so that at no moment could its gleaming surface be seen for a greater distance than a furlong" (1279). Later the "windings become more frequent and intricate, and seemed often as if returning upon themselves, so that the voyager had long lost all idea of direction" (1279). Eventually the traveler "descends" (1280) into an artfully wrought canoe to make the last stage of the journey to Arnheim, to commence the last "rapid descent" (1283) to Ellison's magic world.

Throughout Coleridge's poem, areas of inner and outer space are differentiated. The dome encompasses what is in its interior; it is built on fertile ground "girdled round" with walls and towers; ancient forests enfold sunny spots of greenery; the river that begins above ground runs through caverns measureless to man "down" to the kind of sunless sea that in Poe's story precedes the boat's bursting into the dazzling splendor of Arnheim. From the midst of Coleridge's chasm in the earth (Poe's gorges), a mighty fountain momently was forced to the outer world, throwing up huge fragments of matter whose dancing rocks disturb the river itself. The poet-figure, again, stands alone in the midst of a circle woven three times around him, his worshippers close but also safely outside, protected from his "flashing eyes, his floating hair." The "sunny dome" above the ground is countered by the "caves of ice" within, the solipsistic self and lyric poet sinking into the measureless caverns, while the narrative voice, like the mighty fountain, struggles to make its way to the outer world.

Early in "The Domain of Arnheim" it is said of Ellison that after he came into his incredible fortune, he dispensed enough of it to relatives and individual charities to satisfy his conscience, although he had little faith in the possibility of any improvement "by man himself in the general condition of man" (1271). Having in effect satisfied himself with regard to what the world would deem ethical concerns, he was, says the narrator, "upon the whole, whether happily or unhappily . . . thrown back, in very great measure, upon self" (1271). Again, however, it is necessary to ask of Poe what this self is that Ellison was thrown back upon. The narrator's qualification, "happily or unhappily," is maintained by the sustained tension between the inner state and external space that dominates "Kubla Khan." It is, however, the outside world that, whatever its imperfections, stands between a person and so deep a descent into the submerged self that the individual loses all sense of direction, and the self disintegrates.

Such an immersion in the symbolic caverns of the mind supplies the central image of another of Poe's plague tales, "King Pest." The opening is set in a tavern (reminiscent of Chaucer and Defoe) in which two drunk sailors who have jumped ship find themselves unable to pay their bill and run out into the pestilence-ridden streets. Coming upon a "ghastly-looking building" (244), they break down the door to find themselves in the shop of an undertaker. An open "trap-door" in the room "looked down upon a long range of wine cellars, whose depths the occasional sound of bursting bottles proclaimed to be well stored with their appropriate contents" (245). Descending, they find themselves in the company of the six pests, resurrected corpses, the whole episode much like Alice's journey to the other side of the looking glass, but, of course, even more bizarre.

Just as Poe's "Masque" parodies Boccaccio's frame, if not necessarily directly, "King Pest" virtually mocks the river Alph's journey to a sunless sea. The story is replete with the devices that make Poe a master of the horrible, and his description of plague-devastated London could be read as Defoe's secret nightmares come true—those images of a private horror that H. F. might have recorded but taken pains to exclude from his *Journal* because they reveal too clearly the disordering of the mind that constructs them:

At the epoch of this eventful tale, and periodically, for many years before and after, all England, but more especially the metropolis, resounded with the fearful cry of "Plague!" The city was in a great measure depopulated—and in those horrible regions, in the vicinity of the Thames, where amid the dark, narrow, and filthy lanes and alleys, the Demon of Disease was supposed to have had his nativity, Awe, Terror, and Superstition were alone to be found stalking abroad. (242)

All order had broken down in the city, and crime was rampant—again, Defoe's worst anxieties realized. Not only had the masses of people reverted to a state of nature (actually, in Poe, to the unnatural), but also the supernatural had prevailed. The irrationality of London's population triumphs in "King Pest" as it eschews what Defoe had called "means," the effects of human agency. In Poe's story can be found some of Defoe's ideas and images. Not the plague itself, but the chaos it unleashed were by the "terror-stricken people" less likely to be attributed to the "agency of human hands" than to "Pest-spirits, plague-goblins, and fever-demons" (243).

In this surreal world of London, the horrors of plague are rendered both naturalistic and nightmarishly unreal, the outward signs of a terrified mind. Had the two seamen not been released by drink from ordinary consciousness, they would have been aware that they were wandering into districts of the city "placed *under ban*,"[67] all "persons forbidden under pain of death, to intrude upon their dismal solitude" (242). This official edict is highly ironic, microparasite and macroparasite hardly distinguishable.

This juxtaposition is sustained by Poe. Had the two men

not, indeed, been intoxicated beyond moral sense, their reeling footsteps must have been palsied by the horrors of their situation. The air was cold and misty. The paving-stones, loosened from their beds, lay in wild disorder amid the tall, rank grass, which sprang up around the feet and ankles. *Fallen houses* choked up the streets. The most fetid and poisonous smells everywhere prevailed;—and by the aid of that ghastly light which, even at midnight, never fails to emanate from a vapory and pestilential atmosphere, might be discerned lying in the by-paths and alleys, or rotting in the windowless habitations, the carcass of many a nocturnal plunderer arrested by the hand of the plague in the very perpetration of his robbery. (243–44; emphasis added)

In "King Pest," the plague has moved inward, the whole district of London that had been placed off limits interiorized, Defoe's shut-up houses finally realizing their symbolic potential as figures for the diseased mind. The story effectively transforms the gardens of "Eleanora" and "The Domain of Arnheim" into their opposites, blighted cities whose "fallen houses" are signs of the other, earlier and archetypal fall that pervades Poe's tales. Looked at in the context of the "Domain of Arnheim," the plague goblins are not only the "popular imps of mischief" but also inversions of the "Sylphs, of the Fairies, of the Genii, and of the Gnomes" whose "phantom handiwork" appear responsible for Ellison's creation (1283). The plague goblins, that is, may be the muses in their most demonic and therefore most perverse form.

It is in this interaction of micro- and macroparasites, of internal and external disorder, that the stabilizing influence of positive human action appears most necessary. The disintegration of London has ethical over-tones. As Ellison had noted in the "Domain of Arnheim," a show of order and design is partly pleasing but also partly moral. That in "King Pest" Poe had revised the original phrase "all sense of human feelings" to write instead "moral sense" (243) is arresting. He had shifted from pure subjec-tivity to reach for something less exclusively personal, if still short of the ethical absolutism available to earlier writers. To return again to the "Do-main of Arnheim," Ellison is described as being without the essential flaw that stands in the way of human happiness, but also as one who seeks to rebuild paradise in order to escape the ordinary cares of humanity. His quest involves him in as thorough a retreat from human concerns as Prince Prospero's withdrawing with his followers from the Red Death into the interior space of his abbey.

Poe's plague tales focus on that which makes the myth of paradise so compelling to the human imagination: it is free not only of death but also of ethical concerns for others. Its art, liberated from the didactic, renders the poetry of words as harmonies of music, the dissonances of language disappearing into an imagined perfection. Yet, these palaces of art always threaten to transform themselves into Prospero's abbey or the poisonous streets of Poe's plague-besieged London. In "King Pest" the moral sense counters the solipsistic self, which is itself paralleled by the artist who creates only for art's sake. Neither the individual nor the artist who cut themselves off from the light of common day have a coherent self to sustain. The ethical life is tied to ordinary human concerns, and these were frequently repudiated by the romantic imagination, which thus blocked the way out of the very isolation that, again, "The Domain of Arnheim" metaphorically depicts as "pestilence" (1278). Despite the aesthetic theories of Poe's "The Poetic Principle," its indictment concerning the heresy of the didactic, Poe's stories of pestilence raise another challenge for the artist, who must defend art's right to exist not so much in the ideal republic, but in the midst of plague.

Ibsen's *Ghosts* and the Ghosts
of Ibsen

The theme of contagious, inherited, or pestilential disease links three consecutive plays written by Henrik Ibsen. In *A Doll's House,* Dr. Rank, a secondary but important character, is dying of the final stages of syphilis, the legacy of a profligate father. In *Ghosts,* venereal disease is advanced, as Brian Downs has noted, "into the forefront" of the play, in which Oswald Alving is similarly afflicted.[1] And in *An Enemy of the People,* infected baths that will bring tourists and prosperity to a small Norwegian city threaten widespread disease and place a dissident physician, Thomas Stockmann, in conflict with his entire community. The position of these dramas in Ibsen's canon is important. The playwright himself urged that beginning with *A Doll's House,* his plays be read and comprehended as a group, thereby encouraging his audience and readers to seek thematic unity and continuity among plays that have been distinguished from each other according to whether they treat social issues or the development of the individual. In such a scheme, *An Enemy of the People* is a throwback to an earlier Ibsen. Once again, outraged by the hostile reception of *Ghosts,* he took up his polemic against conventional society.

But despite this connection, *Ghosts* is less frequently linked to the play that follows it than to its predecessor, *A Doll's House.* Helene Alving is interpreted as a Nora who did not slam the door on an intolerable marriage, her son Oswald's illness rendering futile her self-sacrifice. This thematic joining of the two plays results in a neglect of the disease theme that *Ghosts* shares with *An Enemy of the People.* The former is another example of what Brandt has called the socially constructed aspects of sexually transmitted illness, and the latter focuses on questions about how public policy is formulated to cope with disease. They differ, however, in that *Ghosts* is played out in the drawing room of Mrs. Alving, this enclosed space suggestive of her and her son's private psyches. In contrast, *An Enemy of the People* places its action in the social arena as Dr. Stockmann takes on as a personal enemy his town and its citizens, transforming what is at least partially a private war into an abstract confrontation between the individual and the group. This differentiation between the private and the public extends to the distinction that can be made and has been made between two major plays about AIDS, William Hoffman's *As Is* and Larry Kramer's *The Normal Heart*—both of which can be profitably studied in the context of Ibsen. *As Is* is replete with echoes from *Ghosts*, including one of Ibsen's most contro- versial themes, euthanasia; and, as theater critics have already pointed out, the *The Normal Heart* bears strong resemblance to *An Enemy of the People*. A comparison of them should focus on the interaction in their protagonists of the private, even egotistical self, with the committed public activist and reformer.

In *Ghosts*, Oswald Alving has returned from abroad for another of the periodic visits that he has made since being sent away as a small child from the home in which his mother feared he would be morally contaminated by his father. This visit coincides with the opening of an orphanage dedicated to the memory of the profligate Captain Alving, who had died of syphilis. Oswald plans to remain at home this time and it becomes clear that he has plans concerning the maidservant, Regine, whom he does not yet know is his half-sister, her mother having been seduced by Alving. Another visitor to the house is Parson Manders, whom his mother had once loved, and who never ceases to reproach Mrs. Alving for not properly fulfilling her conven- tional role as wife and mother. Oswald too expresses anger toward his mother, his feelings themselves the persistent ghosts of growing up in the Alving household. The climax of the play comes when he discloses to a horrified Mrs. Alving that he too is suffering from syphilis and that his fate is to degenerate into a mindless imbecile, so that her amends for the past and proof of her love will have to be a promise to administer a fatal dose of morphine when obvious signs of dementia appear. When the curtain falls, it is not clear what she will do, call in a doctor or give her son the morphine.

Contemporary critics of Ibsen are less concerned than earlier commen- tators about the accuracy with which Ibsen used syphilis as a dramatic motif because they tacitly follow Raymond Williams's contention that "the inher- ited debt of physical disease is only incidental"[2] to the argument that in *Ghosts*, venereal disease serves primarily as a metaphor for the external forces that have blighted Mrs. Alving's and Oswald's life as effectively as the illness itself. Ronald Gray takes a somewhat different tack, arguing that most of Ibsen's audience is not likely to recognize the medical anomalies in the play:

Few spectators will know whether it is unusual for syphilis to be transmitted only to one child, and not to the other child [Regine] or the mother [Mrs. Alving], whether a man can suffer from the disease for years without its being obvious from his appearance ... whether a sudden outbreak can follow after a complete absence of any signs in childhood, and whether it is normal for only the central nervous system to be attacked. These are improbabilities, according to the experts, but they affect the play only a little.[3]

Agreeing that it may only be incidental to the play's important themes that "the medical verisimilitude of *Ghosts* is pretty thin," Rosebury contends that nonetheless "even in 1880 it ought not to have been hard to come a little closer to probability."[4]

The matter continues to worry some critics, such as Evert Sprinchorn and Michael Meyer, whose relegation of their arguments to footnotes suggests that they agree that the subject of medical accuracy is marginal for interpreting *Ghosts* but at the same time is too intrinsic to the play's structure for the subject to be ignored altogether.[5] Both turn to post-nineteenth-century opinion to ask if Oswald *could* have contracted syphilis from smoking his father's pipe. Meyer, however, introduces what he calls the "far more frightening explanation of Oswald's illness than the usual one," arguing that "Mrs. Alving could have caught syphilis from her husband and passed it on to her son."[6] It is possible to add another speculation to Meyer's suggestion. If Mrs. Alving could be infected but asymptomatic, and if her son Oswald could have remained without visible signs of the illness for so long, then it would seem to follow that critics cannot be so confident that one of the anomalies in Ibsen's treatment of syphilis is that Captain Alving "has also sired the healthy child, Regine, by another mother."[7] That Alving's daughter may also be infected illuminates some of the ironies in Regine's leaving the physically and morally contaminated household of the Alvings to take up a position in a sailor's home and to live out what Gilman has described as the "image of the seductress as the source of pollution."[8]

But even if these speculations are valid, it is still a misjudgment to conclude with Meyer that "Ibsen knew more about medicine than some of his critics."[9] The diseased state of a seemingly uninfected mother who bore a syphilitic child was a matter of puzzlement in the mid-nineteenth century. One physician—as will soon be seen—came up with the answer that would confirm Meyer's suggestion: that the mother could be diseased but asymptomatic and that unless she was infected, her offspring could not be, however sick their father.[10] But even in its time, this to-be-confirmed theory was rejected, and was not validated until authentic diagnostic tests for syphilis were devised. That somehow Ibsen had come in contact with this idea is possible, but it would still be incorrect to believe it conferred on him knowledge that privileges him over his critics. What can be argued, however, is that up to the time when Ibsen wrote *Ghosts* there were many theories about syphilis and its transmission that embroiled physicians of the time in lively debates concerning the very issues pertinent to *Ghosts;* but that in 1880 physicians were dependent upon a patient's symptoms, and the symptomatology of the disease was so varied that it would appear to overlap with most of the illnesses that afflicted humans, giving rise to many contradictory opinions.

Some early theories, again, proved correct. Some, such as the transmission of syphilis from the foetus to the mother, proved entirely wrong (but even at mid-century, physicians were dubious about this possibility). And some issues were clouded because they tended to be approached obliquely —such as the contagiousness of congenital syphilis. The infection of the child blighted from birth with the disease may for the enlightened thinkers of the time have come uncomfortably close to a naturalistic version of the doctrine of original sin. To this day, most books on venereal disease that treat the subject of congenital syphilis remain silent on the infant's infectiousness.[11] That Ibsen may have proven to be correct on such matters as Alving's pipe or, if Meyer is correct in his speculation, Mrs. Alving's being infected but symptom-free, is certainly worth noting. But it may be more profitably argued that the uncertainties surrounding the disease served the playwright well, since he could introduce thematic ambiguities into his play without falsifying reality.

To rely either on modern medicine or on the popular beliefs of Ibsen's time is to neglect the treatises on syphilis available by the time *Ghosts* was written. Two of these have been chosen for discussion here, not because Ibsen necessarily read them, but because they are both important in the lively controversies over syphilis going on in France at mid-century, because they were likely to be known outside of France, because their translation into English reveals just how important the subject was recognized to be— and because, all in all, they indicate that Ibsen did not write his play in a medical vacuum. There were other syphilologists at the time, but Jean Alfred Fournier and Adrien Cullerier are being singled out because they address the very issues that appear in *Ghosts* and that the critics continue to debate. (The work of Philippe Ricord will be significant in the chapter on Brieux and Hawthorne.)

Fournier published many treatises on syphilis, treating one at a time such matters as contagion, heredity, and the infection of what he called "an honest [that is, moral] woman." In 1880, a year before Ibsen wrote *Ghosts,* Fournier delivered in Paris a series of lectures on *Syphilis and Marriage.*

The significance of Fournier's work is not only its content, but also, as the American translator of the published text wrote, its "bringing . . . before the medical profession" an "important subject [that] has been entirely ignored, or only incidentally alluded to, in a majority of our standard text-books." [12] In short, while it is not necessary to view *Ghosts* as a polemical work, its social context should be emphasized, since it was treating the very subject —syphilis and marriage—that was in its time only beginning to receive public attention. Yet syphilis was still a taboo subject that Eugene Brieux was three decades later to present to French audiences with the plea that the taboo and the silence surrounding syphilis and marriage contributed to the spread of the disease. [13]

Cullerier's treatise, translated as an *Atlas of Venereal Diseases* (1868), is distinguished for the doctor's opposition to his colleagues on the subject of whether an uninfected mother could transmit syphilis from father to child. Having observed patients and their children, whom he tracked for many years, Cullerier concluded that the "existence of hereditary syphilis is in-contestable, but it is due to maternal influence alone. The father has nothing to do with it" [14]—that is, an uninfected mother will bear a healthy child however afflicted her husband. Again, Meyer's speculation was part of the mid-nineteenth-century debate, even if Cullerier's ideas were in his own time rejected—even his translator felt compelled to append to that section of the *Atlas* his own disclaimer concerning the requirement that a mother be infected if her child proves to be. [15]

Cullerier is also notable for taking another stand provocative for a read-ing of *Ghosts*. He formed a rigid law that was to prove, in fact, unfounded, that congenital syphilis always "manifests itself during the first twelve months," [16] and that if it were claimed that earlier symptoms had not existed when a young adult was struck with the disease, it was either because such signs had been overlooked or because the patient was falling back on heredity to evade his own responsibility for risking his health and exposing himself to syphilis. If this were not already a startling context for Oswald's thinking that his free living in Paris and Rome was the source of his illness, an idea his mother pushes away by disclosing to him the legacy of his father, Cullerier, who believed that medicine would eventually lay to rest the myth of a late manifestation of congenital syphilis, suggests that the myth might, however, be perpetuated to preserve the peace of an already devastated family.

Indeed, both Fournier and Cullerier are very aware of how diseases are socially constructed. Fournier deliberately uses medical case histories drawn from the upper classes to dispel the widespread idea that syphilis was a disease of the lower classes, and he recognizes that the symptoms of a pure woman may be misdiagnosed either because of the assumption that she could not be ill or in order to protect her and her family (or her unfaithful husband)—such tendencies to falsify or overlook the evidence being damaging to a study of the disease. Cullerier goes even further, implicitly criticizing the sexual double standard for impeding the understanding of sexually transmitted diseases: are we authorized, he asks, "to admit transmission by the father? I think myself that the theory has been too readily accepted, and that it is rather based on moral considerations than on incontestible evidence." [17]

For a study of *Ghosts*, there are other areas treated by Fournier and Cullerier that warrant attention. First and foremost, both of them single out the smoking of pipes in discussions of symptomatology, Fournier supplying a case history with many reverberations for a reading of *Ghosts*, not only concerning the means of transmitting syphilis but also concerning the victimization of a young wife who is virtually a sacrifice to her husband's self-interest and self-gratification:

Another young man belonging to the highest social circles, marries despite my advice, after two years of syphilis. A great smoker, he is often affected with slight labial erosions to which he pays no attention . . . [He] eventually transmits syphilis to his wife, upon whom I afterward discovered an indurated chancre of the lower lip. [18]

Fournier also points to the difficulty in diagnosing early signs of congenital syphilis because of what the French physician calls "one of the most difficult and most delicate points in pathology," that the child's symptoms may be very different from those of the infected parent's or parents', [19] a point that may help address Gray's question concerning the late manifestation of Oswald's disease, the damage to his nervous system being the first manifestation (Oswald does allude to highly unspecific symptoms, the early persistent headaches suffered when a child).

If Ibsen was utilizing the medical possibility that the disease might not become symptomatic until fairly late in the diseased person's life, and if he also played with the possibility of an asymptomatic but diseased mother transmitting the infection, then the path of Regine's life, again, picks up added significance. When Regine leaves the Alving home to take up the life of a hostess in a sailor's home, rejecting Oswald, she hesitates before giving as a reason her unwillingness to nurse an invalid over a long period of time. Brian Downs apparently reads this as Regine "evidently [holding the] error" that "Oswald was capable of communicating his disease," and wonders if Ibsen shared this misconception.[20] It is worth pausing over this question because the difficulty in answering it goes beyond what the medical treatises of Ibsen's or modern times say on the subject. On the whole, the matter was clouded with obscurity, enough so for Fournier to note that the "greatest number of our classic treatises remain absolutely silent upon the question which is about to follow":

When syphilis has contaminated a husband and wife there is a great risk . . . of their child being born tainted with syphilis. Now this infant, supposing it to be syphilitic, evidently carries with it the *dangers of contagion*. [The infection] may radiate from it to the persons who surround it.[21]

That the infectiousness of the child will shortly subside is understood by modern medicine; the subject of prolonged contagion, however, is not one that Fournier pursues.

Now, it will be remembered that Fournier considered the diagnosis of a child not only a very difficult but also a delicate matter, and that it has already been noted that contemporary works on syphilis raise the dangers to the health of the untreated child but, as Fournier would put it, remain absolutely silent about the danger of the child to others. Perhaps Cullerier supplies a hint about the uneasiness that surrounds this matter. When he formulates his "regular law" concerning the baby's first year as "the time for the appearance of hereditary syphilis," he rejects the notion that sooner or later the disease will manifest itself, no child of syphilitic parents ever confident of freedom from the disease. Implicitly, he repudiates not only a medical theory but also the blighting of an innocent child with its parents' misfortune:

There is a great difference between the precision of this law, and the vagueness of most authors who allow the fault or the misfortune of a parent to weigh upon a child during his whole life. It is for future experience to decide whether this is, or is not, an exaggerated pretension.[22]

But it was precisely the idea of inherited sin and guilt that served Ibsen's metaphorical purposes in *Ghosts*. The romantic belief in an infant's innate innocence had never entirely eradicated the idea of original sin, but the more liberal principle may have discouraged writers on syphilis from addressing the possibility of an infected and contagious child. Ibsen, of course, would never adhere to so fundamentalist an idea as original sin, but neither would he embrace the optimistic belief in human perfectibility—about this much his critics are in agreement. For the playwright, other forces in nature and in society were as much impediments to progress and human hopes as the pessimistic religious doctrine had ever been.

Ibsen's pessimism as well as some oblique but noteworthy elements in the play may pertain to Gray's other question, whether Oswald but not Regine would have inherited syphilis. Again, perhaps Regine is infected. And if she is not already, she may soon be. For when she goes to work— euphemistically expressed—as an entertainer in her foster father's home, she will play what the nineteenth century understood to be the prostitute's dangerous role as a means by which venereal disease spread through the society. Ibsen would be indulging in an ironic social judgment if Regine walks out on Oswald only in the end to share his doom.

An awareness of the debates over syphilis in the mid-nineteenth century encourages a look at the real (rather than purely metaphorical) status of syphilis in *Ghosts*. Indeed, Raymond Williams amends his argument on behalf of the metaphor when he concedes that literal syphilis was "for obvious reasons" what "mattered to [Ibsen's] admiring or repelled audience."[23] To understand this critical contradiction, one would have to look forward to some happy day when AIDS will be curable or at least fairly easily treatable, especially in its early stages, which will themselves be readily detectable through diagnostic tests (as syphilis was not when *Ghosts* was written), and then turn back to such plays as *As Is* and *The Normal Heart* and argue that AIDS is merely a metaphor for the diseased perceptions of a homophobic society, such perceptions internalized by a large segment of the gay community. This would give one some notion of what it means to say that syphilis is but a metaphor in *Ghosts*. In fact the real disease and its symbolic manifestations interact throughout Ibsen's play.

Ghosts itself demands that the venereal disease that could not yet be diagnosed or successfully treated be taken seriously, as Ibsen's audience apparently took it. One of its themes, Ibsen critics agree, concerns people's right to experience joy in life, society's attitude towards sexuality an impediment to human happiness. The play describes the beginnings of a sexual revolution, mild, it is true, by today's standards, but real enough for Oswald to outrage Parson Manders and to shake up his mother's view of her marriage when he describes people who form sexual relations outside of sanctioned marriage but far different from the casual contacts associated with prostitution. Admittedly *Ghosts* does not envision, or at least does not even by implication advocate the kind of unbridled sexual freedom the implications of which are treated in both *As Is* and *The Normal Heart*, but the reality of sexually transmitted diseases cannot be separated from increasing sexual freedom.

It is worth noting—again, in the context of what was being argued by nineteenth-century syphilologists—that Ibsen is not as definitive as his critics would have it about how Oswald contracted syphilis. Even if his father's pipe was not the direct cause of his disease, Captain Alving was a negative model for his son, morally contagious—or at least Mrs. Alving thought so. For her, Oswald's disease is itself one of the play's ghosts if in fact her sending her son away proved a futile sacrifice and her dead husband has returned to haunt her through his legacy to their son. Moreover, her son's life abroad suggests that Parson Manders may not be wrong to argue that Captain Alving remains his son's ideal, an argument that suggests multiple levels of real and symbolic contagion. But if Mrs. Alving is not an indirect but a direct source of infection, then her words about wishing to be alone in providing Oswald with his inheritance—"Anything my son gets is to come from me, and that's that" (377)—pick up added irony in an already irony-ridden play.

But Oswald himself thinks at first that his own decision to live in defiance of the puritanical conventions of his time have brought on the illness. His words of remorse—

The incredible truth! This blissfully happy life I'd been living with my friends, I should never have indulged in it. It had been too much for my strength. So it was my own fault, you see! (396)—

were not likely to be lost on Ibsen's audience any more than they are likely to be lost on a contemporary audience that immediately perceives analogies between syphilis in the nineteenth century and AIDS in the twentieth. A lament comparable to Oswald's is uttered by the young man in Brieux's *Damaged Goods* who has similarly joined his comrades to experience a single sexual encounter that, despite earlier precaution, infects him with syphilis—and Brieux may have borrowed from Ibsen on this point. In *Ghosts* Ibsen supplies enough hints about Oswald's earlier symptoms to suggest that congenital syphilis (which Oswald has not yet considered) may have weakened his constitution, but that through his own behavior he had brought the latent disease to an active stage. But *Ghosts* never resolves the matter of *how* Oswald contracted his disease: that Mrs. Alving lays bare his inheritance is not conclusive. It will be remembered that Cullerier labeled as a useful myth the idea of congenital syphilis, since it might bring a modicum of peace to a family already tortured beyond endurance.

There is more to the social context that surrounds the theme of venereal disease in *Ghosts*. Brian Downs has pointed out about its intellectual background that in the decade before Ibsen wrote *Ghosts*, Norway was experiencing much controversy over a disease that afflicted it more than any other European country—leprosy, which was often compared to syphilis. How it was spread and how it was to be contained was of great concern, and after the disease organism was identified by G. A. Hansen, the isolation of infected persons significantly reduced the incidence of the illness.[24] Now neither *Ghosts* nor *An Enemy of the People* raises issues concerning the civil rights of sick and contagious people in the context of society's need to contain a disease, but Ibsen is concerned in both plays with the role of the individual in society, and both plays thereby make possible such an extension of their themes.

Moreover, *Ghosts* does raise specific issues about syphilis transmission, and, again, the whole issue of Engstrand's proposed home for sailors acquires added significance if Regine is understood to have some latent or future relationship to syphilis. When she learns that she is Captain Alving's illegitimate daughter and thus Oswald's half-sister, she reflects that her mother "was that sort" (413), as if contemplating her own heritage. Ibsen's Norwegian text says "Så mor var altså slik en" (so mother was such a *one*), which does not explicitly specify others whom Alving infected when they came into intimate contact with him but may infer a larger group of which Regine's mother was a member. Even if this were not Ibsen's intentions, Engstrand, his sailor's home, and Regine's capitulation to what she takes to be part of her personal inheritance still remain symbolic manifestations of how society perverts human sexuality. But even here, syphilis remained for Ibsen's time too deadly a manifestation of the sexual instinct gone wrong for its reality to be relegated to a literary metaphor.

Ghosts contains its own reminder concerning a propensity to transform a physical reality into mere metaphor. For the play not only takes its images from nature—rain, sun, microparasites—but also draws a clear distinction between the metaphorical vehicle and its referent. The rain with which the play opens and the dismal day that accompanies it represent the social environment in which Mrs. Alving lives and Oswald was raised. But it also stands for the resulting internalization of nature as inner disorder. Parson Manders complains of the rain and is glad to be in a dry room, and Oswald protests against the incessant rain that he construes as a personal persecutor. But Regine, practical and straightforward, that is, unlikely to turn the realm of phenomena into symbols, reminds Manders that the rain is a blessing to the farmers. At the same time *Ghosts* reminds its reader that— to use the words of Coleridge's "Dejection Ode," a poem that not only uses nature as metaphor but is *about* doing so—"we receive but what we give." And, to employ Bruce Kapferer's explanation that it is not nature itself but disordered nature that enters into a conflict with culture,[25] one way of disordering the natural is to relegate physical reality exclusively to metaphoric status. By extension, to look at syphilis in *Ghosts* as *only* metaphor raises a double danger, first to a reading of the play and an understanding of its symbols, and, second, to a world in which sexually communicable diseases pose real and not merely symbolic threats.

Not to belabor the point any further, Ibsen intended that his audience understand venereal disease to be both real and symbolic, just as Blake did when he wrote "London." What Oswald's illness symbolizes has been variously interpreted as "all the determinist forces that crush humanity";[26] as some kind of secular but unspecific version of original sin, a "heritage that gnaws away at the strength of living men";[27] as a warning that the modern age was too optimistic in its belief in progress, thus neglecting "the significance of heredity";[28] and social degeneracy. In defense of the individual, however, Ibsen also depicts through the image of disease the ghosts of outmoded puritanical ideas that formed inherited obstacles to human joy. As Brandt has noted, since the "late nineteenth century, venereal disease has been used as a symbol for a society characterized by a corrupt sexuality . . . a symbol of pollution and contamination, and cited as a sign of deep-seated sexual disorder, a literalization of what was perceived to be a decaying social order." Thus "venereal disease came to be seen as an affliction of those who willfully violated the moral code, a punishment for sexual irre-sponsibility."[29] In suggesting that such an idea was itself sick, and making syphilis a metaphor for such beliefs, Ibsen was turning this social construc-tion of the disease back upon the society that so defined it.

Moreover, syphilis shares with AIDS a long latency period in which the infected person is asymptomatic and thus reality is confounded. Both ill-nesses allow the writer who deals with them to explore a widespread literary theme, the conflict between semblance and actuality. As an Ibsen critic who coins a parody of Kant's categorical imperative has put it, an Ibsen character must obey the injunction to "act so that you *appear* as that which public opinion expects you to be."[30] On the metaphorical level, that is, syphilis in *Ghosts* represents not only what is wrong with the society that impedes the personal development of the individual but also what has as a result gone wrong in the psychic development of that individual who, first, lives accord-ing to such a code, denying the authenticity of self, and, second, internalizes the illiberal principle as a way to live. Oswald's psychological state will be returned to and it will be argued that in *Ghosts* the themes of physical and mental illness, and personal identity, come together.

The matter of personal identity supplies *Ghosts* with many themes, and there is some question as to whether Mrs. Alving or Oswald or both (embroiled in a disturbed mother-son relationship) are Ibsen's main focus of interest. One way to approach this is to start with the customary emphasis on Mrs. Alving, beginning with the significance of her surname, which was originally to supply Ibsen's title for his play. Alving signifies "descended from elves,"[31] and so *Ghosts* too is involved in the theme of the pseudo-earthly paradise.

Ibsen imbued names with great significance; drafts of his plays reveal his constant revising of his characters' names, and many of them contain derivatives of elfland (Alf, the child in *Brand;* Thea Elvsted in *Hedda Gabler,* for example). The Rosmer *name* in *Rosmersholm* helps focus attention on the supernatural creature who lends the play its title. In *Ghosts* Parson Manders asks Oswald if he may call him by his Christian name, ironically sidestepping the dangerous implications of "Alving," and reinforcing his, the clergyman's, interest in bringing the family into line with tradition. And it is the Alving name that adds another dimension to the playwright's claim that after creating Nora he *had* to create Mrs. Alving. It is no accident that Nora is known by her first name, and Helene as *Mrs. Alving.*

The significance of "Alving" is discussed by Maurice Gravier in an essay that argues for the influence on Ibsen of Danish ballads that depict sexual or marital unions between humans and beings from another world. Gravier has argued that these two realms, "Elfarland," or what is more commonly known in English as fairyland, and "Beijarland," the real world or the realm of the social establishment, define the settings and themes of Ibsen's important plays. In the human world is found a society tyrannized by conventions; in elfland, a marginal elite place themselves closer to nature, obeying a very different call.

Reminding his reader of Ibsen's care in choosing names, Gravier says of the Alvings—father and son,

Their nature as elves encourages one and then the other to reject the morality of bigots and puritans and to live according to their impulses and desires. The Alvings certainly belong to Elfland, and Helene, unfortunate wife and mother, tries in vain to draw them into the realm of conventional morality.[32]

Gravier also suggests, almost in passing, that Nora of *A Doll's House* possesses the temperament of an elf.[33] But Gravier does not argue for the direct presence of folklore in *A Doll's House;* nor does he explore what it means that Helene is defined and defines herself as *Mrs.* Alving, that is, the elf's wife.

To place Nora and Mrs. Alving in a world divided between fairyland and human society is to have two folkloristic depictions of woman's role in such a dichotomy, and, by extension, two views of woman's choice in the society Ibsen was writing about. As I have argued elsewhere, Nora is a character based on the widespread Scandinavian (indeed universal) story of the swan maiden, an elf woman—to use Gravier's description—who has been literally trapped in a patriarchically defined world of domestic relations.[34] Usually, the symbolic act of stealing her clothing ties her to her husband's world, and when she rediscovers their whereabouts (i.e., Nora's misplaced dancing dress), she is transformed by putting them on, after which she leaves her home, husband, and children. Ibsen, as is typical in his treatment of folklore themes, inverts the traditional motif: his swan maiden, Nora, does not escape to fairyland (unless, of course, one wants to take an extreme male chauvinistic view of the play), but symbolically acts to acquaint herself with the ordinary world so that she may live in it on some other terms than her society, her husband's appropriated realm, makes possible.

In contrast, Mrs. Alving already inhabits a highly conventional domain, and to the end of the play, she cannot fully shake off its conventions. Indeed, Sprinchorn is correct to say, in a description consistent with Gravier's thesis, that in the last act, she "is a woman torn between two mutually exclusive philosophies: her old one of sacrifice; the new one of joie de vivre."[35] On that will hinge her final act, unknown when the final curtain falls: will she or will she not help her son commit suicide, symbolically returning him to "elfarland," which in the world's folklore and legends is frequently associated with the realm of the dead.

If she does administer the fatal dose, Mrs. Alving will be reversing the role she took on when she married Mr. Alving. For in contrast to the woman who comes from elfland and is trapped by domestic relations (the swan maiden Nora) is the woman, also depicted in the Danish magic ballads on which Gravier bases his analysis, whose role it is to save the elfman. This theme belongs in the ballads to what Per Schelde Jacobsen has called "soul" stories. "The troll," that is, the elfman, "is no longer just nature's tough and powerfully violent representative," but is rather a "pitiful human" who is "trapped inside the troll's body." In this variation of beauty and the beast, the kiss of a pure woman will turn the troll or elfman into a handsome prince. "Once a prince again, he wants to marry his savior."[36] Helene Alving's socially generated frigidity, which supposedly forced her husband to seek his sexual satisfaction elsewhere, is an ironic rendering of this theme and has much to say about the folklore motif that is beyond the scope of this discussion. The very least that can be noted, however, is that Ibsen suggests the impossibility of taming the elfman so long as elfland and the real world remain separate domains, and thus the playwright points the way to a consideration of how thwarted is the quest for self so long as the two realms are sundered. Ibsen has, that is, used folklore and its rendering of the wordly paradise to explore the theme of self-realization that *Ghosts* shares with so many of his works.

There are many versions of an other world in *Ghosts*, and behind them stands once again the archetypal image of Eden and the fall. No Western play written when *Ghosts* was composed could deal with the theme of inherited sin without evoking the idea of original sin and a punishment whose unremitting nature traps generation after generation. It is, moreover, the biblical paradise that supplies *Ghosts* with one of its greatest ironies, and links the folkloristic themes in the play to the naturalistic depiction of syphilis. At one point, Oswald protests against a society that has always defined work as a punishment. That humans must toil in pain for their daily bread is but one of the afflictions that commenced with the fall; and to invoke the one is to imply the others, the most severe of which is human mortality. If people are not killed by some macroparasite or accident, then inevitably their bodies will be prey to disease.

It is for this reason that images of an earthly paradise traditionally promise not only ease and immortality but also exemption from painful, debilitating, and mortal illnesses. It is this that makes Oswald's inheritance of syphilis from his father (whether or not it is transmitted via Mrs. Alving) particularly significant. Elfland, one of the earthly paradises, becomes *the source of,* not the respite from, disease. This irony will be echoed in both *As Is* and *The Normal Heart* as AIDS, often a sexually transmitted disease, is associated with a sexual ideology connected to the other worlds of baths and leather bars in which is sought a pleasure free of conventional morality. Meanwhile, Ibsen's ironic reversals suggest not only that the self cannot be defined in terms of an *un*earthly paradise but also that equally futile is an attempt to civilize the elf-beast, that is, turn Caliban into a prince by teaching him to repress all natural instincts. It is not just that Captain Alving erred in seeking the pure woman who his society encouraged him to believe was his salvation but also that Helene Alving erred in agreeing to take on woman's socially imposed role. One of the ghosts in this play so full of haunted spirits and memories is Oswald's recapitulation of his father's quest and his internalized belief about woman that projects her into the role of redemptress. Oswald tells his mother that Regine "is [his] only hope!"

(400). That Oswald symbolically mixes up his Eves and his Marys in his mistaken perception of Regine, while his father had gotten it right, turns out to make no difference: father and son end up with the same impasse.

There are several ghosts of Eden in Ibsen's play. The most obvious concerns the implied reference to a fall in the diagnosis of the Parisian physician who believes he has identified congenital syphilis and tells Oswald he has been "worm-eaten [ormstukket] since birth" (396). The reference could be to any microparasite, but the circle of associations need not be shrunk very far to invoke an image of a worm-eaten apple, that is, original sin. Then there is Regine's fixation on Oswald's promise to take her to Paris, a theme already treated in an early Ibsen play and developed further when Hilde Wangel and Maja, in *The Master Builder* and *When We Dead Awaken,* similarly reproach the men they believe to have gone back on the promise to reveal all the glory of the world. Nature itself, as Jacobsen indicates, is engaged in a struggle with culture[37] (an expulsion theme writ large), the very collision, again, yielding a disease metaphor as the individual struggles vainly to find an authentic self that accommodates the best of both realms. Conceivably, the incest motif in *Ghosts* as well as in other Ibsen plays suggests a striving for union between two close yet dichotomous halves. And, finally, Paris and Rome with their bohemian aestheticism suggest the partially unreal world of the artist in conflict with philistinism.

The romantic period in which Ibsen wrote was well aware that the quest for the earthly paradise could lead to madness or suicide—or both. It is a sign of Keats's basic attachment to the mundane that he depicts himself in the "Ode to a Nightingale" to be only *half* in love with easeful death. Keats tragically died of the White Plague, tuberculosis, when his genius was just being affirmed in his poems, but the poems themselves speak of emotional health. To pursue the disease metaphor of *Ghosts,* it is necessary to shift from literal disease and its social symbols to the psychological problems also commanding attention in Ibsen's time.

One critic, Derek Russell Davis, holding Ibsen to medical accuracy in *Ghosts,* concludes that the difficulties surrounding a diagnosis of neurosyphilis disappear if for "syphilis" one reads "schizophrenia." In the late nineteenth century, such a diagnosis was unknown, and Oswald's supposed mental illness would have been called secondary dementia, a chronic, incurable, degenerative condition believed to be hereditary. Ibsen might have been acquainted with the Paris psychiatrists who were writing on the subject, and whose theories illuminate the play. Davis builds a persuasive case history of the Alving family pathology—one that all interpreters of the play would do well to read whether or not they accept Davis's diagnosis. In fact, when his essay was anthologized, Davis added a disclaimer, admitting that the term *schizophrenia* had come to be avoided "because it only has meaning in the context of an outmoded theory,"[38] psychiatric emphasis having shifted from the patient's thought disorders to family interaction. This addendum made it easier for Ibsen critics to discard Davis's argument. But he was onto something; it is just unfortunate that his approach has been rejected as thoroughly as he rejected syphilis as the disorder from which Oswald was suffering. Drawing on Paris psychiatrists of Ibsen's time, Davis overlooked the contemporary treatises of syphilologists such as Fournier and Cullerier. To place *Ghosts* in a position to link contemporary explorations of both syphilis and mental illness is to provide additional significance to a major work that probably needs no further arguments for its thematic complexities.

But again, it is virtually a commonplace in criticism of *Ghosts* to read venereal disease as a metaphor for a sick society that stifled the individual. In the words of Parson Manders, "all this demanding to be happy in life" (371) is part of what he sees as the moral decline of his times. The usual view has been well described by John Northam, who argues,

By echoing the terms "inheritance" and "lurks" that Mrs. Alving herself used to describe what she meant by "ghosts" in Act II, [Oswald] gives a wider reference to his disease; it is no longer a single, individual fact, but a fact related to, produced by, those ghosts of dead ideas by which society and, as has been abundantly revealed, even Mrs. Alving, have always been haunted.[39]

That such ghosts will prove to be sources of psychological illness of the sort Davis describes would seem to follow from such a description, not only because of the general conflict between the individual and society, in this play reaching an extreme point, but also because of the specific tension between mother and son portrayed in *Ghosts*.

Congenital syphilis objectifies — almost parodies — the process by which the infant Oswald internalizes his environment, his subsequent psychological development as doomed as his body. It is even possible to draw a parallel between the latency period in syphilis and that period of time between the emotional damage done to a child and the later outbreak of serious mental illness. For example, James Masterson describes adolescent patients suffering from what he calls abandonment depression resulting from the mother's failure to provide emotional support during a critical period of her offspring's early development: "The abandonment feelings then recede into the unconscious where they lie submerged like an abscess, their overwhelming but hidden force observable only through the tenacity and strength of the defense mechanisms used to keep them in check."[40] Oswald, who similarly has endeavored to hold back the physical and psychological fate that overwhelms him, reveals signs of an abandonment depression:

OSWALD: I shouldn't have thought it made much difference to you whether I was around or not.
MRS. ALVING: Have you the heart to say that to your mother, Oswald?
OSWALD: Yet you managed to get on quite well without me before. (394)

Oswald is alluding to his mother's having sent him away as a young child, a reproach she also suffers from Parson Manders, who tells her she has neglected her maternal duties as she had her wifely. She, in turn, had hoped to prevent her son from "breathing the foul air of this polluted house" (376), although she almost welcomes his diseased state as a reason he has returned to her—as dependent as when he was an infant. To say that Masterson could apply his theory to *Ghosts*, in which it is clear that Oswald never achieved healthy individuation, is not to replace the nineteenth-century diagnosis of secondary dementia with Masterson's borderline syndrome so much as to reinforce an argument for evidence of psychological illness in Ibsen's play in which syphilis is thematically implicated.

Many psychological theories bear on the various concepts of the self that this book has been following. Oswald's life can be read as his attempt to become an individual—a persistent theme in the playwright's canon. As Ibsen's biographer Halvdan Koht puts it, Oswald can only " 'realize' " himself by recognizing the "true morality [that] must be found within the individual,"[41] which can only be discovered by discarding the heritage of the past. Once again, Ibsen battles what Sprinchorn calls a "cultural disease"[42] by turning society's concepts against itself. Returning to Brandt's point that for Ibsen's age syphilis was a "symbol of pollution and contamination," a "sign of deep-seated sexual disorder," Ibsen depicts Oswald's disease as ultimately caused by the society that first perverts the sexual instinct and then so interprets the outcome of such a twisting of human nature.

In agreeing that the "central problem" of *Ghosts* "is the problem of personal development,"[43] Ibsen's critics have, again, not always agreed on whose development, Mrs. Alving's or Oswald's, is at stake. Francis Fergusson probably put his finger on the issue when he wrote that "Oswald is, of course, not only a symbol for his mother, but a person in his own right, with his own quest for freedom and release."[44] When Oswald recognizes that his illness has rendered that quest futile, he cries out, "Mother, it's my mind that's given way ... destroyed" (395).[45] At first, his physical and psychological disintegration manifests itself in a rather simple and blatant narcissism, his drive for self-preservation creating a chasm between himself and the world:

You must remember I'm a sick man, Mother. I can't be bothered very much with other people, I've got enough to think of with myself. (416)

But in his self-preoccupation, this narcissism takes a more subtle form, and rather than a chasm between self and other is to be found the blurring of the boundaries that differentiate one's self from another's. In searching for his redemptress, as his father had earlier done in marrying his mother, Oswald can see in Regine nothing more than an extension of his own needs, and, ironically, understands that finally her equally narcissistic preoccupation would have served his own end as she would have willingly administered the fatal dose of morphine rather than be tied to an invalid. And that his mother has thwarted him even in this is all Oswald can think of when he reproaches her for Regine's having left the house:

MRS. ALVING: Regine would never have done it, never.
OSWALD: Regine would have done it. Regine was so marvellously light-hearted. And she'd soon have got bored with looking after an invalid like me.
MRS. ALVING: Then thank God Regine isn't here!
OSWALD: Well then, now you'll have to give me this helping hand, Mother. (420)

But the real horror of Oswald's disease is that before it destroys his body, it will obliterate that already-fragmented self he is so ruthlessly ready to defend, even in the paradoxical act of suicide. It is not death he fears but the possibility of his body surviving for years while his brain is virtually dead. His horror moves the play from the psychological to the philosophical plane and the body-mind problem. Syphilis is attacking Oswald's brain and his regression to idiocy and to the appearance of a "helpless child" is for him "revolting" (418). And Ibsen does describe Oswald's degeneration and dependence on his mother as a parody of the original mother-child bond. Therefore, as Oswald once relied on Mrs. Alving for nurturance, he will now have to rely on her for his death: "I never asked you for life. And what sort of a life is this you've given me? I don't want it! Take it back!" (420).

The theme does not stop with the controversy over euthanasia. In the play *As Is* Rich also asks the only person he can depend on to cooperate in his suicide when his subjective sense of himself as an attractive and hence sexually desirable man is obliterated by the ugly lesions of Kaposi's sarcoma being no longer concealable. But so long as Rich's mind is not affected by

AIDS dementia, he will still possess the intentionality that helps define the self. Self-intervention has been defined as "the assumption of control by [a person] over a line of action that otherwise would have taken a different course. [The person] initiates a new line of behavior which differs from that which normally would have occurred, or aborts his customary way of behaving."[46] Because Rich is still capable of self-intervention, there remains a self to be be preserved, a person to be talked out of suicide.

But when Oswald's mind goes, so does his self, and like Defoe, Ibsen brings to the fore the question of what matters in survival. Unable to make choices, to order his priorities in some ranking of values, Oswald must wrest from his mother *in advance*, while he can, the promise to help him do away with that body that is no longer part of a real self. His situation thus recognized, the debate over what happens when the curtain falls—does Mrs. Alving administer the overdose or not—seems beside the point (in addition to blurring the line between a dramatic production and real events that persist in time and can be speculated about even if outcomes are not known). For the different bases for selfhood will already have ceased to be operative. As a biological entity, Oswald's body, an insufficient criterion for selfhood, will not be "completed by some psychological entity";[47] even if he responds to biological stimuli, he will not experience any mental states, or at least not be aware that he is experiencing them;[48] he will lack self-direction and self-intervention without even experiencing the helplessness that results from knowing he cannot affect outcomes;[49] he probably will not have but certainly will not know he has the subjective feelings and representations that are "a person's fundamental reference point"[50] for locating personal identity. His mental life, which is critical to personal identity, will cease to exist. It is both tragic and paradoxical that what Oswald actually *cares* about in the present comes down to the reality that because the surviving "I" will not be himself in the psychological or philosophical sense, he in the future *will no longer care* whether his body survives or not.

What kind of psychological diagnosis can be applied to Oswald's situation? It is clear that even were Oswald a real person and not a literary character, there would be some disagreement on this point. But what psychiatrist and theorist Arnold Goldberg argues so eloquently about psychiatric theory appears applicable as well to the literary text and the different critical approaches that illuminate it:

Nature does not seem to care how we choose to view it, categorize it, or explain it. Whatever "it" may be, the world comes into being by our own vision of it, and this vision is a product of our theory. Because observations are not distinct from theory, any given chunk of the world will be seen in one way by one theory and in a somewhat different—or perhaps a radically different—way by another. [But] in a given community of persons who share a common language and who are trained to see things in a like way, there will be a high consensus about just what is out there.[51]

The critical debates over *Ghosts* reveal as much about plague as a literary theme as does the play itself. For this reason, the critics (and early syphilologists) rather than the text itself have been the focus of this discussion. Davis's view may not be *the* most accurate reading of Ibsen's play, but it is a significant contribution to the medical and psychological discussion that surrounds *Ghosts*. Davis did not, moreover, have to apologize for his use of *schizophrenia*, even if he subsequently decided not to use it. His later disclaimer and admission of a newer approach to the mental diseases encompassed by the term are not in fact the last word on the subject.[52] In any event, seizing on the label to discredit his argument involves a red herring. His case history is, again, a persuasive picture of family and individual pathology, in which syphilis and mental disease combine to thwart that realization of self held to be Ibsen's persistent concern. To use Goldberg's argument, many views of the individual self are applicable to Ibsen's great play, and these views are neither capable of being translated into each other nor so different as to suggest a futile relativism that defeats theory altogether.

Ibsen's ghosts echo through William M. Hoffman's play *As Is*.[53] Like Oswald, Rich is an artist—a writer rather than a painter—and he has written a book in which, as one of the characters significantly notes, the "main characters are all ghosts" (36). Like Oswald, although in ways barely specified and therefore to a lesser extent, the direction of his life has been influenced by his father. When he tells his lover Saul, "When I was a kid I used to spend all my time in libraries. My childhood was—," he is interrupted with, "If I had a father like yours I would have done the same" (46). Of course Rich's father has not infected him with AIDS. And a mother is mentioned neither in the play nor in Hoffman's preface, which draws on family concerns and influences. The play, that is, is in part about a search for self-identity,[54] but the past is not made up of ghosts that haunt its main character. When *As Is* begins, Rich and Saul are splitting up because Rich has found another lover, Chet. In the course of their bickering over the property they are dividing, Rich almost casually mentions to Saul that he has the early symptoms of the disease that has already killed so many of their friends.

While parents play but a minor role in the development of Hoffman's play, *As Is* contains striking parallels to *Ghosts*, Ibsen's play possibly being encapsulated in what is a minor episode in Hoffman's. In *Ghosts*, Mrs. Alving reproaches Parson Manders for being ineffectual and even rejecting when she turned to him for help after recognizing the debacle that was her marriage. Similarly, in *As Is*, a pregnant woman at an AIDS support group describes what is in essence Mrs. Alving's predicament when she becomes the likely means by which Captain Alving infects his yet-unborn son with the disease from which they both will die.

PWA [PERSON WITH AIDS] 2: . . . These things don't happen in Brewster. Police officers don't shoot up heroin, cops don't come down with the "gay plague" —that's what they call it in Brewster. I can't talk to Bernie. I'll never forgive him. Have a chat with the minister? "Well Reverend Miller, I have this little problem. My husband has AIDS, and I have AIDS, and I'm eight months pregnant, and I . . ." (38)

But the most dramatic similarity between Oswald and Rich is that each appeals to the person closest to him for cooperation in committing suicide at that point when the disease becomes unbearable. Oswald knows from what his doctors have told him that each attack will bring him closer to being the kind of imbecile he cannot bear to contemplate being. To preclude his fate as a preternaturally old man having to be fed and cared for like a baby, he has been hoarding packets of morphine and he appeals to his terrified and resistant mother that when the time comes, she administer the fatal dose. This image of a human being reduced to his diseased body appears in one of the many significant "jokes" in *As Is*: AIDS can, as Rich sardonically relates—also to a horrified relative, his brother—"turn a fruit into a vegetable" (50). He too has tried to hoard doses of a potentially lethal drug, but in the hospital where they are dispensed, the nurse watches to make sure he swallows his pills.

Just as Oswald begs his mother to follow his instructions, so Rich tries to convince Saul to purchase sufficient amounts of Seconal so that when the lesions on his body caused by Kaposi's sarcoma spread above his neck, he can end his life. But whereas *Ghosts* ends on an almost completely hopeless note, it is with regard to the theme of suicide that *As Is* proves life-affirming. Saul first buys and then throws away the Seconal, and promises that he will stay with Rich "as is," which, William Green notes in an essay on the play, is a term used by manufacturers who sell damaged although saleable goods.[55] The play never promises that Rich will survive AIDS, since as in Oswald's case, each attack and hospitalization will bring Rich closer to death. Hoffman's conclusion refuses to flinch from this reality. Still, *As Is* ends more optimistically than *Ghosts:* "Rich should be out of the hospital again in a week or so. For a while. He's a fighter" (58).

Sustaining this contrast between the pessimism of Ibsen's play and the limited optimism of Hoffman's is what might first appear to be an anomalous parallel in the plays' images: the sun in *Ghosts* and neon lights in *As Is.* For Mrs. Alving, the sun is an image of the beauty and joy that make life worth living; the sun also supplies hope, dawn like spring suggesting birth and renewal. But because the sun's daily rising promises a permanence and continuity that often mocks human hopes, it sends her double messages, allowing her to bury her dread and deny the reality of Oswald's prognosis for his own illness. Moreover, in the nineteenth century the sun was a conventional sign of enlightenment, and Mrs. Alving is in sore need of guidance as she must decide whether to seek medical help or administer the fatal drug that will end Oswald's life. In the play's last lines an almost incoherent Oswald begs for the sun, and his mother cannot offer it to him.

The comparable scene and image in *As Is* is more life-sustaining. When Saul reluctantly purchases the Seconal Rich had both begged and demanded he buy, he plans to save some of the pills for his own suicide. But then Saul glimpses in a puddle of water the image of a neon light that prompts him to throw away the drug. He later tells Rich,

In this dirty little puddle was a reflection of the red neon sign. It was beautiful. And the whole street was shining with the incredible colors. They kept changing as the different signs blinked on and off . . . I don't know how long I stood there. A phrase came to my head: "The Lord taketh and the Lord giveth." (55)

This technological rendering of the sun's natural light is a subtle one. Whether Hoffman was bringing Ibsen's play into the modern world or actually exorcising the ghosts of *Ghosts*, his reader is free to contemplate this substitution for Ibsen's sun, an image of light produced by technology. Hoffman's neon light takes on the appeal of the sex shop that it illuminates, symbolizing the freedom of sexual pleasure from nature, from procreation. But the artificial light promises something far more significant than physical joy, as Saul's evocation of God's promise of life indicates. What, after all, is the real hope of the AIDS sufferer? The same hope that sustains sufferers of all disease, relying now more than ever, or so Brandt reminds his readers, on the laboratory of the medical scientist, or on the special expertise of the doctor. Saul throws away the life-taking drug to preserve Rich's life as long as he can because even if there is no magic bullet today, there may be one tomorrow. Science, in the technological guise of a neon light, holds out this promise.

Whatever the direct influence of Ibsen on Hoffman, other significant comparisons between them point to themes inherent in their subject matter rather than a deliberate borrowing by *As Is* from *Ghosts*. The similarities might begin with the folklore that supplied Ibsen with the symbolic elfland that as symbol challenges the real world and its dominant culture. As Per Schelde Jacobsen works out in detail, both in the Danish ballads and in Ibsen's plays, nature and culture (with its subcultures) are delineated by carefully mapped out areas of space.[56] It may seem like a poor and even inappropriate joke to say that fairyland operates in this way in *As Is*, but the play itself does not hesitate to draw on such frames of reference. At one point, when Saul and Rich are embroiled in one of their frequent quarrels, Saul taunts Rich concerning the book the latter is so pleased to have published: "Just how many copies [do] you think a book of 'fairy tales' will sell?" (34). A humorous and ironic return to Eden is provided by Rich, who wonders if there is after death any "place as sweet as this one." He expresses the wish to be cremated, his ashes "to fertizilize the apple tree in the middle of [a] pasture." But his image is also a sign of his fall and his disease: "When you take a bite of an apple from that tree think of me" (56).

In short, one way to read *As Is* is to imagine what Ibsen's play could have been like if it had been written from the perspective of the character who is so important but never actually appears except as one of the many ghosts that haunt the Alving house—Captain Alving, the man from elfland. His point of view only exists in the play to the extent that his wife and would-be redeemer comes to appreciate her part in his sexual promiscuity and understands that by trying to civilize him, she had only succeeded in destroying his (and her own) capacity for joy, their world allowing so little room for personal happiness. A variation on this theme also appears in *As Is*. By his own admission, Saul is the homebody, less inclined to seek other lovers, whereas Rich's sexual promiscuity is part of his resistance to their settled domestic life:

RICH: [We] loved each other. But that wasn't enough for me. I don't think you ever understood this: you weren't my muse, you were . . . *(He searches for the word.)* Saul. *(Saul rises and looks out the window.)* I loved you but I wanted someone to write poems to. During our marriage I had almost stopped writing and felt stifled. . . . (47)

Like Ibsen, who treats the artist and society in many plays, Hoffman takes up the theme of the romantic artist torn between philistine domesticity and creativity, art being traditionally linked to a virtually other world. From the point of view of conventional society, the artist leads an aberrant and hence diseased existence, and the equation of illness with the literary life is a common heritage bequeathed from the nineteenth century to the twentieth. Ibsen's *Ghosts* is a significant contribution to this rendering of the theme. Thomas Mann's *Death in Venice* constitutes perhaps the most profound symbolization of plague in such a context. Hoffmann's addition to this literature extends Mann's treatment, to make explicit how the gay community could readily identify with artists perceived to exist in a subculture.

In treating the artist's search for self-identity and attaching it to Rich's personal quest as a gay man, Hoffman's play almost inevitably raises questions concerning literature's role during plague. To explain, it is useful to place Rich alongside Defoe's narrator in his *Journal of the Plague Year* as well as Blake's speaker in "London." It will be remembered that in both works, these observers of plague wander the streets of London, observing and pitying, but keeping an emotional distance from the pestilence. If "London" is polemical it is because of its commitment to ideals that nonetheless remain disconcertingly abstract. Similarly, Defoe's H. F. had maintained a line between public and private voice, keeping his most personal reactions to the plague hidden from view, in part because the essentially lyric "I" subverts the critical premise that art should move the audience to thought and action. Once *As Is* shifts its focus of interest from AIDS to Rich's search for his self, something similar occurs. To anticipate the discussion of *The Normal Heart*, one way to put this is to argue that Larry Kramer went out of his way to avoid a play like *As Is*, in which, some theater critics argue, Rich could be suffering from almost any fatal disease. No one would have to remind Kramer's audience that the subject of his play is deadly or that the staging must not contribute to the distinction between the play's form, its power to please on one side, and its content, AIDS, on the other. This is not to make invidious comparisons between Hoffman's and Kramer's works but to argue that, together, they reflect the tensions in plague literature — the quest for personal and artistic identity always threatening to remove the work from the social arena.[57]

In what became the preface to his published play,[58] Hoffman describes how he first learned about AIDS while writing an opera libretto, *The Ghosts of Versailles*. (This may explain what appear to be echoes from Ibsen, but also why Hoffman would have an additional reason, beyond subject matter, to associate his own work with *Ghosts*.) He relates that he first viewed as absurd the existence of a disease capable of differentiating on the basis of personal identity, of "distinguishing between homo- and heterosexual men?

Come on" (5). But as he hears of more and more fatalities and close friends who are stricken, and, in addition, learns about his father's cancer and his uncle's stroke—both relatives would die from their illnesses—he responds to his depression as does Defoe's H. F. when he is finally overwhelmed by what he perceives of as a plague intent on destroying an entire population. As "a sort of a therapy," writes Hoffman, "I started to express my feelings on paper" (6).

Unlike H. F., however, Hoffman is ready to go public with his most personal thoughts: "I was willing to go to any lengths for my play, except to imagine myself having AIDS. I was not afraid of contracting the disease through casual physical contact with those who had it. I was well aware that AIDS is transmitted only by an exchange of body fluids. But on a deep irrational level, I was terrified of catching it by identifying with those who had it" (7). It was writing the play itself that helped him work through those feelings, as Defoe suggests that writing in his journal helped H. F. control emotions whose precise nature he never reveals. In terms of this comparison between Hoffman and Defoe, it is noteworthy that Hoffman asks God to protect him as he writes his play. And just as H. F. expresses gratitude to that divine providence that allowed him to survive the plague, Hoffman says of his plea, "He did" (7).

As Is is almost Wordsworthian in its composition. It represents the powerful overflow of emotions through which, as the English poet expresses it, the reader "must necessarily be in some degree enlightened, and his affections ameliorated." Hoffman, however, cannot count on this bridge between writer and audience, and must maintain a balance between self-expression—"And when I'm frightened in this time of trouble, I'm loving to myself" (8)—and a subject that virtually demands that the playwright engage others in some ethically significant fashion. This is a formidable challenge to the writer on plague, and illuminates the tragic irony of *As Is*, which is that precisely at the moment when Rich finally realizes his quest for self, he experiences the first symptom of AIDS, the disease that threatens not only his body but also his newly achieved personal identity, which is deeply implicated in the artist's.

Rich's epiphany returns this discussion to the theme it shares with *Ghosts*, both plays contrasting a plague-ridden world with some version of the earthly paradise. *As Is* not only differentiates the domestic from the artist's realm but also maps out New York so that its various geographic locales stand for different cultures within the city. Hoffman's reviewers have pointed out that the leather bars in which Rich finds sexual partners constitute in themselves a demimonde:[59] they are analogous to the otherworlds Ibsen borrowed from the Danish ballads and other folklore. In Hoffman's play, specific neighborhoods, such as Christopher Street, are associated with the sexual ideology that in a pre-AIDS era was an expression of gay liberation. Proclaimed was a freedom from all ties but those consistent with a pleasure principle. When Saul laments that he misses and used to love "promiscuous sex," Rich amends the adjective "promiscuous" to "nondirective, noncommitted, nonauthoritarian" (28). Whether unconstrained sexual freedom can be equated with joy, however, is a question both *Ghosts* and *As Is* raise. Mrs. Alving's conversion to the joy of life, her awakening to her realization that withholding pleasure from her husband only pushed him back on his asocial inclinations, seems virtually parodied when one of Hoffman's nameless characters tells how "I once picked up a guy [who] liked to be yelled at in German. The only German I know is the 'Ode to Joy' from Beethoven's Ninth," which he then goes on to mock with a combination of curses and high-flown images (21).

The mockery reveals that membership in a counterculture does not guarantee the sought-after freedom to be an individual. In one of the play's multiple conversations (like operatic ensembles), an important rendering of conflicting individuality and communality emerges from the effort of each character to be heard:

CHET: Where's Tribeca?
SAUL: Did you hear me?
RICH: On the isle of Manhattan.
CHET: We're on the isle of Manhattan.
RICH: We are.
LILY: The main characters are all ghosts. (36)

Hoffman's ghosts seem to represent the shadowy selves and aborted relationships that exist in the pseudo-earthly paradises bordered by discrete neighborhoods, inhabited not by persons but by the Clones that are unnamed and undifferentiated characters in the play. That Chet is so intent on locating them, as his complementary character, Regine, was in finding her wonderland in Paris and Rome, draws these characters even closer together: when Rich becomes ill, Chet, his new lover, leaves him as Regine had left Oswald.

In his analysis of Ibsen's folklore sources, Jacobsen has depicted the importance of bridges between symbolically discrete areas of space representing nature and culture.[60] Similarly, bridges constitute a major image in *As Is,* also representing a passage by an individual from one psychological stage to another. Rich describes his lonely childhood, his "desperate" (46) need to find people like himself, as well as a time when he rejected the role of "your typical office-worker-slash-writer" (47), grew a beard, and wore sandals so that he would be fired and could just write. But neither living with a steady Saul nor total freedom from human commitment proved satisfying: selfhood could be achieved neither through nor without ties to some other person. It was when he was running on the East River Drive on a dark night that

I came from the darkness into the light. I'm running downtown and I make this bend and out of nowhere straight up aheaa is the Manhattan Bridge and then the Brooklyn Bridge, one after another, and my earphones are playing Handel's *Royal Fireworks Music*. It can't get better than this, I know it. I'm running and crying from gratitude. I came from the darkness into the light. (47)

Jacobsen has suggested that in light of the significantly delineated neighborhoods of *As Is*, the bridges offer a potential for Rich to achieve his identity by breaking free of the exclusive ghettos inhabited by a large segment of the gay community.[61] Again, it is thus tragic in the classical sense that after this *self*-recognition scene, Rich experiences the first symptoms of AIDS.

It is difficult, however, to think that Hoffman created this tragic moment for its own poignant sake. Realistically, it was within the subcultural space of geographically segregated neighborhoods that AIDS was most prevalent. As one of the hospice workers says in the play, "I've worked with thirty-five people altogether. About a third of them had AIDS. It *is* the Village" (37). Rich's experience of a secure self-image, which then makes it possible for him authentically to bond with another human being, Saul, is poetically expressed in beautiful images of lit-up bridges and evocations of Handel's music before which discretely bound-off areas evaporate. This is not to say that individual epiphanies do not occur, but that for the artist the stark distinction between beauty and truth is always close at hand, although it is tempting to transform what Poe called the poetry of words into pure music. The light and music imagery in the scene in which Rich sees the bridges can also be found in a conversation between Rich and Chet (with a sarcastic remark thrown in by Saul) on a poem Rich has written:

CHET: There's a line of your poem I don't understand.
RICH: Only one? I have no idea what any of it means.
CHET: "The final waning moon . . ."
SAUL: Don't smile.
RICH: "And the coming of the light."
CHET: I love the way it sounds. (35)

In 1985 AIDS had indeed appeared to differentiate one group from another, gay men from the rest of society, and by Hoffman's own description of how he came to write his play, the disease was going to have a great impact on the self-awareness of those who had escaped infection. Again, *As Is* is by critical consensus a far less polemical play than *The Normal Heart*, which appeared at the same time. Nonetheless, in Hoffman's drama can be found the tension that makes *As Is* another ghost of the romantic tradition. The writer must choose between the personal and the lyric transfused with light and music, whose meaning is subordinate to its sound, or the social and dramatic, which plague would seem to demand.[62] But so long as such tension forms a dramatic motif, the play—even if not overtly polemical—remains anchored in the social world.

Ghosts is far less polemical than is *An Enemy of the People*, in which Ibsen not only divides public from private but also distinguishes the literally pestilential baths from the metaphorical disease from which Dr. Thomas Stockmann comes to decide his whole town and ultimately the entire modern world is suffering. This conversion of plague to social ill was, however, part of the radical revolutionary tradition of the middle and late nineteenth century. As Virchow writes in his essay on "Diseases of the People" (1849), as "individuals have their somatic and psychic diseases, which but represent the expression of the normal laws of life and thought under abnormal conditions, so also do we see somatic and psychic diseases in populations and nations."[63] Thus, says Virchow, "we may be allowed to speak of the health and disease of the people in an abstract manner." Do we not, he asks,

always find the diseases of the populace traceable to defects in society? No matter whether meteorological conditions, general cosmic changes and such are inculpated, never do these in themselves make epidemics, they only induce them whenever, through poor social conditions, the people have lived under abnormal conditions for a long time.[64]

Thus for Virchow the ills that inspired the European revolutions of 1848 and the epidemics of cholera during that time are intrinsically related. And such are the assumptions behind Stockmann's excoriation of his community: its infected water system is both real and a symbol of a deeper, widespread spiritual infection.

Whereas *An Enemy of the People* supports such an equation between literal and social epidemics, it also challenges the idea that the masses can be trusted to remedy their ills. And, in celebrating the reformer's individual conscience, the play draws a very fine line between an aristocracy of the intellect and blatant egotism.[65] As a physician, Stockmann had practised medicine in a rural section of Norway so remote from the culture of the city as to extract from him the observation that the people there would have been served better by a veterinarian than a doctor. And lest there be some misunderstanding of his intentions, Stockmann's denigration of the folk who were romantically exalted in his time is emphasized by the unambiguous animal imagery he employs to portray the common people, typified by his town's citizenry, which deems him the enemy when he brings them a truth they would prefer not to have. But until his discovery of that truth, Stockmann is delighted that his brother, the mayor of the community they grew up in, has brought him back from the country and guaranteed his income by putting him in charge of public health.

The town is facing economic problems, and its only hope is the baths that have been turned into a spa to attract visitors. During the previous year, however, Stockmann had noticed that "there were a number of curious cases of sickness among the visitors ... typhoid and gastric fever" (38; tyføse og gastriske tilfeller), his juxtaposition of an infectious disease with the milder and more general designation of stomach complaints perhaps being Ibsen's way of expressing the interaction between an individual and hence personal disorder and an epidemic that implicates an entire community. At first Stockmann thought the tourists had brought the infections with them, but, beginning to doubt that the problem had been in that sense carried in from outside, he set about analyzing the water, discovering that industrial wastes from his own father-in-law's tannery were serious pollutants:

DR. STOCKMANN: The whole establishment [the baths] is a whited poisoned sepulchre, I tell you! A most serious danger to health! All that filth up at Mölledal, where there's such an awful stench—it's all seeping into the pipes that lead to the pump-room! And that same damned, poisonous muck is seeping out on the beach as well! (38)

Naively, Stockmann expects to be treated as a hero by the municipal government, the liberal newspaper to which he is accustomed to contributing articles, and the townspeople. With feigned modesty he protests that he not be rewarded with "a parade or a banquet or a presentation" (80). Little by little, however, he discovers that to one extent or another, personal self-interest, either economic or ideological, turns the entire community against him, even the warring segments within it, when he delivers his message that all the town has to offer "those poor invalids who come to [it] in good faith and pay good money hoping to get their health back" is the "water's poison"

(54). The doctrine of self-preservation enunciated by Defoe's H. F. and Boccaccio's brigada has evolved into a social Darwinian struggle: as the newspaper publisher, Hovstad, says of his own apostasy from his liberal ideals, "That's the law of nature. Every animal must fight for survival" (121).

As he realizes the position he is in, Stockmann's stake in cleaning up the polluted baths shifts to the more evangelical aim of reforming the town: "It's no longer just the water-supply and the sewers now. No, the whole community needs cleaning up, disinfecting" (67). Ibsen's audience has no need to ponder these disease images: Stockmann's metaphor is hardly subtle as he lashes out at a town meeting:

When a place has become riddled with lies, who cares if it's destroyed? I say it should simply be razed to the ground! And all the people living by these lies should be wiped out, like vermin! You'll have the whole country infested in the end, so eventually the whole country deserves to be destroyed. And if it ever comes to that, then I'd say with all my heart: let it all be destroyed, let all its people be wiped out! (102)

To a now-generalized image of plague Stockmann has added the element of contagion. Moreover—to use the bubonic plague as a context here even if such was not Ibsen's intent—in his anger, Stockmann invokes the animal imagery that he uses to differentiate the masses from the intellectual elite with whom he identifies himself (but of which he can find no other example in the municipality's power structure). He has, in effect, conflated the rats and fleas that carry plague with the human beings that are then infected, and he would exterminate the latter as readily as the former: "I love this town so much that I'd rather destroy it than see it prosper on a lie" (102).

An Enemy of the People belongs to the literarature of civil disobedience, harking back at least as far as Sophocles's *Antigone* and carrying forward to, among other dramas, Bolt's portrayal of his "hero of selfhood," Thomas More. As in *Ghosts,* Ibsen continues to attack outmoded ideas, doctrines inherited from forefathers, the most dangerous among them, according to Stockmann, being the idea that the ignorant masses "are the very essence of the people"—that they "*are* the people" and "have the same right to criticize and to approve, to govern and to counsel as the few intellectually distinguished people" (98). The play was written after the public's outraged response to *Ghosts,* with its treatment of the still-taboo subject of syphilis. As Arno K. Lepke has written, "the first draft of *An Enemy of the People* was written by an irate man rising spontaneously to defend his authentic self. . . . Yet, after two revisions of the original draft, the final version of the play presents Doctor Stockmann as a highly questionable, blundering, paradoxical, and almost foolish rebel."[66] Perhaps another way to put this is to say that *An Enemy of the People* more fully explores the contradictions surrounding heroes and heroines of selfhood, who are deliberately or unwittingly transformed in literature into illiberal aristocrats, such contradictions being not always apprehended or appreciated by a would-be liberal audience.

An Enemy of the People may therefore not be as "*straightforwardly* polemical*" as Robert Brustein claims it is.[67] Looked at this way, moreover, the play appears less anachronistic in the Ibsen canon. For example, Michael Meyer's biography separates "The Critic of Society" from the succeeding "Explorer of the Unconscious," the chronology of Ibsen's plays locating *An Enemy of the People* in the latter category.[68] It does not, of course, explore the unconscious in the way that its predecessor, *Ghosts*, does, but it does investigate the problem of personal identity that is deeply implicated in the idea of an unconscious. *An Enemy of the People* reveals how difficult it is to separate the communal being, the social critic, from the individual whose conscience cannot be neatly disentangled from unconscious motivation.

The ambiguities surrounding Stockmann emerge, again, from the extension of the law of nature, or self-preservation, to social and economic survival, and beyond that to the inner realm of a defended self-esteem. A telling example is Stockmann's father-in-law, Morten Kill, probably the most repellent character in the play. It is his factory that has polluted the town's water supply; and when rumors of the pollution spread, he buys up the baths' stock very cheaply, effectively blackmailing Stockmann because it is then Mrs. Stockmann's inheritance that will be lost or will appreciate depending upon what her husband decides to do in his fight with the town. But in his opposition to Stockmann and his determination to stifle the truth about the pollution, Morten Kill is also concerned to preserve his good "name" (117), his reputation in the town upon which his sense of his own personal identity and standing in posterity rest.

To depict so many levels of self-interest in his characters Ibsen had to have contemplated how tenuous the line is between conscience and sheer egotism. In *An Enemy of the People,* only two characters come close to acting without a personal stake in outcomes. Stockmann's daughter, Petra, is one of Ibsen's true idealists, committed to the truth for its own sake. Thus she condemns the journalist Hovstad for pandering to his public's taste for cheap literature, rejecting his explanation that an editor can't always do what he wants, and that if he wants "to win people over to certain liberal and progressive ideas, it's no good scaring them all off" (72). She also rejects her would-be suitor when it becomes clear that his support for her father has to do with Hovstad's interest in her rather than the truth. But then, her defense of her father is difficult to disentangle from his "public-spirited action" (73). If this personal concern for Stockmann, this love for a parent, compromises Petra's own dedication to the truth, it would appear that only to that extent is she a not wholly disinterested supporter of Stockmann's cause.

A more purely disinterested character is the sea captain Horster. Like Captain Don Pedro Menendez in the last and most misanthropic book of *Gulliver's Travels,* who out of sheer benevolence (what Camus in *The Plague* will designate as common decency) comes to Gulliver's aid, Horster offers Stockmann whatever help he can. The captain is on his way to America—a weak symbol in Ibsen for human freedom—and when Stockmann appears unable to combat the resources the town has marshalled against him, Horster offers the Stockmann family passage at the cost of some trouble to himself. But because the vessel belongs to another, Horster's generosity loses him his position. At that point, he offers Stockmann shelter in his house, that piece of private property over which he exercises complete control. This relationship of private ownership to individual rights has already been taken up in the discussion of Defoe's *Journal of the Plague Year.* For Ibsen, who was financially dependent on sales of his books, the response to *Ghosts* must have been a sharp reminder that free speech and artistic freedom were often dependent on economic self-sufficiency.

Clearly, then, Ibsen addresses the matter of what it is that is to be preserved in the individual's survival of an infectious microparasite or of a macroparasite in the guise of society itself. Self-preservation is perceived to transcend the merely physical, and what was philosophically never a simple matter—what it is to be a self—becomes still more complex. When Stockmann protests against having to "put [his] personal advantage before my most sacred convictions" (67), he appears to believe that these two areas, practical concerns and conscience, are capable of being easily differentiated. On the surface, he seems to be fulfilling the conditions for ethical behavior enunciated by Kant, that he act for the sake of duty alone. But when his father-in-law, with whom Stockmann may have more in common than he would like to think, comments, "Your conscience must be in pretty good shape today, I imagine," Stockmann answers simply, "Yes, it is" (116). But his simple response is also part of his denial in himself of what he attributes to others. When his brother, the mayor, admits that he helped to financially support Stockmann and his family due to his hope that "I might be able to some extent to hold you in check," Stockmann is outraged: "What's that? It was only your own interests. . . !" (56). That the satisfaction he himself takes in his own good conscience might similarly constitute his own interests and thus subvert the purity of his acts is not a possibility Stockmann ever faces.

Although Stockmann's egotism is only a part of who he is, self-interest consistently infuses his concerns for others. To say *contaminates* this concern might be too strong, but it would add another layer of meaning to Ibsen's use of pollution and illness as motifs in the play. So long as Stockmann opposes the idea that as a public employee he has "no right to express any opinion that conflicts with that of [his] superiors" (59), he is heroic in his championship of free speech. Moreover, so long as he enjoys company and proves a genial host, he is no aloof reformer, but a companionable citizen, delighting in the town he claims to love and in the company of people to whom he feels connected, expressing a healthy tie to an extended human community. Even the pleasure he takes in Hovstad's praise for his report on the baths as an "absolute masterpiece"—"Yes, isn't it? Well, I'm very pleased, very pleased" (66)—can be read as his expressing a normal human requirement for positive mirroring by his environment. There is nothing suspect in his feeling that it is a "wonderful thing" to be able to "feel that one's been of some service to one's home town and fellow citizens" (41), or to stand "shoulder to shoulder in the brotherhood of one's fellow citizen!" (53).

But this communal bonding is countered by Stockmann's extreme individualism. While it may be repressive to say, as his brother does, that the "individual must be ready to subordinate himself to the community as a whole" (30), it is also a problem that Stockmann acknowledges no limits and proclaims the freedom "to speak [his] mind about any damn' thing under the sun" (59). His evangelical zeal makes him arrogant, and as Hovstad wryly says about his contribution to the *People's Tribune*, Stockmann is given to dropping the paper a line whenever "he wants to get any particular home-truths off his chest" (24). According to the mayor, Stockmann is not, moreover, inclined to share the credit for the development of the baths, even with a brother (26–27). And in the event that the mayor's view be suspect, Stockmann is hardly a disinterested scientist in his investigations of the water supply. That the discovery of the contamination was made by him—"I've made [it], yes" (37)—is a matter he relishes, so that his subsequent disclaimers of personal recognition are rendered suspect. And, finally, in the area of family, a place that almost guarantees a playwright the audience's good feelings, Stockmann's words may subvert the impression attached to the good husband and father. When he is exhorted to curb his zeal for his family's sake, he replies, "My family's got nothing to do with anybody but me!" (60), as if his family consisted not of independent agents but only of extensions of himself. Ibsen may have wanted to soften the implications of Stockmann's words, because at the very end of the play, the doctor proclaims his isolation at the very moment that he can luxuriate in the emotional protection of a family both loving and ironically indulgent:

DR. STOCKMANN: . . . The thing is, you see, that the strongest man in the world is the man who stands alone.
MRS. STOCKMANN [*smiles and shakes her head*]: Oh, Thomas, Thomas—!
PETRA [*bravely, grasping his hands*]: Father! (126)

And thus it is as one deeply invested in those "others" that constitute family, rather than as consummate egotist, that Stockmann is last seen in the play, Ibsen having avoided rather than resolved the major philosophical problem in his play.

The centrality of Stockmann's individualism in the play minimizes the theme of pestilence, which is less central to *An Enemy of the People* than syphilis is to *Ghosts*. Stockmann might have taken on his town concerning many issues, and his regular contributions to the liberal press suggest that he did. But although Ibsen's creation of an intellectual aristocrat was not intrinsically connected to the disease motif, one way to describe aristocracy is by its ever-constant attempt to ward off the contamination of the crowd. In a century that began with a romantic exaltation of the folk and concluded with artists inhabiting ivory towers, this nobility belongs as much to the artistic as to the political realm. As Stockmann says, "If only I knew where there was a primeval forest or a little South Sea island going cheap" (108), he seems unaware of the ironic ring to his own words: even the primitivistic dream of the earthly paradise is tied to private property.

By portraying his embattlement with society over *Ghosts* in *An Enemy of the People*, Ibsen has in part shifted the later drama away from its social problem towards an allegory of the artist's plight. The play reveals how the individual's self-definition parallels the artist's. Ibsen's play, that is, is not entirely focused on how a community deals with a plague and the extent to which self-esteem becomes another manifestation of self-preservation: it also asks implicit questions about who the writer's audience is perceived to be. The matter is thus more complex than indicated by the theater reviewer who perceived the parallels between Thomas Stockmann and Ned Weeks in Larry Kramer's play *The Normal Heart*: each is "meant to appear two-sided, correct in his analysis of the crisis and the need for radical action" but "also shrill, intolerant and unbearable."[69] Ibsen's and Kramer's plays have a great deal in common, but no theme unites them as significantly as the perplexing dilemma concerning how to separate the reformer's zeal on behalf of humanity from the necessity of preserving an ego that must defend itself against hostile others. Inevitably, this problem becomes implicated in the playwright's relationship to those who view and review plays.

In Kramer's play, Ned Weeks is one of the organizers of what *The Normal Heart* does not name but that critics and audience recognize as the Gay Men's Health Crisis, created to fight AIDS in many ways, one of which is to force public officials to confront the reality of the disease on all fronts, medical, social, and political. Ned, however, is a very strident activist, offending not only those outside but also those within the organization. Moreover, he has joined with a polio-crippled physician, Emma, to spread the word to the gay community that they must refrain from sex, which Emma is convinced is the way the disease is being spread. Thus Ned threatens not only the pleasure-seeking aspect of gay life but also its very ideology, an ideology in which sexual freedom—that is, promiscuity—has come to equal freedom per se—that is, the freedom for gay men to be homosexual without the censure or prejudice of their families, their employers, or the society at large. This equation and its implications for gay identity is one that Ned resists, with the result that in the end he is expelled from the organization he had helped to found.[70] Parallel to this social theme in *The Normal Heart* is Ned's love for Felix, who has AIDS, their relationship being similar to that between Rich and Saul in *As Is*.

In his foreword to *The Normal Heart*, Joseph Papp writes that in his "moralistic fervor, Larry Kramer is a first cousin to nineteenth-century Ibsen" (29). *An Enemy of the People* and *The Normal Heart* might be better described, however, as fraternal twins, the similarities between them striking,[71] and the differences noteworthy. In both plays brothers play an important part, although the mayor and Thomas Stockmann are essentially antagonists, whereas Ned and Ben Weeks deeply love each other. The sibling relationships nonetheless sustain the parallels between Ibsen's and Kramer's works. In each play one brother is an important person in the established society, a mayor or partner in a large law firm. In contrast, his rebellious brother is judged deviant by the society epitomized by that establishment, either because of a refusal to conform to the majority will, sexual preference, or both. To differing degrees, the conventional brother helps financially to sustain the other one, but the emotional support that Stockmann and Ned seek is either denied or only ambivalently granted. It is the mayor who joins with the town in designating Stockmann an enemy of the people; Ben and Ned Weeks, because their mutual love does not bridge the gap between straight and gay identity (at least, not until the symbolic end of the play), also disagree over which one is the antagonist:

BEN: You make me sound like I'm the enemy.
NED: I'm beginning to think that you and your straight world are our enemy. (71)

At this moment what is implicit in Ibsen's play is articulated in Kramer's: it is the conventional brother rather than the rebellious one who is the enemy of the people, and in each play it is a real or threatened plague that brings this reality to the surface.

Whereas Stockmann's brother, a government official, represents authority per se, so that only the aristocracy of the intellect advocated by Ibsen might depose him, Ben Weeks's very liberalism pushes Ned towards a similar position. Ben says that he cannot commit his law firm to support the organization Ned is helping to found to battle AIDS because he alone cannot speak for a democratic institution with an elected board of directors, a claim to which Ned replies, "I think I like elitism better" (45). But what Ned really needs from Ben is positive mirroring, which would necessitate Ben's retreating from his long-held position that homosexuality is an illness. And when Ben protests that his acceptance of Ned as a psychological equal will not help to save Ned's dying friends, Ned responds, "Funny—that's exactly what I think will help save my dying friends" (70). More perhaps than in any other literary work treated in this book, the social construction of a disease is held to be directly implicated in its epidemiology. It will be remembered that Defoe's H. F. had painted a pragmatic but nonetheless chilling portrait of a natural selection by which plague killed off in largest numbers those persons, the poor, who during the pestilence constituted the greatest potential threat to London's stability. So does AIDS promise to reduce substantially a large segment of the population perceived to be made up of deviant others by those who view it from the outside, and *The Normal Heart* confronts this issue directly, highlighting it when Ben resists admitting his at-least-partial connection with those who think in such terms.

In *An Enemy of the People*, plague is more potential than actual despite the outbreak of gastric disorders and typhoid the year before the action actually begins. But in *The Normal Heart*, the increasing incidence of AIDS is marked by the statistics that were kept track of during the play's run and painted on the theater wall: Kramer writes, as "the Center for Disease Control revised all figures regularly, so did we, crossing out old numbers and placing the new figure just beneath it" (19). In both dramas pestilential baths figure as the locus of infection, and in both, the threat to the city's tourism if the infectious disease receives widespread publicity has a significant impact on public policy. In *The Normal Heart*, this aspect of the problem is muted, since the mayor of New York is depicted as having varying motives for downplaying AIDS, and, in any event, the city's denial that it is experiencing what the play deems a "plague" (40) extends to many groups, the most noteworthy, ironically, being the very people most afflicted at the time the play appeared in 1985. In contrast, tourism is of course the aggravating element in what appears to have been Stockmann's almost chronic conflict with his town.

On the other side, in *An Enemy of the People* the baths do not carry the same symbolic weight they have in *The Normal Heart*, where they are associated with the gay sexual ideology from which Ned Weeks dissents. He becomes a virtual pariah when he not only brings the bad news of the play's doctor, Emma Brookner, that the only way for gay men to protect themselves from the mysterious and fatal disease is to become sexually abstinent, but also challenges the gay community to decide whether sexual identity in general, and promiscuous sexual activity in particular is that by which they wish to be identified. If, then, the baths constitute a gay man's earthly paradise, then Kramer is able to make his point by the ironic twist that disease originates *from* the pseudoparadise, no longer a retreat from the literal and symbolic ills of the world. In both Ibsen and Kramer, baths intended to be physically and spiritually cleansing prove a source of infection: spas intended to be communal gathering places in both end as sources of contagion and, ultimately, human isolation. And in both plays, doubt concerning the validity of the claims made about the baths' infectiousness subvert the reforming efforts of the main character.

Like *An Enemy of the People*, written—at the beginning, at least—to assuage some of Ibsen's fury over the popular reception of *Ghosts*, *The Normal Heart* has its autobiographical roots in Larry Kramer's role in helping to create the Gay Men's Health Crisis as well as in his indignation at being expelled from it for ideological and tactical differences. *The Normal Heart*, however, is more precise in its treatment of disease than *An Enemy of the People*, less capable of being translated into an allegory of the private conscience or the artist's separation from society, because the historical moment is more central to Kramer's drama. AIDS is portrayed as having acted as a catalyst both inside and outside of the gay community, forcing into the open what had remained segregated from the general view. Ned describes a meeting with an old friend who screams at him, "You're giving away all our secrets, you're painting us as sick, you're destroying homosexuality"—and then tries to slug him, "right there in the subway. Under Bloomingdale's" (66–67). This reference to upper-middle-class New York's shopping paradise is thematically significant. AIDS unites, both as victims and as fighters of the disease, groups that had earlier disclaimed each other, for example, transvestites and "Brooks Brothers" types (54). The latter remain skittish about their own visibility, worried, for example, that they might lose their jobs. The infighting that goes on in *The Normal Heart* is more complex than that in *An Enemy of the People*, in which Stockmann has the entire community against him, including those who at least in principle should have been on his own side. Of course, Ned Weeks will face the same outcome, in part because of the personality characteristics he shares with Stockmann, but the conflicts within Ned's activist organization are historically grounded.

Additionally, Kramer portrays how the severity of AIDS was forcing philanthropically inclined persons (such as Ben Weeks) to face their attitudes about gay life as they decided how far they would go to support the fight against a disease that was so far not immediately threatening them. But the incipient epidemic was also forcing gays to concern themselves with their image in the straight world. They could not merely slough off as prejudice views that could influence the battle against AIDS. As a result— or so the play suggests—they had to deal with the extent to which others' perceptions of them affected their self-esteem. Again, another kind of survival was at issue. The confrontation between Ben and Ned on this point is a poignant one in which the development of the integrated self is depicted as requiring the affirmation of important others. When Ned lashes out at Ben—

You still think I'm sick, and I simply cannot allow that any longer. I will not speak to you again until you accept me as your equal. Your healthy equal. Your brother! (71)—

the dramatic confrontation is not between two ideas but between two people who love each other and each of whose self is implicated in the other's. Ben is paradoxically both correct and significantly in error when he challenges Ned to define himself without his, Ben's, acquiescence to this self-definition.

To deal with the historical moment in which a private struggle for self-identity emerged because a plague forced it into the open, Kramer keeps most of his play in the public sphere. Unlike Ibsen's Dr. Stockmann, who works alone in his study until, with the help of a laboratory, he confirms his hypotheses about the infected baths, Kramer's Dr. Emma Brookner fights the disease and what she takes to be its source without needing to have her theories validated. Herself a survivor of polio, which crippled her only three months before the preventive vaccine was found, Emma has no reason to trust time. She diagnoses those who have AIDS, tells their friends and relatives that loved ones are going to die, and ferociously prods Ned into spreading her word about sexual infectiousness. Eventually, despite the conviction that activist physicians are derided as nuts, she agrees to testify before a governmental commission, confronting her peers with her fury and her frustration, literally throwing at them the records of her AIDS patients:

We are enduring an epidemic of death. Women have been discovered to have it in Africa—where it is clearly transmitted heterosexually. It is only a question of time. We could all be dead before you do anything. You want my patients? Take them! TAKE THEM! . . . Just do something for them! (109)

In her strident urgency she mirrors Ned; together, as physician and writer, they play the parts combined in Dr. Stockmann.

Equally public are the scenes in *The Normal Heart* that take place in newspaper and governmental offices. Ned and his eventual lover and AIDS patient, Felix, first meet in the offices of the *Times*. Felix cannot write about AIDS in a newspaper that chooses to relegate the new disease to back pages, and only occasionally at that; his sphere is, he self-deprecatingly admits, fashion and entertainment. Like Ibsen's Hovstad (and perhaps Porter's Miranda), he keeps his job by keeping his readers amused and informed on matters particularly trivial in the face of plague; and like Hovstad—if far more sympathetic—he experiences little conflict between the potential power of the pen and the way he actually uses his.

For Ned, the newspaper is hostile to gays and to his own crusade against AIDS, but nowhere near as antagonistic as the mayor's office. The scene that takes place in a "meeting room in City Hall" (81), a "basement room that hasn't been used in years" (82), parallels Stockmann's failed attempt in a similar environment to persuade the town to adopt his position with regard to the baths. Similarly, Ned cannot convince the mayor's assistant, Hiram, that there is "an epidemic going on" (87). The verbal melee that takes place in *The Normal Heart* differs from that in *An Enemy of the People* mainly in that the in-group fighting in the former is so pronounced that Hiram is able to demand, "If so many of you are so upset about what's happening, why do I only hear from this loudmouth?"—to which Ned replies, "That's a very good question" (89). After more furious exchanges, Ned yells imprecations after all of them, the mayor's representative and his own fellow fighters against AIDS.

The scene ends with the stage direction, "He is all alone" (91), possibly echoing the end of *An Enemy of the People* and Stockmann's proclamation about those who must fight by themselves. But *The Normal Heart* does not, in fact, conclude with Ned alone. In addition to what is played out in public space, Ned's private drama reinforces some of the play's major and some-times only implied themes concerning the relationship of self-identity to human bonding. In both Kramer's and Hoffman's plays, the main character is able to make a genuine commitment to another, entering a one-on-one relationship that negates the sexual ideology of promiscuity that had emo-tionally separated men before the contagiousness of AIDS literally did so.

But here the two playwrights skirt a dangerous area that Camus avowedly eschews when the narrator of *The Plague* admits—in a passage that will be quoted again in the discussion of the novel—that what is "true of all the evils in the world is true of plague as well. It helps men to rise above themselves. All the same, when you see the misery it brings, you'd need to be a madman, or a coward, or stone blind, to give in tamely to the plague" (115). One way to give in tamely is to romanticize pestilence, and both Hoffman and Kramer come perilously close to doing so when their lovers are drawn closer together because one of the pair has AIDS. But when at Felix's deathbed appear both Ben and Emma, a larger and more symbolic hope seems to find expression, that the marriage between Ned and Felix prefigures a union between seemingly disparate worlds—the straight and the gay, the scientifically medical, and the compassionately human.

The Normal Heart draws not only its title but also an essential theme from W. H. Auden's poem, "September 1, 1939," two stanzas of which preface Kramer's play. The verses contrast the abstract—universal love, the state, the citizen, the sensual man in the street—with concrete persons, the "we," the first person plural selves, who must "love one another or die" (9). In *The Normal Heart*, a plea that AIDS patients be treated as more than diseased bodies emerges from Emma Brookner's rehearsing the variations on hospital care, from the research institutions for whom the patient is a statistic to the liberal "square, righteous, superior" staff of the hospital "embarrassed by this disease and this entire epidemic" (92). She thinks that medical expertise joined to human compassion is almost entirely lacking in her profession, and part of her tirade concerning the scientist's quest for personal glory points back, once again, at the contradictions in Ibsen's play. According to the mayor, his brother, Dr. Stockmann, is reluctant to share the honor attached to developing the baths, and this basking in self-love extends, as was seen, to his pleasure in being the one to discover the pollution in them. Similarly, according to Kramer's Emma, researchers who reduce human sufferers to laboratory animals in the first place will not in the end make their results public until they are guaranteed personal renown.

Here, the private ego is displayed in a more ominous light than in Ibsen's play. AIDS is a real and deadly disease, not Kramer's literary invention, and any secrecy concerning medical discoveries will result in people dying. Emma may be plagued with a suspicion that the three months that elapsed between her being struck with polio and the appearance of a vaccine had to do with such a quest for personal recognition.[72] The irony here is that the theme concerning the private ego is not restricted by *The Normal Heart* to the medical profession,[73] which, aside from Emma's example, is portrayed unfavorably, but extends to the play's protagonist.

As both activist and egotist, Ned Weeks resembles and at the same time differs from Ibsen's Stockmann. Ned recognizes that his coworkers against AIDS believe he is using the fight to "make [himself] into a celebrity" (73). On the face of it, this is an easy charge to refute; Ned passionately believes his own battle cry, that "every gay man who refuses to come forward now and fight to save his own life is truly helping to kill the rest of us" (73). But he does not face up to this problematic connection between self-preservation and the common good; and by extension, he is on philosophically weaker grounds when confronting the accusation that he is "self-serving" (73), an indictment that becomes particularly complex when taken literally. With love, not anger, Felix points out to Ned that he is a fighter who loves a fight, and therefore that he is enjoying the battles in which he is engaged. Felix's observation parallels Morten Kill's wry comment that Stockmann is enjoying the pleasure of his own conscience. Whether it then follows that Ned is "on a colossal ego trip" (113), as charged in the accusing writ that virtually drums him out of the activist group he helped create, involves a question raised in both Ibsen's and Kramer's work.

Does self-gratification contaminate the fight for the right cause? And does this philosophical conundrum lead nowhere but to the claim that unless the individual adapts to the general will, he does no more than stroke his own conscience for the pleasure that yields? In Kramer's play, it is

Bruce, a handsome man who draws followers with his good looks and nonconfrontative personality rather than with his ideas, who reads out the indictment against Ned drawn up by the organization intent on ridding themselves of their rebel. That Bruce had once been a Green Beret is a point that had already been emphasized in the play: he was a fighter but also one who followed orders, who conformed for the sake of the group. Significantly, in his comeback to those ready to expel him from their ranks, Ned employs a military metaphor: "I want to be defined" as "one of the men who fought the war" (115). But it is not true that he is willing to be a mere private in the army: he is adamant in defining the precise nature of the enemy, directing the battle, and at least verbally court-martialing anyone who gets out of line. His sharp tongue and his inclination to burst into angry print at the slightest provocation (just as Stockmann writes for the *People's Tribune* whenever he has a "truth" to convey) create tactical difficulties for himself and for others, and sometimes he seems to win battles at the expense of the war itself, which, on the other side, is escalating as ideological opponents fight among themselves. Ned pays the price of isolation, begging not to be "shut out" by the others but left, nonetheless, like Stockmann, "standing alone" in his fight (115).

The Normal Heart has been praised for transcending its own imperfections in "its sense of urgency, necessity, a *cause*."[74] But it has also, with *As Is*, been faulted for "stumbling" on "the real issue now at stake for gay men —the question of who they are," while failing to take this subject anywhere significant.[75] This chapter has suggested that for Ibsen, Hoffman, and Kramer, matters of personal identity are crucial, but that all three face the difficulty of defining the self in a modern world. When Ned Weeks pleads that gays who identify themselves with their sexuality commit a kind of self-genocide, he stops short of suggesting that AIDS is a symbol of that fate. For Ned, for Kramer, this modern plague is too real and devastating to be turned into a metaphor; moreover, such an analogy would smack of the fruits of sin. Yet it is also true that in few literary works is the urgency surrounding a disease linked so emphatically to questions concerning identity.

In creating a modern Dr. Stockmann in Ned Weeks, Kramer underscores the significant problem raised by a play whose intent is openly propagandistic, which is how to present its social concerns without falsifying larger, more abstract concerns about what it means to be human and what it means to be a particular kind of human being. If both Ibsen and Kramer wrote their plays to work out private indignation, they might still have come to recognize the full extent of the ego's stake in the battles undertaken by the individual, and this understanding may have resulted in plays that are part self-confession. At the end of each drama, the protagonist's semi-isolation points to an ultimate lack of resolution. The final curtain finds Stockmann basking in the indulgent love of Catherine and Petra; Ned is last seen embraced by his brother Ben, with whom he is personally reunited despite their differences. Finally, Kramer must take his solution from Auden's poem: there are no abstractions, only people who suffer, and some who love.

If *The Normal Heart* succeeds in rousing some of its audience to action, it is probably not only because of the well-handled propaganda cited by some reviewers, nor the old-fashioned aim of enlightening and informing as well as entertaining praised by others, but also because Ned Weeks's passionate attachments to real people may inspire where ideas themselves falter. But can any writer trust his rhetorical aims to such emotional engagement? When Felix confesses—

You know my fantasy has always been to go away and live by the ocean and write twenty-four novels, living with someone just like you with all these books who of course will be right there beside me writing your own twenty-four novels (49)—

he is sharing with Ned an image of the artist's paradise in which writers have no need to ask such a question.

Microparasites, Macroparasites, and the Spanish Influenza

The influenza pandemic of 1918 has been called by one of its historians "the most appalling epidemic since the Middle Ages,"[1] but, according to another who has studied it, the "average college graduate born since 1918 literally knows more about the Black Death of the fourteenth century" than about the epidemic.[2] The disease came to be called the Spanish influenza and sometimes, more colorfully and perhaps more insidiously, the Spanish Lady, the feminization of influenza perhaps not as dangerous as the portrayal of syphilis as a woman, but nonetheless contributing to the stereotype of woman as polluter. In any event, there is indeed a glaring disparity between the dramatic possibilities of describing the pandemic and the relatively slight impact it has made on the consciousness of the world and of the United States, where it coincided with America's entry into World War I. And this disparity has caused puzzlement:

The important and almost incomprehensible fact about Spanish influenza is that it killed millions upon millions of people in a year or less. Nothing else—no infection, no war, no famine—has ever killed so many in as short a period. And yet it has never inspired awe, not in 1918 and not since.[3]

If it does exist for some as a "folk memory," it has nonetheless failed to produce any enduring folklore, for it has been claimed that the "Spanish Lady inspired no songs, no legends, no work of art."[4] In American literature, however, the influenza pandemic has provided at least two authors, Wallace Stegner and Katherine Anne Porter, with major subject matter and themes for fiction. The former has used the outbreak of influenza as a motif in several works, one of which, his "Chip off the Old Block," is on its way to becoming a classic short story. The latter's novella, *Pale Horse, Pale Rider*, is acknowledged to be "one of the twentieth century's masterpieces of short fiction," a work that also provides the historian with a "most accurate depiction of American society in the fall of 1918," synthesizing what otherwise could be gleaned only from the popular press.[5]

Both Stegner and Porter make use of the coincidence of two of what each author would call plagues, the war and the flu, a conjunction that supplies a blatant instance of McNeill's depiction of human life as caught between macro- and microparasites, it being an additional point of interest that the influenza epidemic would strike hardest at the same segment of the American population as would the war. As Alfred Crosby has described it,

The interweaving of the war and the pandemic make what from a distance of a half-century seems to be a pattern of complete insanity. On September 11 Washington officials disclosed to reporters their fear that Spanish influenza had arrived, and on the next day thirteen million men of precisely the ages most liable to die of Spanish influenza and its complications lined up all over the United States and crammed into city halls, post offices, and school houses to register for the draft.[6]

In Stegner's work, war and flu spell the end of the American dream, whose demise renders futile the attempt to achieve a personal identity that presupposes its existence. For Porter, who depicts the ironic death of a soldier, not from wounds suffered in battle but from influenza, the disease has a broader and more existential symbolism where it comes to her heroine's quest for self-definition. For despite the existence in *Pale Horse, Pale Rider* of religious themes in which some readers find Porter's belief in personal redemption, the American scene depicted in her novella comes very close to resembling the absurd world of Camus's *The Plague*.

Wallace Stegner tells the story of twelve-year-old Chet Mason, who becomes the man of the house when his father, mother, and brother—all ill of influenza—are taken to their town's makeshift hospital. His father's condition is complicated by frostbite incurred during a journey to purchase the whisky believed to be an effective medicine for flu. While his family is recovering, Chet remains in contact with the infirmary, supplies it with the excess milk piling up at his house, hunts for meat as food, wards off with a gun the half-breed Louis Treat and an unnamed companion intent on stealing the brew, sells the liquor for more money than his father would have charged, and, when the end of World War I is announced, holds a party to which he invites neighbors who were spared during the epidemic or were already released from the infirmary. At this celebration the whisky is imbibed freely, and in the midst of the merrymaking, Chet's father returns home and angrily confronts his son, accusing him of mishandling affairs while the family was away.

There are two ways for a reader to experience Chet's encounter with the pandemic believed to have killed over twenty million people throughout the world and to have infected about five times that number, the infection rather than its threatening fatality being central to Stegner's themes, since in this story no important character dies of the flu. The episode appears in Stegner's saga of the Mason family, *The Big Rock Candy Mountain,* and is alluded to again in its sequel *Recapitulation.* It also exists as a separately published short story. The context supplied by the novels reveals Chet to be a relatively minor character compared to his father and brother, but only in the novels is it clear how pervasive are Stegner's metaphors of disease. *The Big Rock Candy Mountain* begins with the early life of Chet's mother and the death of his grandmother from what appears to be tuberculosis and thematically concludes with the death of Chet's mother from cancer and with the impact of her illness and death on her husband and surviving son, Bruce. For by this time, Chet too is dead, his earlier triumph during the epidemic rendered ironically futile not only because he escaped the flu only prematurely to die of pneumonia while still a young man, but also because of the bleakness of his young manhood and the hopelessness of his future. As Stegner critics suggest, the Mason family deaths parallel the demise of the myths upon which America was supposedly built.[7] There is a bitter irony that Chet's end comes about through the transformation of nature into a commercial venture by the society that trapped his father in the perpetual quest for the quick buck:

If Chet had not been generous and good-natured, he would not have worked up a sweat on a cold and windy day, helping dig somebody's car out of the snow at the Ecker ski-jumping hill outside of Park City. If he had been born luckier, he would have waited to catch pneumonia until after antibiotics had tamed it. Being generous, unlucky, and ill-timed, he dug and pushed, he got overheated, he fell sick and he died within six days. . . . Then he escaped from his future, which was drab, and his marriage, which was in trouble, and abandoned to others the daughter he had conceived before he was legally a man. . . . Like his catch-up reading, his instruction in real life had much ground to cover in only a little time.[8]

In effect, the brevity of Chet's final illness mirrors his life, and, significantly, the short tale Stegner carved out of his long novel commences with a passage about time:

Sitting alone looking at the red eyes of the parlor heater, Chet thought how fast things happened. One day the flu hit. Two days after that his father left for Montana to get a load of whisky to sell for medicine. The next night he got back in the midst of a blizzard with his hands and feet frozen, bringing a sick homesteader he had picked up on the road; and now this morning all of them, the homesteader, his father, his mother, his brother Bruce were loaded in a sled and hauled to the schoolhouse-hospital. (205)

The requirements of short fiction necessitate such condensation of events, and in "Chip off the Old Block," genre actually duplicates the quick course of the disease, and, symbolically, the brief span of a human life. Such a connection between form and content is implied in Stegner's 1989 foreword to his *Collected Stories*. He describes how "increasingly, in [his] own writing the novel has tended to swallow and absorb potential stories," how he "found fairly early that even stories begun without the intention of being anything but independent tended to cluster, wanting to be part of something longer" (x-xi).

In life as well, incidents become part of what will hopefully constitute the extended biography of the individual self. As the celebrity queried about his feelings about having reached a quite advanced age replied, he felt very well considering the alternative.[9] One wants to survive, to make each event part of something longer. Mortality in general and plague in particular threaten this hopefulness. The rapidity of Chet's sudden passage from youth to young adulthood in the short story, and the successive failures of the generations of Masons are—as in all family sagas—actually condensed in Stegner's long novels. Time bears an uneasy relationship to narrative, and, again, genre itself mirrors history, the relation of incident to the larger picture. The promise and collapse in rapid succession of the American dream parallel Chet's story, which is but part of the family chronicle treated in the novels. Similarly, in Europe, where World War I had crushed hopes that the Congress of Vienna marked the end of such global battles, the apparent progress of a century was suddenly rendered a mere illusion. The appearance and disappearance of the influenza pandemic that came to be known as the Spanish Lady, virtually personified the grim reality of the era, joining with the war to mock the human hope to achieve that which endures.

To read "Chip off the Old Block" outside *The Big Rock Candy Mountain* is, however, to view Stegner's metaphors of disease through a more optimistic lens, to avoid learning that Chet was untouched by the influenza epidemic and its often-fatal respiratory complications only to succumb in early adulthood to pneumonia at that very time when the early hopefulness of his life was past and the discovery of antibiotics was not far off. Time creates in Stegner's work the gap between promise and reality, but in this story, despite its explicit introduction, time can be ignored. There are, in addition, formal benefits to reading the story in isolation, for by itself it obviates the criticism that has been leveled at *The Big Rock Candy Mountain*, that whatever its power, it is structurally flawed, lacking a consistent focus of interest (is it primarily about the patriarch Bo Mason or about his son Bruce, and in either case, why does the novel begin and end with the lives and deaths of Bruce's grandmother and mother, with so much of the narrative being about his mother's life?); without a consistent point of view; and deficient in the literary use of "myth, symbol, current psychology, or neo-theology"[10] that are among the elements of a great novel. Joseph Warren Beach has asked of this novel, "what of the distinctive pleasure which one takes in a work of art?" and he continues with gentle reproach that Stegner, committed to realism, "refrains from using the 'distortions' of art, and . . . does not greatly command the finer tools of irony, suggestion, pathos, fancy, or intellectual abstraction, which variously serve in the masters to give esthetic point to a neutral subject."[11]

By itself, "Chip off the Old Block" meets these objections and is a satisfying work. It has a consistent focus of both interest and point of view, Chet himself, and it employs the art of fiction to write about the impact of a plague on the developing identity of the young boy. There is no doubt that for the youth the influenza epidemic has accelerated the inexorable movement towards adult responsibility and adult consciousness. One of Chet's activities during his lonely hours is to write a story in which a young explorer encounters many dangers, among which are menacing snakes he significantly mislabels "boy constructors" (211). From the real perils he faces, and from the narrative he invents, Chet creates his own rite of passage.

Stegner's depiction of influenza and its impact on a small western American town[12] is accurate. For example, Chet wonders at his father's contracting flu, he being a man "who seldom got anything and was tougher than boiled owl" (205). In fact, Chet's father is particularly ill, and it is reported to his anxious son that at one point his survival had been in doubt. That influenza hit hardest such a man, in the age group of twenty to forty, who, because he lived in a rural area isolated from the illnesses prevalent in the cities and thus had not built up many antibodies to disease, is part of the history of the 1918 pandemic. McNeill contends that when a population is depleted of persons in such an age group, its leaders and most productive workers, the community is likely to suffer a greater demoralization than when the very young or the very old suffer the highest mortality rate.[13] Again, the age group described by McNeill corresponds to that of the soldiers likely to be lost in the war that was at that time still raging. But it is Katherine Anne Porter, not Stegner, who makes use of that coincidence.

Moreover, Stegner's story combines naturalistic detail with popular belief, such as the relationship of plague to sin (more about that shortly). Finally, "Chip off the Old Block" is almost a perfect rendering of McNeill's description of human life participating in a universal food chain in which one creature feeds off another and normal existence is capable of being expressed in images of hunting, warfare, and disease. At one point Chet affirms his ability to take care of himself while alone by reporting, "I shot rabbits all last fall for Mrs. Rieger. . . . She's 'nemic and has to eat rabbits and prairie chickens and stuff. She lent me the shotgun and bought the shells" (207). And at the conclusion to the story, when the struggle between father and son reaches a boiling point, the angry but also proud parent invokes a cannibalistic figure of speech to proclaim of his son, "He'd eat me if I made a pass at him" (219). If the generation gap is, as Stegner's critics argue, a primary theme in his fiction, then fathers themselves are macroparasites against which sons must defend themselves, and Bo Mason's imagery could extend from the universal but naturalistic food chain to the myth of Cronos, who literally swallowed his own children in order not to be symbolically swallowed by them.

Indeed, the structure of "Chip off the Old Block" persistently involves the interaction of micro- and macroparasites. Stegner draws heavily on the coincidence of World War I and the influenza epidemic:[14] it is the war rather than the pandemic that one of his characters labels a "plague" (216). Thus the "emancipation" of Chet's father from the "dread sickness" is writ symbolically large in the "emancipation of the entire world" (216). Chet himself had been entrusted to "hold the fort" (205) of the familial house, and had warded off the invasion of Louis Treat. And, of course, the father-son relationship is depicted as it often is in literature, as an archetypal battle. When Bo Mason berates Chet for wasting the whisky he had almost died to procure—"Will you please tell me why in the name of Christ you invited that God-damned windbag and all the rest of those sponges over here to drink up my whiskey?"—Chet declines to "defend himself." "The war was over," he says, taking the offensive. "I asked them over to celebrate" (217).

Stegner employs a biting irony when the elder Mason invokes Christ and God in proclaiming his patriarchal right of property, for this family can be read as a figure for American society, oscillating as it does between nurturing generosity (feeding) and exploitation (eating). Chet selflessly hunts animals for the woman whose anemia requires meat; he unquestioningly acts as part of the community in donating bedding to the hastily constructed infirmary; he takes the initiative in donating milk that collects and that will go sour if not used. But he also luxuriates in the increased self-esteem he enjoys after selling the supposedly medicinal whisky for even more profit than his father expected to make. What the pestilence has done is to bring into sharp relief the contradictory elements intrinsic to American life. And as Chet crosses the line from youth to adulthood, he carries with him these conflicting reactions to the plague-created crisis:

"People wanted [the whisky] for medicine," Chet said. "Should I've let them die with the flu? They came here wanting to buy it and I sold it. I thought that was what it was for." (218)

His father articulates an older, but no less contradictory ethic that eschews price gouging: " 'You didn't have any business selling anything,' he said. 'And then you overcharge people' " (218).

Stegner's ironic perspective on the relation of business to crisis appears reflected in one of the townspeople, Vickers, who comes to collect the bedding for the infirmary and stays to buy some whisky. As he and Chet negotiate the price of four dollars or four-fifty for a bottle, "Vickers's face was expressionless. 'Sure it isn't five? I wouldn't want to cheat you' " (206). When Chet sets the price at four-fifty, Vickers buys twenty-seven dollars worth and asks with what is presumably both an approving and knowing laugh, "What are you going to do with that extra three dollars?" (206). On a larger plane, the cost of things threatens to spill over into a major social problem, and one of the characters in the story recognizes that the community will be put to a test both as individuals and as a group concerning how far it is willing to go to help those left helpless by the death of the persons who were their support.

He wouldn't be surprised if the destitute and friendless were found in every home in town, adopted and cared for by friends. They might have to build an institution to house the derelict and the bereaved. (212)

Stegner is considered a regional writer, a describer of the American West compounded of raw nature and legend, the writer invoking and at the same time debunking traditional myths. The town in which the Masons reside is no Eden, but the image of an earlier paradise is implied when the same character worries that after the epidemic, "the town would never be the same" (212). "Chip off the Old Block" employs images of a fall and of an expulsion, both of which inform the themes involved in Chet's maturity and his defense of his own disobedience when confronting a threateningly punitive patriarch, his father. Much later, in *Recapitulation*, Bruce Mason contemplates the search for a new Eden:

But Paradise. . . . He feels that quiet back lawn of the city of his youth as a green sanctuary full of a remote peace. "Paradise is an Arab idea," he says. "Semitic, anyway. It's a garden, always a garden. They put a wall around it because that's how their minds work, they're inward-turning, not outward-turning."

"Paradise," he concludes, is, however, "safe, not exciting," like the "lawns of his youth."[15] This nostalgia for security illuminates "Chip off the Old Block." It is out of the relative security of childhood that Chet is about to be thrust as he confronts the epidemic.

Chet, who "resolved to be a son his parents could be proud of" (210), stands at a boundary not only between the world of children and that of adults, but also between a safety perhaps as illusory as paradise itself and adventure, symbolic of the promise that will be extinguished with his life. The boundaries that separate the ideal and the real are also those that separate nature from culture, and it is here that the story of the "boy constructor," the tale Chet writes for himself, picks up significance, for it is about the quest for a "lost city" of gold. Even Chet's title, "The Curse of the Tapajós" (211), contains echoes of the punishment motif attached to the fall. First the young author "*hunts* up a promising locale" (210; emphasis added), which he finds in an uncivilized tributary of the Amazon. He then "created a tall, handsome young explorer and a halfbreed guide very like Louis Treat," the predator whom Chet runs out of the Mason family home with a gun. Later, when his fictional counterpart must not only dodge the snakes too "thick" (undoubtedly in both size and number) to handle, but also evade the half-breed guide "who was constantly trying to poison the flour or stab his employer in his tent at midnight," Chet begins to wonder at his own story and to ask himself "why the explorer didn't shoot the guide" (211). Now Chet is stymied by his own tale, whose ending he cannot yet glimpse, and intuitively he collapses predators and infectious disease into a collective vision: "And then suddenly the explorer reeled and fell, mysteriously stricken, and the halfbreed guide, smiling with sinister satisfaction, disappeared quietly into the jungle" (211).

The explorer, Chet's persona, probably refrains from killing the halfbreed because of Chet's natural identification with the menacing guide (who may also be a figure of his father). Like Caliban, Louis Treat is an image of the wild man, neither pure nature nor assimilated to culture. Chet remembers what his father had told him, that "you could trust an Indian, if he was your friend, and you could trust a white man sometimes, if money wasn't involved, and you could trust a Chink more than either, but you couldn't trust a halfbreed" (208). In this ethnic and ethical scale is laid out the history and the paradoxes of the American scene, a scale that, in a time of plague, picks up particularly disturbing reverberations. Nature, like Indians, could be trusted if its benign face was turned toward one (as it never is in a time of pestilence); and culture, in some high form, such as that represented by China, held out at least the possibility of a social ideal. Neither nature nor culture in their pure forms match the reality of America. In another Stegner short story, "The Chink," an inhabitant of the town in which the Mason boys live, Mah Li, is from the point of view of its inhabitants as much an "other" as if he were not human, "as much outside human society as an animal would have been." The narrator, this time Bruce Mason, tells how "I loved Mah Li as I loved [a] colt, but neither was part of the life that seemed meaningful at the time" (191).

In a disquieting fashion, Stegner reveals the parallels between the supposedly civilized white man, who *sells* medicine, and the half-breed who tries to steal it. Like Caliban, who uses the language Prospero has taught him only to curse his master and wish a visitation of the Red Plague upon him, Chet's half-breed guide is associated with the "curse" of the Tapajós, slinking away as the explorer-hero is mysteriously stricken with illness. Chet has difficulty fathoming his own tale and its meaning:

It was going to be hard to figure out how his hero escaped. Maybe he was just stunned, not killed. Maybe a girl could find him there, and nurse him back to health. . . . (211)

Just as the expulsion from Eden is sometimes joined to the promise of a female redemptress with her heel on the neck of the deceitful serpent,[16] so is the curse of the Tapajós and the jungle full of snakes mitigated by the healing presence of a young girl. This female function is exemplified, significantly, during the party to celebrate the end of the war, during which one of the guests makes two toasts, the first being to "those heroic laddies in khaki who looked undaunted into the eyes of death and saved this galorious empire from the rapacious Huns" (214–15). It is only through aggression that men can achieve selfhood in the terms established by patriarchal culture, and at one point Chet revises his story and imagines that in the jungle there is a "beautiful and ragged girl, kept in durance vile by some tribe of pigmies or spider men or something," so that he would need to "rescue" her and "confound [her] captors" (212). Consistent with such an image of female helplessness is the other toast, made to "those gems of purest ray serene, those unfailing companions on life's bitter pilgrimage, the ladies" (215). The possible blurring of "laddies" and "ladies" paradoxically only serves to intensify the distinction made in the toasts.

In "Chip off the Old Block," the nurturing woman is Chet's mother, mediator between the boy and the fearsome patriarch, Bo Mason. Her role is echoed by another female character, Mrs. Chance, who in the face of Bo Mason's anger pulls her husband away from the party with a "quick pleading smile" (217) that virtually epitomizes woman's function in the aggressively interactive world of men. But the importance of Chet's mother extends beyond the traditional parallels between the good mother archetype and the gentler side of human culture. In Stegner's story, the maternal figure also suggests an artistic ideal, although one more likely thwarted than fulfilled in time of plague. The relation of gender to the redeeming potentialities of language can only be apprehended, however, after recognizing communication itself to be one of Stegner's themes in "Chip off the Old Block."

By writing so much of what he only partially comprehends in his own story, Chet, as youthful author, represents the uncertainties of an authorial voice. In this way, Stegner may join Boccaccio and Poe in confronting the marginality of literature, Stegner perhaps formulating a new metaphor: the author as half-breed, inherently "other" in the practical world yet necessary because it is the coherence of language that bestows structure on the incoherence of events. The difficulties surrounding language become motifs woven through "Chip off the Old Block." For example, when Louis Treat faces Chet in his attempt to take the whisky away from the young boy by pretending he had been sent to fetch medicine for the community, he tries to reduce the struggle between them to one of mere language: " 'We 'ave been sent,' Louis said; 'You do not understan' w'at I mean' "—to which Chet replies, " 'I understand all right' " (209). But Chet's composition, the story within Stegner's story, suggests that narrative can only struggle to comprehend and be comprehended. Chet will never develop sufficient self to grasp the possibilities of his own symbolic autobiography, which is probably why—to invoke Stegner's metaphors of disease—he will eventually succumb to infection. For he *is* a chip off the old block, and his life will end, as the passage from *Recapitulation* suggests, as an unfinished story.

"Chip off the Old Block" parodies the literary endeavor itself in the person of a character nicknamed Dictionary Chance because "he strung off such jaw-breaking words" (211). He is described at one point as "voluble to the last" (217), and it is he who takes upon himself the role of bombastic party speechmaker and who makes a defense of Chet's celebratory party when Bo Mason's son stands silent before his angry parent. A survivor of the flu himself, Chance had also brought Chet the frightening news that his father almost died as well as the reassuring news that Bo Mason did recover.

Chance's connection with language points to how plague strikes at verbal communication itself, a theme that Camus insistently and profoundly explores in *The Plague*. Stegner, like the French author, creates a world in which surviving the influenza epidemic is as arbitrary as dying from it. That is why Dictionary Chance, whose name signifies not only a capricious universe but also the tenuous relationship of language to events, does not tell Chet his father is all right before he tells Chet that Bo Mason almost died: words can be as confused and confusing as events.

It is therefore only an added irony that Chance does not see matters this way and that there is a darker side to eloquence, for he depicts a world in which epidemics are part of some horrific moral order. Like a pompous preacher he instructs Chet to "mark [his] words" (212) and heed his prophesy that the epidemic signals the decline of the town. Chet listens to Chance "tell [stories] about the Death Ward" (212), but these prove to be moral exempla. On one side Chance tries to be kind to the young boy who is alone, tries to substitute as father, playing the part of good father in contrast to Bo Mason's wielding of power over his son. But all Chance really does is manipulate words for authority where the elder Mason is more likely to exploit the paternal role and the privilege he assumes with it.

Like some kind of hell-and-damnation preacher—he is described as dominating the Mason kitchen like an "evangelist" (215)—Chance associates the pestilence with sin and punishment. Describing the horrors of the makeshift infirmary, he refers with disgust to a "hard to kill" townsman whose incontinence, the result of his illness, necessitated that his bed be cleaned six times a day.

"I hesitate to say before the young what went on in that ward. Shameful, even though the man was sick." His tongue ticked against his teeth, and his eyebrows raised at Chet. "They cleaned his bed six times a day," he said, and pressed his lips together. "It makes a man wonder about God's wisdom," he said. "A man like that, his morals are as loose as his bowels." (213)

Stegner's imagery involves not only language but also the mechanics of articulation as well as the gap between the mouth that moves and the silence that is always, in this story, ominous. Chet writes his story with "his lips together in concentration" (210); he "gnawed his pencil" (211) as a sign of his struggling over his tale of the Tapajós. Chance's tongue ticks against his teeth and he presses his lips together in a sign of moral disapproval when he describes the incontinent influenza patient. There is a distinction drawn between the party guests who imbibed Bo Mason's whisky and "smacked their lips" (214) in noisy pleasure, and the "moment of complete silence" (216) that follows Bo's return home and his obvious displeasure.

Although Chance's wife, elsewhere described as "incoherent" (214) and portrayed at one point as crying "every time she spoke" (211), protests against her husband's harsh view of the ill man, Chance wagers "that a man as loose and discombobulated as that doesn't live through this epidemic" (213). It is telling that Chance's so-called eloquence should always hover on the verge of becoming a kind of verbal diarrhea: Bo Mason contemptuously dismisses him as a "windbag" (217). At the same time, it is Chance whose dissonant volubility expresses the ambivalence of his community. He links the influenza epidemic, the "terrors of the plague" (214), with the "dread plague of war" (216), but it is only the former that he views in terms of a moral and social decline. As influenza attacks his microcosmic world, he envisions his town as irrevocably changed by the epidemic, a fallen place. His choice of words suggests equivocality: he "wouldn't be surprised" if the destitute were found in every home; the town "might" have to build institutions to house them (212). Bo Mason may be correct in repudiating Chance's verbiage, but his dismissal picks up disturbing intimations if it can be read as applicable to the narrative voice itself.

Having created a youthful persona whose use of language falls short of what in any event he can only imperfectly comprehend, a patriarch who almost deliberately surrounds himself with his family's silence, and a parody of the writer who distorts language because his own vision is sometimes clear and sometimes twisted, Stegner is hard pressed to create a model character who can uphold language, and—by extension—literature. In the end, he may have taken recourse to a device used by many male writers who wish to create a fictional perspective that is both within and outside the dominant society: he creates a symbol for literature out of the female voice.

At the beginning of "Chip off the Old Block," Chet has received his father's instructions, expressed negatively in terms of what his son should *not* do, as well as his mother's "words," a "solemn burden on his mind" (205). Mrs. Mason is more than mother: she stands as a verbal intermediary between father and son, concerned to explain the husband who "didn't understand" (219) his son and who in any event will not "admit he was wrong" (219). As mediator, she hopes to close the gap that separates father from son. But the mother who can use language to break through silence must remain subordinate to the husband she must interpret and in effect give shape to. In contrast to Mrs. Chance's wordless tears, language is available to Chet's mother but the only time when she is named in the story she is called "Sis" (216), a diminutive that reduces the matriarch to the role of another child. Ultimately, the only real metaphors available to the re-demptive female are those of a man's world. It is his mother who metaphor-ically draws on a world of aggressors when she tells Chet to "hold the fort" (205) while the family struggles with influenza.

"Chip off the Old Block," like its miniature analogue "The Curse of the Tapajós," ends inconclusively. Chet's parents are proud of him, but the tensions within the family are as unresolved as the fate of Chet's imagined hero-explorer; no one can see the direction of his or her personal narrative. In the end, Chet's experience with plague is that of an author for whom plot and language remain uncertain in a world embroiled in a persistent struggle to ward off micro- and macroparasites.

According to Crosby, *Pale Horse, Pale Rider* lacks attention outside of literature courses because "it is about a person undergoing a traumatic experience as the result of something most people do not recognize as having been of much importance: the 1918 pandemic of Spanish influ-enza."[17] When the novella begins, Miranda experiences the first symptoms of flu; at the end, she emerges transformed as a person from a long bout with the illness. In between, as her headaches increase and she becomes convinced that something terrible and perhaps fatal is about to befall her, her increasingly tenuous connection to external reality brings into sharp relief her struggle for other kinds of survival. But even those likely to teach Porter's novella do not appear to view Miranda's illness as critical to a reading of it. Usually the disease is treated as but a metaphor: the "influenza epidemic is also, of course, the physical counterpart of the illness of society at war."[18] As is true of Stegner's story, however, it is the coexistence of micro- and macroparsites that lends *Pale Horse, Pale Rider* its thematic intricacy and depth.

The structure of *Pale Horse, Pale Rider* can be described in two ways, one of them having to do with the external events surrounding Miranda's fight with influenza, the other with a series of dreams and visions, among them what Porter later described as the "Beatific Vision, the strange rapture that occurs, and maybe more often than we can ever know, just before death,"[19] a religious concept that has strong psychological significance for Miranda's attempt to achieve personal identity in the face of threats to her body and to her striving to maintain individuality. Miranda's delirium during the flu allows the reader the sense of experiencing a character's struggle for self-hood from within that place where the struggle is actually taking place, the unconscious. The perspectives of "Chip off the Old Block" and *Pale Horse,*

Pale Rider, that is, are quite different. Stegner's young Chet projects his developing self onto the narrative he invents of the young explorer who falls stricken with a mysterious disease in a jungle he cannot imagine his way out of. Miranda's self remains internalized, persistently subjective. She too has visions of a jungle, a "writhing terribly alive and secret place of death" (299), and part of the ambiguity surrounding her recovery from influenza, her sense that in being alive she had been "condemned" to the "dull world" whose efforts "to set her once more safely in the road . . . would [only] lead her again to death" (314), has to do with whether she too is trapped in her symbolic jungle.

Miranda is a young journalist who with a female coworker named Towney (she writes the town gossip column) had once suppressed a story about a scandalous elopement in order to protect the reputation of a young woman and her family. When another paper was therefore able to scoop the story, Miranda was demoted from reporter to theater reviewer. Even her profession, that is, can be conceived of in terms of hostile invasions of people against others: the young woman who had attempted a flight to freedom is described as "recaptured" (274). Miranda's unwillingness to participate in this mutual aggression makes her susceptible to attack: her illness is both real and historically based in the 1918 pandemic but also a sign of her alienation in her world. The very place in which she lives, an impersonal rooming house, can hardly be called home, nor can it promise another home to be shared with Adam, the young soldier who takes up a brief occupancy there until he is sent overseas to serve with the ground troops, his coming back a "returned hero" (283) unlikely. Despite this unfriendly place in which they meet, however, Miranda and Adam try to escape the real world for the brief few days in which she pretends to hope. But it is difficult to maintain her illusions: " 'I don't want to love,' she would think in spite of herself, 'not Adam, there is no time and we are not ready for it and yet this is all we have' " (292). Their situation is glossed by Camus's *The Plague,* in which the narrator relates how "plague had gradually killed off in all of us the faculty" of love, "since love asks something of the future, and nothing was left us but a series of present moments" (165). But even such precious moments are cut short when Miranda collapses with flu. It is Adam who nurses her through the night before she enters the hospital, perhaps contracting the illness in that time, for it is he who dies—not of war, but influenza. Miranda must face a life without her Ferdinand, not in the brave new world of Shakespeare's heroine, but in what she perceives to be a "world" in which there is "too much of everything" threatening and hostile.

Wanting only to sit down and die, she can be contrasted with Miranda of *The Tempest,* and perhaps for this reason it is significant that she also wants to lose her memory and "forget [her] own name" (289).

An important feature of *Pale Horse, Pale Rider* that sets it apart from other works of plague literature is that it is written by a woman about a woman. Miranda must not only establish her individual self in a world resistant to its development but also affirm a female identity. Gender plays an obviously important thematic part in the story, war particularly differentiating male and female roles. One of the characters, Miranda's coworker Chuck, is particularly important in this sense. His own lung disease disqualifies him for battle, a matter about which he is particularly defensive. It is he who vehemently protests against what he views as the feminization of war:

"It was Florence Nightingale ruined wars. . . . What's the idea of petting soldiers and binding up their wounds and soothing their fevered brows? That's not war. Let 'em perish where they fall. That's what they're there for." (286–87)

At the same time, from the male-dominated view of his own culture, Chuck exhibits sex role confusion. Miranda is demoted from reporter to a "routine female" job (275) when she is made theater critic, the very position Chuck wants. And although he maintains a hard attitude toward a war he cannot fight in, in his own personal war with an alcoholic father, Chuck evidences the same kind of softness that had led Miranda to suppress the story of the elopement.

Meanwhile, Miranda's reluctant contribution to the war effort involves participation in areas filled with woman's work, such as rolling bandages, knitting socks and sweaters for the troops, visiting the wounded in hospitals, or attending social events in which, for example, women dance with lonely soldiers and generally provide companionship for them. When Towney is found knitting a rose-colored garment, Miranda asks her what soldier would be the recipient of this gift with such a sprightly (and, implicitly, decidedly feminine) color, to which Towney replies, "Like hell. . . . I'm making this for myself" (275). In general, however, Towney does not allow this minor rebellion to interfere with her doing what was expected of a woman during the war. In contrast, Miranda's resistance presages a conflict with Adam had they ever had the time for their relationship to develop. Several example could be cited, but one telling one should make the point clear. Adam knows very well that Miranda does not easily wear woman's role:

"I can see you knitting socks," he said. "That would be just your speed. You know perfectly well you can't knit."

"I do worse," she said, soberly; "I write pieces advising other young women to knit and roll bandages and do without sugar and help win the war."

"Oh, well," said Adam, with the easy *masculine* morals in such questions, "that's merely your job, that doesn't count." (281; italics added)

The final ambiguity is hardly accidental. What does not count? That Miranda urges other women to knit rather than knitting herself, or her job, her source of her meager income but, nonetheless, her independence?

Miranda has been held to be typical of Porter's female protagonists in illustrating

a basic psychological conflict ... [between] a desire, on the one hand, for the independence and freedom to pursue art or principle regardless of social convention, and, on the other, a desire for the love and security inherent in the traditional roles of wife and mother.[20]

Adam's death from influenza not only deprives Miranda of his love and the possibility of fulfilling such traditional roles, but it also, and perhaps more significantly, thwarts Miranda's ability to work through her ambivalence.

In an important letter, Porter responded to an essay about her work she professes to have loved but whose basic tenet she attacks thoroughly, rejecting both Freud himself and any Freudian theory (such as female penis envy) that would result in the idea that what Miranda wants in *Pale Horse, Pale Rider* is to be a man. It is, writes Porter,

almost impossible for any woman to convince any man that this is false. ... What [women] really want, I think, is not a change of sex, but a change of the limited conditions of their lives which have been imposed because of their sexual function. ... A woman who knows how to be a woman not only needs and must have an active force of character and mind, but she has invariably, I have never known it to fail, an intense self-respect, precisely for *herself*, her attributes and functions as a female. ... What she wants is the right *really* to be a woman, and not a kind of image doing and saying what she is expected to say by a man who is only afraid of one thing from her—that one day she will forget and tell him the truth!

Porter continues with a point quite significant for a reading of *Pale Horse, Pale Rider,* because it suggests that Adam's nursing of Miranda through their last night together may be the only ministering to her needs that he could ever really be capable of, his concern for her body's health, however tender, being another manifestation of the sexual desire that draws him to her. To provide in addition any essential support for her attempts to establish an autonomous female identity would require a transcendence of gender conflicts he could never achieve. Porter writes in the same letter,

I know that when a woman loves a man, she builds him up and supports him and helps him in every possible way to live. . . . I never knew a man who loved a woman enough for this. He cannot help it, it is his deepest instinct to destroy, quite often subtly, insidiously, but constantly and endlessly, her very center of being, her confidence in herself as woman.[21]

One of the poignant aspects of *Pale Horse, Pale Rider* is that Adam and Miranda seek to *know each other* during their brief time together. Again, a tender and caring person, Adam is nonetheless stereotypically masculine. He wants to be an engineer and does not read much beyond engineering textbooks. He loves driving his roadster very fast and sailing a boat. He would have preferred to be a pilot than part of the ground troops, but he had given in to his mother's hysterical fear, she, implicitly typical of a woman, not realizing that flying is safer than what he is fated to do.

During his talking about himself, "Miranda knew he was trying to tell her what kind of person he was when he had his machinery with him. She felt she knew pretty well what kind of person he was" (287). But when he says he wants to know about her, her answer is significantly vague: "There's nothing to tell, after all, if it ends now, for all this time I was getting ready for something that was going to happen later, when the time came. So now it's nothing much" (302). They are "two persons named Adam and Miranda" (280), but he knows far better than she who he is. Her identity is less clear to her precisely because she is a woman. And when, during an "instant that was a lifetime," she is struck by "the certain, the overwhelming and awful knowledge that there was nothing at all ahead for Adam and for her" (291), the insight may go beyond the war and the plague of influenza. In a work of fiction whose essential theme is *survival*, what is at risk for Miranda is that in any permanent union with Adam, she could not preserve a hard-won female identity.

It is survival itself that creates a thematic conjunction out of the historical coincidence of World War I and the influenza pandemic, both of which were conflated in the popular imagination. Plagues are often blamed by some people on others, who become scapegoats, as the Black Death was attributed to Jews who poisoned drinking water, or AIDS to female poisoners[22] or white scientists committing genocide against black people. In *Pale Horse, Pale Rider*, influenza is discussed as an instance of germ warfare by the Germans against the Americans, the conversations betraying an insularity that ignores the prevalence of the illness throughout the world. The reportage is evocative of Defoe's account in his *Journal* of the kind of ignorant superstition the poor in particular were prone to. In Porter's work, a more sophisticated class becomes the carrier of rumors:

"They *say*," said Towney, "that it is really caused by germs brought by a German ship to Boston, a camouflaged ship, naturally, it didn't come in under its own colors" (284; italics added)

At first she pretends to think the report "ridiculous," but as she continues, the space between herself and the "they" whose beliefs she is reporting narrows:

"They think the germs were sprayed over the city—it started in Boston, you know —and somebody reported seeing a strange, thick, greasy-looking cloud float up out of Boston Harbor and spread slowly all over that end of town. I think it was an old woman who saw it." (284)

Miranda also absorbs the local folklore, for she too has merged in her conscious mind the plagues of war and influenza, tracing the start of her bad headache to the beginning of the war (274). Her doctor has a German-sounding name, Hildesheim, and while she is delirious in the hospital, the physician becomes transformed in her vision into a killer, "his face a skull beneath his German helmet, carrying a naked infant writhing on the point of his bayonet, and a huge stone pot marked Poison in Gothic letters" (309). But for Miranda, the confrontation with an enemy other is also an extension of a widespread indifference shown by people to each other, fear of contagion during plague thus being merely a literalization of a prevalent human alienation. When Adam returns Miranda to her room after an evening together, she is surprised that he watches her up the stairs:

Miranda hardly ever saw anyone look back after he had said good-by. She could not help turning sometimes for one glimpse more of the person she had been talking with, as if that would save too rude and too sudden a snapping of even the lightest bond. But people hurried away, their faces already changed, fixed, in their straining towards their next stopping place, already absorbed in planning their next act or encounter. (284)

It is only an additional irony that Miranda's focal point for a generalized social paranoia, Dr. Hildesheim, should be the one to preserve the life about which she is so ambivalent but which she cannot give up. Miranda's drive for physical survival is portrayed at the beginning of the story in the first of her visionary experiences—this one in a dream. It is here that she appears as the rider on a pale horse engaged in a race against another rider —death—that she is determined to win: "I'm not going with you this time —ride on!" (270). When she thinks of the miracle of meeting Adam, it is in terms of their being "alive and on the earth at the same moment" (280). The two of them engage in conversation about their health, for example the dangers of smoking, and Miranda is filled with wonder that despite the perils of war he faces in just a few days, he "looked so clear and fresh, and he had never had a pain in his life" (282), not knowing, of course, that this is precisely the profile of the person attacked most violently by the influenza. In contrast, she, whose way of life involved "unnatural hours, eating casually at dirty little restaurants, drinking bad coffee all night, and smoking too much," strives successfully during her illness "to keep her small hold on the life of human beings . . . no matter what" (307), to the point that she cannot submit to her beatific vision of pure being, instead living to join the "dead and withered things that believed themselves alive" (314).

But the struggle merely to exist goes beyond Miranda's health, for her entire life is engaged

in a continual effort to bring together and unite firmly the disturbing oppositions in her day-to-day existence, where survival, she could see clearly, had become a series of feats of sleight of hand. (271)

At one point she asks Adam, "Don't you love being alive?" (302). But there is something hysterical in the question, because for Miranda, being alive is to engage in the unremitting effort to remain fit enough to live, the "disturbing oppositions" in her life being not only the conflict between herself and her environment but also the conflict between her instinct for survival and a very pronounced death wish. Part of Miranda's struggle has to do with her resistance to the forms of society, supposedly constructed to insure individual survival but inevitably antithetical to the self's endeavor to preserve itself.

That is, the social contract is as thematically important to *Pale Horse, Pale Rider* as it is to Defoe's *Journal of a Plague Year*. In theory, the contract is an antithesis to chaos and a reference point for civic duty, which is itself a possible antidote to a person's alienating fear of others in the world. In times of plague — as has already been argued — the tensions in the social contract emerge to disclose the separateness of human beings, fear of contagion — again — literalizing an essential antipathy toward others, or, at best, a drive toward self-preservation that under stress alienates even well-meaning individuals. But whereas works such as Defoe's *Journal* affirm the viability of the social contract, *Pale Horse, Pale Rider* looks at it from the opposite point of view. The collective itself becomes a macroparasite against which the individual needs protection. It is interesting in this regard to note David Richter's suggestion that the name of Miranda's "respectable and suspicious" landlady is Miss Hobbe, for in this work in which names are so important, the landlady's name

recalls that of the seventeenth-century English philosopher, Thomas Hobbes, who postulated that man originally inhabited no peaceful Eden, but a land of perpetual warfare, where every man's hand was against every man, and where life was "solitary, poor, nasty, brutish, and short."[23]

Richter's suggestion reinforces the parallels between Miss Hobbe's rooming house and the state whose preservation was the point of the Hobbesian conception of the social contract. For although the good of the individual is inferred by the agreement people enter into for mutual protection, individual needs rarely prevail. When, for example, Miranda asks for better curtains than the thin ones that do not adequately keep the light out of her room in the morning, she is promised new ones that do not, however, appear. And when Miss Hobbe learns that Miranda has influenza, she orders the ill woman back to bed immediately, not for Miranda's good but for the protection of herself and her other tenants. She is determined that Miranda be sent to the hospital without delay, and protests,

I tell you, they must come for her *now*, or I'll put her on the sidewalk. . . . I tell you, this is a plague, a plague, my God, and I've got a houseful of people to think about! (299)

That Miss Hobbe's house cannot support itself, that is, "was not paying" (298), may symbolize the precariousness of the state based on the social contract, whose initial premise is the war of all against all. Only the force of punishment (a symbolic as well as real eviction) can guarantee the conformity of a person to the requirements of the group and preserve the abstract whole.

In Miranda's delirious vision, the hospital becomes a place to which criminals are sent, the plague a crime rather than the traditional punishment for one, and the health care workers "executioners" (309) in league with death itself. The old man in the next bed who dies of influenza appears to her a pitiable criminal being dragged away protesting that the "crime of which he was accused did not merit the punishment he was about to receive" (308). In her delirium, Miranda conflates original sin, the fruits of which are plague and death, with the unknown sin of the individual against an order from which the person is essentially alienated. As the "executioners" advance, the

soiled cracked bowls of the old man's hands were held before him beseechingly as a beggar's as he said, "Before God I am not guilty," but they held his arms and drew him onward, passed, and were gone. (309)

Miranda and Towney are very conscious of punishments meted out in a world in which individual initiative is discouraged. When they had suppressed the news story of the elopement (a symbol of personal choice whose

punishment was to be public scandal), they had been virtually court-mar-
tialed, their ranks broken. Having "taken their punishment together, [they]
had been degraded publicly to routine female jobs" (275). This juxtaposition of punishment and gender creates an added level to the conflict between individual and society, here disclosed as a confrontation between the
female condemned and the patriarchal sentencer. Miranda, as already noted,
comes out of her bout with influenza to think of herself as "condemned"
to live.

The male representatives of the persecuting and prosecuting state are
both insignificant and powerfully insidious—the Liberty Bond salesmen.
Miranda's fear is that she will be punished for her failure to buy one.
Richter has pointed out that "the name of the bond is an irony Porter did
not have to invent." [24] In terms of a social contract, there is additional irony
attached to the word *bond* (which Porter later uses to describe the weak
relationship Miranda has to the men who return her after a date to her
rooming house). The war against Germany presumably represents a solely
external threat, the war bond drive the intended mutual cooperation of
American citizens to win that war. Instead, those in charge of selling bonds
engage in internal warfare, become the aggressors, another group of invading macroparasites against which Miranda feels as helpless as against war
and influenza. The man who issues unspecified threats if she does not
purchase a bond is an apt candidate for Hobbes's nasty and brutish human
being, an enemy attacker or criminal in the war against his own kind: he
had a stony stare, "really viciously cold, the kind of thing you might expect
to meet behind a pistol in a deserted corner" (272). Miranda and he face
each other as enemies, one of them trying in self-protection to avoid the
inevitable confrontation. "Usually she did not notice [him and his partner]
at all until their determination to be seen was greater than her determination
not to see them" (271). It is only a sardonic feature of this symbolic military
engagement that her antagonists invoke the common struggle in which
supposedly they are all embattled as part of their attack: "We're having a
war, and some people are buying Liberty Bonds and others just don't seem
to get around to it" (272). Miranda remains "desperately silent," trying to
decide on some tactical defense, her words to herself creating an ambiguity
about just which battle she is contemplating:

[Miranda] thought, "Suppose I were not a coward, but said what I really thought?
Suppose I said to hell with this filthy war?" (273)

The entire world of *Pale Horse, Pale Rider* seems made up of macroparasites.[25] Miranda thinks about the invasion of her private territory at work:

"reminded of the way all sorts of persons sat upon her desk at the newspaper office," she wonders *"why* won't they sit in the chair?" (271). Her job as theater reviewer breaks out as another kind of war, one in which she is both aggressor and attacked. Her reviews of performers are, she realizes, an assault not only on their performances but also on their selves, and she wishes they did not care what she thought. It is when she understands how badly she has hurt someone with a review that she decides, in a weary gesture of identification, that she wishes to die. The object of her review, in turn, says he is "going to take the goof who wrote that piece up the alley and bop him in the nose" (287). When he actually threatens physical violence, he is driven off by Miranda's friends as if repulsed in battle, but not until his own bellicosity is revealed. A seeming antithesis to this pitiable figure turns out to be as pathetic but also insidiously macroparasitic. This is Chuck's alcoholic father, who "beamed upon [his son] with the bleariest eye of paternal affection while he took his last nickel" (286). Porter's story shares with Stegner's the image of the universal food chain, as Miranda describes another bond salesman: "Just another nasty old man who would like to see the young ones killed; . . . the tom-cats try to eat the little tom-kittens, you know" (294). In such a world only survival counts. It is because Chuck cannot fight the war and therefore need not live through it (although, ironically, he has to worry about his lung disease) that it ceases to mean anything to him: "I don't care how [the war] started or when it ends. . . . I'm not going to be there" (290).

But among the different kinds of survival dealt with in *Pale Horse, Pale Rider,* survival of the individual self prevails as that under which all other survivals are subsumed. That Porter is portraying Miranda's striving toward selfhood is a point about which most Porter critics agree. Robert Penn Warren contends that there is in the story a "paradoxical problem of definition," a "delicate balancing of rival considerations."[26] Philip Yannella has given Miranda's conflicts an historical context, noting that 1918 was a "crucial year in the history of modern selfhood" and that Porter's novella makes some "acute observations about the attrition of nineteenth-century definitions of selfhood, the development of the twentieth-century self, and the failure of the twentieth-century self to establish suitable patterns of behavior."[27] Thus, according to Thomas Walsh, influenza does not so much cause Miranda's despair as bring "to the surface" what already "lay submerged in her character."[28] The specific rooting of Miranda's problem in her southern origins is added by James Johnson, who says that in Porter's fiction is found the theme of the "individual within [her] heritage." Related themes are cultural displacement and, finally, a slavery to nature and "sub-jugation to a human fate" that dooms a Porter character to "suffering and disappointment."[29]

But the quest for self in *Pale Horse, Pale Rider* exists as a theme very much as Miranda herself exists, on "multiple planes" (304) of being. But "planes" is perhaps inadequate to Porter's own purposes as Miranda experiences "tough filaments of memory and hope pulling taut backwards and forwards holding her upright between them" (304). Her predicament is more complex than such an image suggests, involving paradoxes whose elements are difficult to separate. As Richter points out, for Miranda "to summon the will to live that will enable her to survive her illness, she must detach herself from all the values that have given her life meaning and, though she ultimately survives, she pays a price that may not be worth the empty life she regains."[30] Miranda is transformed from a potentially loving young woman to one who subsists on her own indifference. What can be inferred from Richter's argument is that *Pale Horse, Pale Rider* addresses the difficult philosophical issue of just what survives in survival. The novella, that is, raises the body-mind problem. Porter is not, of course, a systematic philosopher, and the problem is depicted not through logical analysis but through the images and visions that make up Miranda's conscious and unconscious responses to both body and mind.

One result of Miranda's illness is that it allows her out-of-body experi-ences. While she lies ill in the rooming house, she has one of her visions, imagining herself sailing into a jungle that—it has already been noted—represents death. The jungle probably also represents her unconscious, in which unformulated terrors and her persistently resisted death wish are revealed. The language of her vision includes words and phrases such as "screaming," "bellow of voices all crying together," "a writhing terribly alive and secret place of death," "danger, danger, danger," and "war, war, war" (299). Miranda's reaction is not to recoil, however, but eagerly to meet these dangers, and in a moment of dissociation one part of her observes the other:

Without surprise, watching from her pillow, she saw herself run swiftly down this gangplank to the slanting deck, and standing there, she leaned on the rail and waved gaily to herself in bed, and the slender ship spread its wings and sailed away into the jungle. (299)

Later, in the hospital, Miranda experiences a more intense form of dissocia-tion, the struggle between a death instinct and the will to survive described in an image of fission:

Her mind, split in two, acknowledged and denied what she saw in the one instant, for across an abyss of complaining darkness her reasoning coherent self watched the strange frenzy of the other coldly, reluctant to admit the truth of its visions, its tenacious remorses and despairs. (310)

It is at this point that she approaches what Porter was to call her beatific vision, which Miranda responds to "with serene rapture as if some promise made to her had been kept long after she had ceased to hope for it" (311). What she envisions are "pure identities," without material bodies (although, of course, Porter must use the language of bodies to describe them) and without the conflicts that can result in a mind that "split in two."

Their faces were transfigured, each in its own beauty, beyond what she remembered of them, their eyes were clear and untroubled as good weather, and they cast no shadows. They were pure identities and she knew them every one without calling their names or remembering what relation she bore to them. (311)

That Miranda thinks she knows them is susceptible to several explanations, but clearly they correspond to very deep wishes on her part to be free of the "disturbing oppositions" that engage her in her unremitting struggle merely to exist. That her visions are "pure identities" means of course that they are free of personal identity, for it is the survival of her individual self that causes Miranda the most difficulty. What Georges Rey says in his essay "Survival" supplies an interesting commentary on *Pale Horse, Pale Rider,* supplying it with the philosophical context it evokes. Rey writes that the "possibility of an *entirely* disembodied, yet still somehow *personal, existence* seems simply capricious: idle 'image mongery.' "

We are led, then, both by the presuppositions and by the failure of a purely psychological criterion, to our bodies. We were really led there already by considerations of the causal basis of our survival at a given time. . . . We might have been led there independently by even a casual inspection of the notion of a person: whatever the details, such creatures consist at least of a complex of capacities, abilities, dispositions; and, as such, as many writers have rightly insisted, they cannot float about somehow unanchored in space and time.[31]

And, indeed, through the ministering of doctors and nurses as well as through the tenacity of her own will, Miranda comes out of her ecstasy and, as John Donne's famous poem describes the ecstatic out-of-body experience, *descends* to her body.

The body supplies *Pale Horse, Pale Rider* with much of its imagery, for Porter is always specific about the concrete details of her characters' physical existence in their environment. Miranda's conflict is as immaterial as the mind itself, but her emotional withdrawal from a hopeful commitment to her world is described in specifically physical terms: "her hardened, indifferent heart shuddered in despair at itself, because before it had been tender and capable of love." Earlier her body had been foreign to her. She had even asked herself, "Do I even walk about in my own skin or is it something I have borrowed to spare my modesty?" (270). Adam's very health causes her to think of his body as a monster, an image she also evokes for herself, but from a different emotional perspective, Miranda being estranged from her body whereas Adam is comfortable in his. In the hospital, Miranda experiences not relief but entrapment when she recovers from influenza, thinking how

The body is a curious monster, no place to live in, how could anyone feel at home there? Is it possible I can ever accustom myself to this place? . . . Miranda looked about her with the covertly hostile eyes of an alien who does not like the country in which he finds himself. (313)

For Adam, it is the body that is tantamount to personal identity. When Miranda, who is profoundly depressed by the war, tells him that it is what war "does to the mind and the heart" that is so awful, adding, "you can't separate these two—what it does to them is worse than what it can do to the body," Adam pragmatically replies, "The mind and the heart sometimes get another chance, but if anything happens to the poor old human frame, why, it's just out of luck, that's all" (294). Richter points out that the tragic ending to *Pale Horse, Pale Rider* rests on the irony that "contrary to what Adam thinks, the body may well 'get another chance,' but the heart and mind, once altered, are changed forever." [32] This is perhaps another way to say that for Adam philosophical issues of personal identity are not important, whereas for Miranda they had been critical. She has, in short, resolved the problem of survival by, in the end, adopting Adam's view and abandoning the quest for self-definition. The body that was once alien to her because she sought an identity that was more than it alone could supply is now all she has—or wants.

Richter's argument that Miranda summons the will to survive at the expense of the values she had lived by—that is, in effect, by abandoning that self that is more than just body—touches on another plane of meaning in *Pale Horse, Pale Rider*. The story is illuminated by a concept of selfhood that comes from self psychologist Douglas Detrick, who parallels the tension between the individual and the group with the historical evolution of the unconscious:

I believe that until the modern era, the archetypal collective unconscious organization was more or less adequate for humans both in the cultural and personal domain. However, this organization was slowly undermined over the last two millennia by the expansion of the personal unconscious.[33]

Among the forces that Miranda must ward off to preserve her personal identity are the archetypes that make up her heritage. According to Robert Penn Warren, Miranda's final insights become her personal myth, and she "must live by her own myth. But she must earn her myth in the process of living."[34] Such a reading may, however, be too optimistic, for the dual plagues of war and influenza may indicate that in her culture, Miranda must learn to live without myths.

If, as Thomas Loe contends, Miranda's visionary experiences involve a symbolic "journey of initiation, necessarily internal,"[35] then Miranda is on an archetypal quest to free herself of archetypes. The very opening of the story reveals the tension between the constraints of a heritage and the striving of the individual. In Miranda's first dream, a sign of the onset of influenza, she "knew she was in her bed, but not the bed she had lain down in" earlier. She was in a "room she had known somewhere," and she feels the need to get up, to leave while some unknown *they* "are all quiet." But she cannot at first find her (again, vaguely described) "things," that which is hers alone: "Things have a will of their own in this place and hide where they like." An ambivalent fondness for and rejection of those who crowd upon her, her past and still too much a part of her present, become mixed up with images of death and survival, illustrating Detrick's concept of a struggle between the archetypal and personal unconscious:

Faces will beam, asking, Where are you going, What are you doing, What are you thinking, How do you feel, Why do you say such things, What do you mean? . . . How I have loved this house in the morning before we are all awake and tangled together like badly cast fishing lines. Too many people have been born here, and have wept too much here, and have laughed too much, and have been too angry and outrageous with each other here. Too many have died in this bed already, there are far too many ancestral bones propped up on the mantelpieces, there have been too damned many antimacassars in this house, she said loudly, and oh, what accumulation of storied dust never allowed to settle in peace for one moment. (269)

The passage seems almost an extension of sections in *Old Mortality* in which Miranda, who had when too young entered into an unfortunate marriage (this is not mentioned in *Pale Horse, Pale Rider*), visits her southern home:

"Ah, the family," [her cousin Eva] said, releasing her breath and sitting back quietly, "the whole hideous institution should be wiped from the face of the earth. It is the root of all human wrongs." . . . [Miranda] felt a vague distaste for seeing cousins. She did not want any more ties with this house, she was going to leave it, and she was not going back to her husband's family either. . . . She knew now why she had run away to marriage, and she knew that she was going to run away from marriage, and she was not going to stay in any place with anyone that threatened to forbid her making her own discoveries, that said "No" to her. (217, 220)

And yet Miranda asks in *Pale Horse, Pale Rider* about that which anchors her in a concrete world of familiar realities—her grandfather, great-aunt, cousins, a decrepit hound, and silver kitten—"What else besides them did I have in the world?" (270). When she thinks she is going to die, she wonders if she should go home: "It's a respectable old custom to inflict your death on the family if you can manage it" (298).

One way to define the conflict in Miranda's relationship with Adam is to realize that he represents a series of archetypes, whereas she struggles to free herself of the archaic organization of her world. They are, as earlier noted, two persons *named* Adam and Miranda (280). As Adam's name suggests, he is the first man, an original (Richter points out the significance of his surname, *bar*-clay).[36] Like Adam in Genesis, Adam Barclay is doomed to fall, "not for any woman, being beyond experience already, committed without any knowledge or act to his own death" (284). He is also archetypally American, a Protestant (Miranda is Catholic), as well as a model for the American soldier. "He was wearing his new uniform [which is custom made to fit him exactly], and he was all olive and tan and tawny, hay colored and sand colored from hair to boots" (278). Stereotypically masculine, he is one of those concerned that wearing a wristwatch (as soldiers had to) would make him a sissy. But he is also a figure of the saintly martyr, and in one of Miranda's visions, they are both shot through with arrows of death, he perishing while she is cheated of this release. Perceived by Miranda to be pure, "all the way through, flawless, complete, as the sacrificial lamb must be" (295), he represents all the soldiers that were to die at the front. And only a few words later, she hopes they "don't come to a mud puddle" (295), for he will carry her over it like the archetypical courtier.

Not that Adam wears his archetypes comfortably. He is described as "infinitely buttoned, strapped, harnessed into a uniform as tough and unyielding in cut as a strait jacket" (279). But then, that is the point about past heritages: in their repressiveness they are never easy to bear. But only Miranda seems to know this. Her very name—borrowed from Shakespeare[37]—promises her release from the burden of her past, represented in part by cousins named Eva and Maria. In these names, of course, are the most basic Western archetypes of woman, the temptress and the redemptress, the one causing the fall, the other the archetype of the good mother who redeems the world after the sin of her counterpart. But Shakespeare had created in *The Tempest* not only the possibility of a brave new world but also a woman free of the archetypal dichotomies implied by Eve and Mary: Miranda, innocent and uncorrupted to the end. To repeat a passage already quoted, it is when Porter's Miranda can no longer bear the world she lives in and wants only to sit down and die that she despairingly says, "I wish I could lose my memory and forget my own name" (289). Shakespeare's Miranda will remain free of Caliban and the Red Plague with which he curses her father; Porter's Miranda will succumb to pestilence. When she emerges from her physical crisis, there will be no "more war, no more plague" (317) but also, in the most profound sense, no more Miranda.

It is therefore quite significant that it is Towney who comes to the hospital when Miranda is ready to be released, and that at this point Porter's reader is reminded of Towney's real name, Mary Townsend. And it is as Mary that Miranda addresses her, longing for some spiritual anchor in the world that she can no longer provide for herself: "Do you suppose, Mary . . . I could have my old room back again?" (316). Mary reassures her that her possessions had been stored with Miss Hobbe, a symbolic confirmation that Miranda has given up striving for individuation. And when the nurse informs her that the taxi that will take her away from the hospital is waiting, "there was Mary. Ready to go" (317).

Interpretations of the conclusion to *Pale Horse, Pale Rider* vary from the extremely pessimistic, to the neutral or mildly hopeful, to the affirmation of Miranda's spiritual rebirth.[38] The story does end with a validation of Eudora Welty's conviction that time is the critical theme in Porter's fiction: the last sentence reads, "Now there would be time for everything" (317)—even, supposedly, time for Miranda to begin again to recreate her self, although Porter critics frequently point out that *Pale Horse, Pale Rider* is the last of the author's Miranda stories. But, in fact, time did play an important part in this piece of fiction that has its roots in Porter's own struggle to survive influenza during the pandemic of 1918. For after almost twenty years, Porter turned her bout with an almost fatal illness into the work considered her masterpiece. Interestingly enough, she writes in a letter to Robert Penn Warren that she is searching for another title; but the title she retained after obvious contemplation may supply *Pale Horse, Pale Rider* with its most obvious hopefulness.

On the night before she enters the hospital, Miranda tells Adam she knows "an old spiritual," which she begins to recite: "Pale horse, pale rider, done taken my lover away" (303). He responds that he had heard it sung by the black workers in Texas oil fields, and reminds her that there are "about forty verses, the rider done taken away mammy, pappy, brother, sister, the whole family besides the lover." Miranda corrects him:

"But not the singer, not yet," said Miranda. "Death always leaves one singer to mourn. 'Death,' " she sang, " 'oh, leave one singer to mourn—.' " (304)

This image of an enduring art that in its own way recreates the world can be found in *Old Mortality,* in which Miranda and her cousin Maria attend concerts and theaters to discover that there

was then a life beyond a life in this world, as well as in the next; such episodes confirmed for the little girls the nobility of human feeling, the divinity of man's vision of the unseen, the importance of life and death, the depths of the human heart, the romantic value of tragedy. (179)

There are correspondences between this passage and Porter's description of a transcendent beatific vision. And while there is nothing romantic about influenza in *Pale Horse, Pale Rider,* there is in it an expression of the romantic value of tragedy, the word *tragedy* itself inferring not only a catastrophic event but also its rendering through an artistic genre. Like the monument to the surviving singer in "Pale Horse, Pale Rider," that is, the spiritual itself, Porter's novella is a testament to that which can survive even plague, that for which there might always be time, perhaps even enduring through time—the literature of plague.

SIX

Plague, Physician, Writer, and the Poison Damsel

When Fournier published his book on *Syphilis and Marriage* in 1880, he had several purposes. Like his other treatises on venereal disease, this one provided medical education. The important discoveries concerning the diagnosis and treatment of syphilis were yet to occur, and Fournier's careful look at and classification of symptoms and patterns of transmission —many of his conclusions arrived at deductively—were being communicated to physicians who would encounter and attempt to treat the disease. The book could also educate that segment of the general public that would read it, ironically the same group that he was depicting as more dangerous in the spread of the disease than it as a class wished to admit to itself. For Fournier was also addressing a virtually taboo subject, shifting the site of the disease from the streets and their vices to the bedrooms of respectable households. The doctor's role was no longer restricted to that of healer. Unlike the speaker in Blake's "London," who from an objective distance remarks on the plague that blights the "marriage hearse," the physician that Fournier addresses must be directly concerned that a bridegroom might "give a virtuous young woman the pox as a wedding present."[1] In asking the question, what conditions ought the groom "fulfill, medically, in order that we may be justified in permitting him to marry," or "conversely, in what conditions will it be our duty to defer or even absolutely interdict the marriage"?[2] Fournier implicates the medical profession not only in the course of the marriage and its issue, and in ethical (eventually, in legal) dilemmas, but also in matters of conscience ordinarily dealt with by the clergy. Moreover, the physician's examining room had been extended to the arena of public health; inevitably this involved the doctor in conflicts concerning individual patients, the larger circle of people around them, and society as a whole.

For all of these reasons, Fournier was also attempting to change the public image of the syphilitic, the middle- or upper-class patient he was regularly seeing being one whose need to maintain privacy and avoid scandal was not only acute but also capable of being achieved. But this demand for concealment by respectable people as well as the hypocrisy that governed their sexual lives made them especially insidious spreaders of the disease. Again, these classes were then, as they probably are now, the same ones likely to read books about the diseases that plagued them, to be educated by such reading, and in turn to educate their families. A major source of the problem, they constituted a potentially major source of the solution. Fournier's work is intended as a guide to insure healthy marriages and families, and its immediate translation into English indicates that its public usefulness was quickly recognized outside of France.

This brief survey of Fournier's intentions is based not only on *Syphilis and Marriage*—invoked earlier to identify controversies prevalent when Ibsen wrote *Ghosts*—but also on a dramatic work often mentioned in connection with Ibsen's, a play that virtually dramatizes Fournier's profile of the "new" syphilitic: Eugene Brieux's *Damaged Goods*, whose French title, *Les Avariés* is a term that euphemistically identifies a syphilitic patient as well as morally and socially designating him as "damaged." The first and third of its three acts take place in the offices of its main character, a doctor, the second act in the home of a family devastated by his advice having gone unheeded. The doctor had diagnosed the medical condition of one George Dumont to be syphilis, and had dissuaded the young man, who was about to be married, from committing suicide by assuring him that his disease had a 95 percent chance of cure. But when, following upon his relief, George is informed that he must postpone his wedding for three or four years, since it is likely if not definite that he will infect his wife, the young man seizes on the off-chance that this will not happen and proceeds with the marriage. For he has also contracted to buy a notary's practice, for which his prospective bride's dowry is necessary. Moreover, he is overwhelmed with his own sense of not deserving what had happened to him, for, or so he argues, compared to many other men of his generation, he had practised what his age might have considered safe sex. He had restricted himself to the wife of a best friend he knew to be faithful in the marriage, and to a young woman whose family enjoyed the economic privileges of the relationship and hence carefully guarded her on behalf of her sexual partner and benefactor. George claims indignantly, as if he were victim rather than accomplice in his own plight, that it was only a single encounter with a woman whose sexual history should have made him particularly careful that had brought him to his present condition. The doctor wryly responds that one careless instance was sufficient. In any event, George defies medical advice and takes matters into his own hands: drawing, ironically enough, on a more respectable plague, tuberculosis, he finds in vague respiratory symptoms an excuse to postpone his marriage for six months and then pronounces himself cured and ready to wed.

Act 2 finds the married couple a year later, lamenting the absence of their three-month-old daughter, who, in accord with the traditions of their class, is in the charge of a wet nurse. But then disquieting news reaches Dumont. His mother accompanies both nurse and infant to her son's home after learning that the nurse has probably been infected by the baby, who has visible if relatively minor symptoms of congenital syphilis, such as a rash and pimples in her mouth and throat. The same doctor who had diagnosed George is called to the house, and he and the grandmother are embroiled in a verbal battle over the well-being of the nurse (or future nurses) versus that of the child, who—or so its family believes—might not survive if bottle fed according to the doctor's instructions. The father and grandmother are immune to moral issues, although sensitive to the possibility of a lawsuit, several nurses having already been awarded large settlements by the courts for having contracted syphilis from infected infants nursing at their breasts. Moreover, a new law has made doctors who knowingly neglect to warn such nurses if they are in danger also liable to suit, so what is essentially a moral issue is now also a legal one. The Dumonts pay off their nurse, who has now cunningly understood how she can use her situation to get money but has not grasped the full danger to her health. She leaves, but not before the young Mrs. Dumont discovers the truth, act 2 ending with her histrionically "shrieking like a mad woman" at her husband, "Don't touch me! Don't touch me!" (234).

Act 3 returns the audience to the doctor's office, this time in a hospital, where the younger Mrs. Dumont's father, M. Loches, arrives to procure a certificate testifying to his son-in-law's condition prior to marriage so that his daughter can obtain a divorce. The doctor refuses to comply on several grounds. The first has to do with the confidentiality George can expect from his physician.[3] The second involves the doctor's disagreement concerning the divorce being in the best interest of the family in general, the young woman in particular. The third concerns his indictment that the father must accept some of the responsibility for the debacle, since he had made many inquiries about his future son-in-law's character and income, but none about his health. And when all arguments fail, the doctor asks Loches if he is in a position to judge the young man: had he never exposed himself to the danger of contracting syphilis? If uninfected, could he claim more than luck where his son-in-law had been unlucky?

Come, come, let us have a little plain speaking! I should like to know how many of these rigid moralists, who are so choked with their middle-class prudery that they dare not mention the name syphilis, or when they bring themselves to speak of it do so with expressions of every sort of disgust, and treat its victims as criminals, have never run the risk of contracting it themselves? It is those alone who have the right to talk. How many do you think there are? Four out of a thousand? (241)

Persuading the man that his daughter can construct a good marriage out of the present debacle, that "there is much truth in the saying that reformed rakes make the best husbands," that "we will make sure that when they are reunited their next child shall be healthy and vigorous" (242), the doctor draws the father, a legislator, into his vision of a more enlightened society. This, perhaps, explains the "we" ("nous nous arrangerons" [85]) who will insure the well-being of future generations, educating the public about syphilis as a medical disease while addressing the moral issue, which does not rest on any inherent sinfulness attached to sex but rather on hypocritical sexual behavior. To this end, the doctor introduces one of his patients, a prostitute, whose story presents her as a stereotypical fallen woman, victim of her society, thwarted in her striving towards respectability, paying men back for her misery by, at this point, willfully spreading the disease with which she has been afflicted. When Loches excoriates her for being a poisoner, the doctor must remind him that she had herself first been poisoned. In effect, Blake's harlot has finally been allowed to speak for herself.[4]

As a problem play, *Damaged Goods* announces its content to the audience when it is addressed by the theater manager before the curtain goes up: "The object of this play is a study of the disease of syphilis and its bearing on marriage" (186). By substituting the word "object" for the French "sujet" (3), the English version emphasizes the rhetorical *aim* of the drama, the intention both to promote social reform and to educate the audience about the individual's role in the spread of syphilis, as well as to provide advice about how persons might protect themselves and those they are concerned about. When the doctor reproves Loches for failing to investigate the health of his future son-in-law as carefully as he had investigated his character and his finances, Brieux is sending a message directly to every father in the audience concerning his daughter's future.

The playwright is drawing on the traditional advantage of literature in describing a social problem or making an ethical point over other forms of writing because literature alone has pleasure as its means and can give flesh to abstract ideas by way of characters whose actions will affect outcomes. Brieux dedicates his play to Fournier in a brief letter that prefaces his text:

Monsieur,

I request your permission to dedicate this play to you. Most of the ideas that it attempts to popularize are yours.

I believe, with you, that syphilis will lose much of its gravity when one dares to speak openly of a sickness [mal] that is not a shame nor a punishment and when those who are infected [atteints], knowing what misery [malheurs] they are capable of spreading, are more aware of their responsibilities towards others and towards themselves.

Believe, Monsieur, my respectful sympathy. . . .(3)[5]

Brieux's use of the word "sympathie" indicates more than his agreement with the renowned syphilologist's views on the disease. Rather, he suggests an inherent identification between himself and Fournier, who is represented in the play as an unnamed physician known variously as "le docteur" and "le medicin," which terms emphasize his role as an abstract representative of his profession. Brieux is, in effect, putting Fournier on stage, supplying him with a medium that promises a wider public than his books alone could hope to gain.

In this way Brieux and Fournier, playwright and physician, exchange identities. The writer becomes healer, and—conversely—the doctor as literary character becomes one who uses *words* rather than dispenses medicines to heal private and public disease. As noted in the earlier discussion on Chaucer, the psychological function of the doctor is traditional, and, according to McNeill, was even more so when the medical profession was ineffective against diseases and epidemics. But *Damaged Goods* appeared at a time when the very advances in medicine complicated the physician's role. The play stood at the threshold of crucial scientific discoveries: identifying the spirochete that causes syphilis, devising a reliable test for it (the Wassermann test), and developing effective antibiotics whose side effects did not threaten to be almost as bad as the disease itself. But such progress postdates *Damaged Goods,* and Brieux's physician can be accused of being too cavalier, too optimistic about the ease with which George might be healed. But, again, Brieux's doctor is not primarily dispensing medical treatment. The prescription that the he writes for George Dumont in the first act is a miniature text, a symbol of the play.

For it is language itself, its use and misuse, that supplies *Damaged Goods* with one of its major themes. People who shamelessly entered into the most immoral sexual relations insisted on surrounding the "act that reproduces life by the means of love" with a "gigantic conspiracy of silence" (249). The same persons who took their children to music halls where they were exposed to the most licentious language and acts yet adhered to some ignorant preconception of childhood innocence and would not "let [their offspring] hear a word spoken seriously on the subject of the great act of love" (249), thus denying sex education a role in the schools. It is because he "was afraid to tell" (248) his father that he had syphilis that a young man consulted medical quacks, the disease having progressed very far before he came under the care of Brieux's hero-doctor.

But adults were also shielded from reality, from the language of disease. George's father had owned a small provincial paper and George admits that had they "ever printed that word"—*syphilis*—they would have lost their readers, although that same readership was hungry for "novels about adultery" (194). In a scene reminiscent of the encounter between Dr. Stockmann and Hovstad, George insists that the press must conform to public taste. Thus the word *syphilis* is taboo, and what the doctor insists is that the disease cease to be treated like a mysterious evil the very name of which cannot be pronounced. The "ignorance in which the public is kept of the real nature and of the consequences of this disease helps to aggravate and to spread it" (248). It is the contagiousness of this concept as much as the illness itself that the doctor attacks when he responds to Loches's demand for his complicity in divorce proceedings.

Few things exasperate me more than that term "shameful disease," which you used just now. This disease is like all other diseases: it is one of our afflictions. There is no shame in being wretched—even if one deserves to be so. (241)

What he calls for is some "plain speaking" concerning those who "dare not mention the name syphilis" or speak of it with "every sort of disgust" and "treat victims as criminals," as if they themselves "have never run the risk of contracting it themselves" (241). It is neither morality nor divine judgment that separate the sick from the well—just luck in the past and possibly education and understanding in the present.

But in the isolated realm of the syphilis patient, the words from outside are as afflicting as the microparasites that destroy from within: the *record* of syphilis proves more incurable than the disease itself. When the doctor tries to talk Loches out of separating his daughter from her husband, he argues that this father has failed to consider that his "daughter has been exposed to the infection," and that a statement to that effect "will be officially registered in the papers of the case" (238). But his daughter's ensuing inability to remarry is nothing compared to the effect of public record on his granddaughter, whose inheritance will be to endure a double infection:

Indeed! you think that this poor little thing has not been unlucky enough in her start in life? She has been blighted physically: you wish besides to stamp her indelibly with the legal proof of congenital syphilis? (238)

This family's misfortune threatens to dissolve into words, into story, and against Loches's threat to kill his son-in-law and his confidence that he will be acquitted, the doctor counters, "Yes; but [only] after the public narration of all your troubles ["la révélation publique" (81)]. The scandal and the misfortune will be so much the greater, that is all" (239).

It is thus in a realm of language rather than science that Brieux's doctor moves. It is what his patients say to him, not their physical symptoms, that allows him to know "better than anyone" (189) what constitutes the morals of his time. And when George begs for assurance that he can look forward to cure and eventually to marriage, the doctor answers, "Je vous le jure," (13), the translation, "I give you my word on it" (193), true to the spirit rather than the letter of the French text. For in *Damaged Goods*, the doctor must counter words with words, and when George repeats some erroneous information he has been told is true, the doctor, part in mockery and part in frustration, can only mimic, "You have been told! You have been told!" (193; "On vous avait dit. . . . On vous avait dit!" [14]).

It is as a debater rather than a physician that the doctor confronts Loches, significantly a deputy for his town famous because he is a "regular orator" (235). At first, refusing Loches his request for documentary evidence to use in the divorce, the doctor is reluctant to engage in controversy with his opponent, but he eventually concedes: "Since I have let myself in for it, I may as well explain my position" (238). Once having prevailed with Loches, the doctor must tell the father, at a loss as to how to "persuade" his daughter "to return to her husband," that there are "arguments that you can use" (242). His ability to sway George had been unfortunately undermined by another syphilologist, Ricord, who, if Brieux's presentation is accurate, apparently differed with Fournier about the inevitability of contagion. Although Brieux's doctor responds to his patient, "I will answer you" (201), he cannot muster the irrefutable facts of science to sustain the rhetoric that is almost by default his strongest weapon. When the prospective groom argues that not only his future happiness but also his economic well-being is at issue, his position is thrown back at him with the implications of his words:

DOCTOR: . . . I can easily show you the way out of the difficulty. Get into touch with some rich man, do everything you can to gain his confidence, and when you have succeeded, rook him of all he has.
GEORGE: I'm not in the mood for joking.
DOCTOR: I'm not joking. To rob that man, or even to murder him, would not be a greater crime than you would commit in marrying a young girl in good health to

get hold of her dowry, if to do so you expose her to the terrible consequences of the disease you would give her. (197–98)

At those times when he is most discouraged about how to halt the spread of syphilis, it is his failure with language that overwhelms the doctor. Coming to examine the infected Dumont infant and recognizing George, he exclaims, "You married and had a child after all I *said* to you" (217; italics added). But George's predicament is not the doctor's first discouragement, and he had earlier admitted to the prospective bridegroom that he was ineffectual with other patients:

I am almost afraid of not having been persuasive enough. I feel as though in spite of everything I were in some sort the cause of their misery. I ought to prevent such misery. . . . Give me your word that you will break off your engagement. (200)

But more often than not, the self-interest of the syphilitic patient would prove insurmountable, impervious to the logic of the disease and its epidemiology. What he cannot expect to achieve with George, the doctor may with Loches—outraged father, true, but also legislator entrusted with public welfare. And so he will move Loches to action not with words but, finally, with what the doctor alone can provide, a parade of the hapless and helpless victims of syphilis and their devastated families: the father whose son waited perhaps too long to admit to his family that he was sick; or the poverty-stricken woman who suffers the disease passed on by her now-dead husband and, lacking both money and time off from work for treatment, remains without even the luxury of outrage enjoyed by the bourgeois Mrs. Dumont, who can indulge in screams of horror and fury, and who has her father to fight for and protect her.

But the most important case history for the doctor's argument is the prostitute who is "at once the product and the cause" (253) of so many social ills, her potential for spreading syphilis the result not of her fallen nature but of her own victimization. Her narrative is typical, an account of a maidservant being seduced by her master, whose wife then turns her out on the streets. Ironically, the prostitute has the ambition to be an actress, to make of the stage rather than the streets a livelihood. As a ruse to elicit her life's history, the doctor informs her that Loches can help her realize her goals, when, in fact, it is the doctor himself who supplies the dramatic arena on which she may act out her narrative. More literally, Brieux as playwright transforms the prostitute's dream into actuality: he provides her with a stage, a script, and even—in the person of his doctor—a director.

It is at this point that the doctor and the playwright, whose identities had been merged throughout the play, diverge, the rhetorical aims of the play not entirely consistent with the power of art. Since *Damaged Goods* is the very antithesis of art for art's sake, Brieux must confront the limitations of his medium, which can aim at reform but not assure it. Thus the playwright must constantly gauge his own rhetorical effectiveness. About the prostitute's story, the doctor asks Loches, "Was I not right to keep that confession for the end?" (253). For it is on Loches the legislator rather than on either doctor or playwright that the power to make changes rests. To the prostitute's own words, the doctor has "nothing more to say" ("rien à ajouter" [101]), passing rhetoric back to the person in whose domain it really belongs: "But if you [Loches] give a thought or two to what you have just seen when you are sitting in the [legislative] Chamber, we shall not have wasted our time" (253–54).

Such a separation between the devices of art and the realities of science and action apparently frustrated Brieux's translator, who seems to have found the playwright's language more suited to lectures on venereal disease than to a play based on them. For despite McNeill's claim that the "learned discussion of syphilis was as florid as the symptoms of the disease itself when new,"[6] the French text is matter-of-fact, often more so than the English version, to which is added the metaphor that stands behind the title *Damaged Goods*. That is, to the case histories of syphilitics, which are the last ploy by Brieux's doctor to persuade those capable of action to act, are added the verbally induced images capable of eliciting the sympathies of the audience that was experiencing a play, not listening to Doctor Fournier lecture on syphilis and marriage. When the doctor proposes to Loches that he meet some of his patients, he assures the deputy that their physical condition will not shock him. Brieux's words are straightforward:

Rassurez-vous, je ménagerai vos nerfs, aucun de ceux et de celles que vous allez voir n'a de tare apparente. Je m'étais dit hier: "Enfin, voilà un député qui va prendre en main la cause qui nous est chère. . . ." Je m'étais trompe. Vous veniez pour un autre sujet. Tant pis. (87–88)

(Be assured, I will spare your nerves; none of those you are going to see have obvious symptoms. I said to myself yesterday, "Finally, here is a deputy who will take up the cause that is to us so dear." I was mistaken. You came for another reason. Too bad.)[7]

The version of this passage in the translated play not only supplies the strategies of literary language but also draws attention to what it conceives of as its own contribution to Brieux's work:

To outward appearance [these patients] have nothing the matter with them. They are not bad cases; they are simply the damaged goods of our great human cargo. I merely wished to give you food for reflection, not a lesson in pathology. (244)

The shifting relationship between physician and writer, as well as the comparison between Brieux and his English translator, ultimately rests in *Damaged Goods* on differences in language. The artist's *self* is always at stake in writing about plague—rhetoric and art, means and ends frequently in conflict. The way words are used as persuasive devices and the role of persuasion itself in *Damaged Goods* have to do with the playwright's self-definition as social critic and artist, the language of each not always compatible. In the play, this concern is expressed in the doctor's own struggle to define his role. When George Dumont implores him to prescribe a treatment for syphilis that works more rapidly than the ones he presently has at his disposal, the doctor responds that the days of miracles are past.

DOCTOR: ... I am a physician, nothing but a physician. ...
GEORGE: No, no! You are more than a physician: you are a confessor as well. You are not only a man of science. You can't observe me as you would something in your laboratory and then simply say: "You have this, science says that. Now be off with you!" My whole life depends upon you. (197)

George is correct: Brieux's doctor is more than a physician. And he may be a confessor as well. But the "more" that he is is a rhetorician, and his words may be no more immediately consoling to his patients than the limited cures he offers. His predicament has already been seen in Kramer's *The Normal Heart*. Like Brieux's physician, Dr. Emma Brookner has something compelling to say, and in both cases the doctors' words have to do with the sexually transmitted diseases they are diagnosing and—to vastly different degrees of success—treating. The content of these doctors' argument is likely to be disregarded by the very persons they most want to reach. In both plays, the limitations of medicine, the absence of an easy cure, call into play the powers of language—which the writer must direct either towards social reality or towards helping to create, if unwittingly, the illusions out of which humans build their fantasies.

Moreover, doctors themselves may contribute to the dangerous social construction of the diseases that plague their patients. When George Dumont reveals obvious signs of ignoring the doctor's advice, the latter tries yet another persuasive tack to convince the young man of his fiancée's danger:

... Take this book—it is my master's work—here, read for yourself, I have marked the passage. You won't read it? Then I will. *(He reads passionately.)* "I have seen an unfortunate young woman changed by this disease into the likeness of a beast." (202)

"J'ai eu le spectacle d'une malheureuse jeune femme convertie en un véritable monstre par le fait d'une syphilide phagédénique." (25)

Between "beast" and "monstre" as an image of a syphilis-infected woman there is not much to choose from. Outside of the romantic celebration of nature, for example Wordsworth's description of "glad animal movements" in "Tintern Abbey," the likening of people to beasts carries with it a strong condemnation and the assumption that they have lost or surrendered their moral selves. But why should the woman ravaged by syphilis be assumed to be less than human, even, as a monster, outside of nature itself? Especially if she is a victim rather than perpetrator of the disease? There are traditional and dangerous assumptions behind the doctor's image that he seems unwittingly to perpetrate.

Thus his simile for syphilis effectively personifies the disease as a woman:

. . . I have one thing that I always tell my patients: if I could I would paste it up at every street corner. "Syphilis is like a woman whose temper is roused by the feeling that her power is disdained. It is terrible only to those who think it insignificant, not to those who know its dangers." (242–43)

"La syphilis est une impérieuse personne qui ne veut pas qu'on méconnaisse sa puissance. Elle est terrible pour qui la croit insignifiante et bénigne pour qui sait combien elle est dangereuse. Elle est comme certaines femmes, elle ne se fâche que si on la néglige." (85)

The feminization of the disease carries with it implications that the play bears out. Just as the disease must be controlled, so must women be—or protected, which is but the other side of the coin.

The female characters in this play are recognizable stereotypes, and it is telling that in the French edition, the cast of characters segregates male and female players, the women listed after the men. The young Mrs. Dumont is a naive woman about whose fate the male characters—her fiancé and eventual husband, her father, and the doctor—are embroiled in arguments. That she has given birth to an infant daughter only extends her role in the play, since the vulnerability of helpless female citizens is supposed to elicit the protectiveness of patriarchal society. Thus the syphilitic widow who appears in act 3 is passive, helpless, and totally dependent on the doctor's skill and direction. On another side, when George's wife does finally learn the truth, her unleashed fury likens her to her angry mother-in-law, whose self-interest, pettiness, and intense emotions surrounding her granddaughter make it impossible to elicit rational thought from her in the matter of dealing prudently with the family predicament. And the wet nurse is merely a cunning, lower-class version of the older woman. Finally, although Brieux obviously meant to arouse sympathy for the infected prostitute, what he also conveys is that men, in whose hands rest the laws of society and the forms of its institutions, would do well to protect themselves—of course by enlightened means—against her dangers.

Thus metaphor and gender combine in *Damaged Goods* with sinister results, since social assumptions about women tend to obliterate the distance between Brieux's metaphor for syphilis and its referent. The young and naive Mrs. Dumont and the anything-but-innocent prostitute are morally and socially polar opposites. Yet both are infected with syphilis and are thus both carriers of the disease. Actually, the play hedges this point and it is never definite that George's wife is infected. To return to the earlier discussion of *Ghosts,* French syphilologists were debating the very question of whether an uninfected mother would or could give birth to a diseased child. That George will almost certainly infect his wife is the doctor's primary concern; the danger to their children becomes an important but additional argument.

But if a virtuous woman could carry the disease as readily as a prostitute, a widow infecting a new and healthy husband, for example, then what M. Loches says of the whore is equally applicable to his daughter, that these miserable women are veritable poisoners ("ces misérable femmes [sont] véritables empoisonneuses" [94]).[8] Despite their shared victimization, then, both Mrs. Dumont and the prostitute are dangerous—if to statistically differing degrees. Add to this initial ambiguity that Brieux's virtual personification of the disease as a woman may be—as will soon appear to be the case—conventional, then what *Damaged Goods* constructs is another portrait of the poison damsel, a legendary figure evoked by Loches's contemptuous use of the word "empoisonneuses."

It is the poison damsel who supplies a contextual framework for Nathaniel Hawthorne's renowned and enigmatic story, "Rappaccini's Daughter."[9] Many of its puzzling features have been explained by Carol Marie Bensick, who argues that it is syphilis and not some mysterious disease or generalized evil that is at issue in a tale in which the rivalry between two doctors blights the hopes of one's would-be protégé, Giovanni, and kills the other's daughter, Beatrice. Bensick's argument is a strong one, carefully documented, and the following discussion will follow its assumptions and conclusions, stressing perhaps more than she, however, the image and significance of the polluted and polluting woman epitomized in the poison damsel legend.

In the *Gesta Romanorum*, the Queen of the North, bearing a grudge against Alexander the Great, "nourished her daughter from the cradle upon a certain kind of deadly poison," and when the child grew up, the queen sent her daughter as a gift to Alexander. But his tutor Aristotle at once perceived the danger posed by the young woman and arranged to have her kissed by a condemned prisoner, who immediately died. The deadly girl was summarily returned to her mother.[10] In "Rappaccini's Daughter" a slightly altered variant of the legend is attributed to "an old classic author" who euphemizes the sexual connotations of other variants and tells of

an Indian prince, who sent a beautiful woman as a present to Alexander the Great. She was as lovely as the dawn, and gorgeous as the sunset; but what especially distinguished her was a certain rich perfume in her breath—richer than a garden of Persian roses. Alexander, as was natural to a youthful conqueror, fell in love at first sight with this magnificent stranger. But a certain sage physician, happening to be present, discovered a terrible secret in regard to her. (117)

In his evocation of the "sage physician," Dr. Baglioni is preparing Giovanni for his own part in protecting the young man from Beatrice's socalled poisonousness.[11] But the substitution of doctor for philosopher also helps point "Rappaccini's Daughter" away from a generalized theme often treated by Hawthorne, the crimes committed by science against the human heart, toward a specific and historically based depiction of physical disease and cure. The connection between the poison damsel and medicinal healing might have come to the author from various sources, one of which has recently been argued to be a Renaissance text, Timothy Bright's *Treatise on Melancholy*, which describes how poisons coexist in nature with "wholesome fruit and soveraigne medicine."[12] Bright's analogue to the poison damsel legend would be the account of how certain persons in Italy (where Hawthorne's story takes place) "did without hurt sucke the poyson of vipers, and without perill did usually hunt them."[13]

Before turning to "Rappaccini's Daughter," it will be useful to pursue some of these associations. First is the account of persons who immunize themselves against vipers by gradually imbibing their poison. The poison damsel's story has been studied in detail by N. M. Penzer, whose search for meanings in widely disseminated folktales and legends is usually attached to his interest in how they traveled from their point of origin, which he believes to be India. Thus Penzer rejects the idea that the poison damsel's meaning can be traced to venereal diseases because of his conviction that syphilis appeared in India only after the story was long established there. But his denial of a specific connection does not preclude Penzer's tracing noteworthy connections among poison damsels, venereal disease, serpents, and traditions of women as polluters. For example, he discusses the *vagina dentata* motif, the belief held by many peoples that some women have teeth in their vaginas and that men who have intercourse with them will be castrated.[14] To extend Penzer's references, Apaches also tell stories of Vulva Women and the ingenuity of men who insert wooden sticks into their genitals, breaking off the threatening teeth and rendering them harmless.[15] Similar stories depict poisonous female characters, for example, Rattlesnake Woman, who first ingests the venom of her natural mate, then metamorphoses into a beautiful woman, attracts men, and kills them by transferring the poison to them.[16] If men resist her, she will die of the venom she has accumulated. Corollary stories, less well known, are told by women, who complain of being invaded by vaginal serpents: "The animals enter the female reproductive system, where they may hatch a whole litter and mutilate or kill the woman, or (in one text) they may merely wriggle around in her vagina and drive her crazy."[17] That gynecological disorders and venereal diseases may contribute to such tales adds a fascinatingly realistic layer of meaning to what is a virtually endlessly provocative symbolism.

Moreover, if Hawthorne did read Bright's treatise on melancholy, it might have reminded him of another, the more renowned seventeenth-century *Anatomy of Melancholy* by Robert Burton, in which the story is told of a lamia (a snake woman) who married a philosophy student, Lycius, his teacher Apollonius Tyanaeus attending their wedding to expose the bride as evil illusion, at which disclosure she vanishes. One of Hawthorne's sources for "Rappaccini's Daughter" is Keats's rendition of this anecdote in his own poem "Lamia."[18] Hawthorne is, however, unlikely to have realized that his own substitution of physicians for philosophers would have touched one of Keats's major concerns. Having decided against being a surgeon after his training at Guy's Hospital, Keats turned to writing poetry and was thereafter torn between medicine and literature—to use the words of one of his letters, between women who had cancers and Petrarchan coronals.[19] In one of his last poems, "The Fall of Hyperion," he asks if poets might not be physicians to all men. For the English poet, sometimes the muse herself might as well have been a poison damsel, substituting the illusion of pleasure for the reality of a world of real diseases, one in which the "fever and the fret" of life causes men to "sit and hear each other groan"—a world where

palsy shakes a few, sad, last gray hairs,
Where youth grows pale, and spectre-thin, and dies.

("Ode to a Nightingale")

The realistic medical basis for their themes strengthens the connection between Hawthorne and Keats. In "La Belle Dame sans Merci," the narrator perceives that the knight who has loved the mysterious temptress is wasting away:

I see a lily on thy brow
    With anguish moist and fever dew,
And on thy cheeks a fading rose
    Fast withereth too.

The White Plague, tuberculosis, the disease from which Keats died, may stand behind this image, which may have been borrowed by Hawthorne for "Rappaccini's Daughter." Often described as feverish, Giovanni—perhaps as a result of disordered senses—believes he sees the withering of a fresh bouquet of flowers being held by Beatrice Rappaccini.

Strikingly, Hawthorne, too, had contemplated a career in medicine, if only to reject outright the idea that he would derive his living from other people's miseries,[20] in contrast to Keats, who thought being a poet was self-indulgent because people *needed* doctors. Despite this difference, the two writers shared a concern for art's role in a world in which it was losing ground almost in proportion to the growing influence of science and medicine. Keats's poems and Hawthorne's tales are linked not only by common literary sources and images borrowed by Hawthorne from his English romantic predecessor, but also by their shared literary motifs, again, grounded in medicine.

Because of its frequently shifting narrative perspective, events and characters being depicted not necessarily as they are but rather as what one character or another thinks they are, "Rappaccini's Daughter" is difficult to summarize. Its basic plot, however, resembles such stories as that of the lamia or poison damsel. Early in the sixteenth century, one Giovanni Guasconti comes from Naples to Padua in order to attend the university famed for its medical studies. From his lodgings he is able to observe a lush and strange garden with exotic and unusual herbs and flowers, the gardeners who tend the plants proving to be one of the university's most renowned if unorthodox professors of medicine, Giacomo Rappaccini, and his daughter Beatrice, close to her father in learning and the possession of arcane knowledge. Giovanni notices, however, that the father tends the plants from a slight distance as if afraid of their influence on him, whereas Beatrice has no fear of the blooms and moves about and handles them as if attached to them by a special sympathy. He also believes he has witnessed from his window above the garden several strange events: that a bouquet of fresh flowers that he throws down to Beatrice has withered in her arms, and that a lizard and an insect that have come close enough to Beatrice for her to breathe upon them have died. From then on a mingled desire and revulsion intensify Giovanni's attraction to and obsession with Beatrice. His ambivalence is fueled by the mixed signals he receives from another physician, Pietro Baglioni. It is Dr. Baglioni who characterizes Dr. Rappaccini for Giovanni, claiming that his rival cares more for science than human life and would sacrifice anyone—his daughter and Giovanni included—"for the sake of adding so much as a grain of mustard seed to the great heap of his accumulated knowledge" (99–100). The narrator, whose point of view is distinct from the characters, and should not be taken for granted to be that of Hawthorne, comments,

The youth might have taken Baglioni's opinions with many grains of allowance, had he known that there was a professional warfare of long continuance between him and Doctor Rappaccini, in which the latter was generally thought to have gained the advantage. If the reader be inclined to judge for himself, we refer him to certain black-letter tracts on both sides, preserved in the medical department of the University of Padua. (100)

The controversy divides Baglioni, a traditional Galenist who adheres to taditionally approved methods of curing disease, from Rappaccini, an empiricist and follower of Paracelsus, who experiments with drugs distilled from the blooms in his garden, concocting toxic brews to fight the systemic poisons that he believes make people ill. Rappaccini is credited with some near-miraculous cures, admits his rival, although he, Baglioni, believes that these are the "work of chance" (100). Here is a noteworthy difference between Brieux's play and Hawthorne's story. Brieux treats the transmission of syphilis as a social problem, arguing that in a large number of cases only chance separates the infected from the uninfected. Treatment of the disease is handled in the play as if it were a simple matter. In Hawthorne's reconstructed Italian Renaissance, the source of disease (whether or not it is syphilis) recedes into the background, and the cure is a matter of either science or chance, depending upon whether this is seen from the view of Rappaccini or Baglioni.

It is Baglioni who tells Giovanni the story of the poison damsel and of the sage physician who discovered her terrible secret; and playing on Giovanni's suspicions, his growing propensity to believe that the beautiful Beatrice is tainted with moral as well as physical evil, Baglioni suggests that "the poisoner Rappaccini" has created a daughter "poisonous as she is beautiful" (118). But he also claims to possess the antidote to Rappaccini's vile brews, one "little sip" of which "would have rendered the most virulent poisons of the Borgias innocuous" (119). He encourages Giovanni to feed his medicine to Beatrice and await the effects, which turn out to be her swift death: "As poison had been life, so the powerful antidote was death" (127–28). The young woman dies with an enigmatic reproach to Giovanni: "Oh, was there not, from the first, more poison in thy nature than in mine?" (127). And as she dies before her father and lover,

Professor Pietro Baglioni looked forth from the window, and called loudly, in a tone of triumph mixed with horror, to the thunder-stricken man of science,

"Rappaccini! Rappaccini! And is *this* the upshot of your experiment!" (128)

The story, again, follows a well-known narrative pattern. A young man finds himself torn between his attraction to a beautiful but strange and perhaps dangerous woman, on one side, and a wise man, often a philosopher or priest, intent on saving him from her, on the other. Hawthorne's story plays a significant variation on this narrative pattern by, again, assigning the role of philosopher or priest to a doctor—indeed, two doctors, who represent radically different approaches to medicine. That one of them is the father of the possibly dangerous young woman is consistent with the world's folklore and legends, where many tales involve a male protagonist who enters into a relationship with an ogre's daughter. Dr. Rappaccini is to Beatrice, for example, as Aeetes is to Medea, another enchantress schooled in poisons. Moreover, whereas Lycius and Alexander find no evil in the lamia or the poison damsel until the philosophers alert them to danger, Giovanni's assessment of Beatrice rests, as Bensick argues in convincing detail, on why Giovanni is predisposed to distrust the beautiful young woman.

Bensick's study, itself an intriguing narrative that moves towards rather than begins with the startling idea that syphilis supplies a major clue to the story's meaning, is not the only work on "Rappaccini's Daughter" to shift interpretation away from the story as an allegory of science versus imagination to a focus on the specific medical controversies that inform Hawthorne's tale. From other Hawthorne critics one learns that the practice of medicine was undergoing significant changes in the nineteenth century and supplied many contentious disputes with which the author was familiar.[21] It has been argued that there were six significant areas in which doctors were severely criticized, only two of which are absent from "Rappaccini's Daughter": the love of gold that characterizes Chaucer's physician, and the lack of respect towards death implicated in vivisection. The four interrelated indictments of the medical profession reflected in "Rappaccini's Daughter" are the indifference to life supposedly characteristic of Rappaccini but ultimately of Baglioni as well, since being proven correct is for both of them more important than human health or concerns; the preoccupation with an opportunity to enhance personal reputation even if at the patient's expense (a theme discussed earlier with regard to *The Normal Heart*); the seemingly heartless experimenting on people to prove new theories, science counting more than cure; and the internecine squabbles that pitted doctors against each other as Rappaccini and Baglioni were, their disagreements further undermining the public's confidence.[22]

An unwitting pun is employed by M. D. Uroff when he writes that when the public "looked at the profession as a whole, they were apt to say, 'A plague on both your houses.' "[23] Although Uroff does not say so, the many plagues suffered in the United States in the nineteenth century—for example smallpox, typhus, yellow fever, cholera—would have been a spur to, pressure on, experimentation by, and criticism of the medical profession. Ironically, a legacy of controls instituted because of concerns over what patients might or might not endure is today contended by some to be a worse evil, because treatments that show promise are either withheld or restricted to small control groups until their effectiveness can be solidly demonstrated, while people with little to lose are denied their possible effectiveness and die. Hawthorne's story is an early example of the search for the magic bullet, and, ironically, Rappaccini's garden, the "Eden" to which the story frequently refers, an allusion that has lent itself to a variety of interpretations of Hawthorne's use of the garden motif,[24] is akin to a medical laboratory, making it a unique rendition of the earthly paradise theme in plague literature. This point will be returned to.

Uroff points out that in Hawthorne's time, the medical profession in Massachusetts "was in a state of flux over licensing practices, educational requirements and the large number of charlatans who dispensed cures."[25] One of the strongest debates concerned the confrontation between allopathic and homeopathic practices of medicine, the former based on traditional medical procedures of the sort advocated by Baglioni, the latter represented by Rappaccini:

Homeopathic doctors regarded disease not as a separate entity affecting a specific organ but as a derangement of the "immaterial vital principle" pervading and animating the body. This vital principle, homeopaths believed, had the capacity to expel morbid disturbances but its natural tendency to restoration was temporarily paralyzed by disease. To start the curative process, homeopathic practitioners afflicted the system with a more intense but similar disease whose presence spurred the vital principle to new efforts.[26]

And as Bensick notes as an addition to this way of reading Hawthorne's tale, an instance of the "immemorial conflict between the Galenists and the Paracelsians, the dogmatics and the empiricists" was the enormous controversies over innoculation in the eighteenth century, controversies with which, again, Hawthorne was familiar. Innoculation may make itself felt in his story by way of Rappaccini's theories, innoculation being, as Bensick points out, a "literal application of the principle that like cures like."[27]

This recent critical emphasis on the particulars of medical practice reflected in "Rappaccini's Daughter," when added to the historical specificity of names, locales, and other details in the story, supplies further weight to Bensick's argument that even the disease in question is specific, and is syphilis:

A naturalistic account of the poison plot of "Rappaccini's Daughter," then, goes something like this. Like his suppressed prototype Paracelsus, who wrote on syphilis, and like Giacomo Berengario da Carpi, who is implied in the tale's allusion to Cellini [who made the artful vial that held the supposed antidote that would cure Beatrice], Rappaccini has a special interest in the treatment of syphilis. He is using the Paracelsian emphasis on experiment as well as the Paracelsian principle that like cures like in his research into poison as a possible cure for syphilis. Rappaccini's interest in syphilis may have begun because he himself is a sufferer [he is always described in the story as ill]; or, just as likely, he may have contracted syphilis while engaged in the study of it. Then also, he may have a special interest in the disease because his daughter has a latent case. Or it may be that Beatrice was born sound but that he has innoculated her with poisons designed to immunize her to syphilis, so that at his death she will be in no danger of ever contracting the disease of the age [the Renaissance].[28]

Bensick's argument is further strengthened by a book she has located but did not use in her study.[29] Two years before Hawthorne's story first appeared (1844), a translation of Philippe Ricord's treatise on syphilis was published in Philadelphia, its very title striking because of the emphasis on experimentation and innoculation: *A Practical Treatise on Venereal Diseases; or, Critical and Experimental Researches on Innoculation, Applied to the Study of These Affections* (1842). Like the works of other nineteenth-century French

syphilologists, Ricord's is a storage house of medical and sociological information about venereal disease, much of it validating McNeill's contention,
already quoted in the discussion of Brieux, that there was a correlation
between the "florid" descriptions of syphilis after it first appeared and the
learned discussions that ensued. Early in Ricord's book, among his "General Remarks," is a piece of legendary history about syphilis that is not only
perhaps more florid than most, but also brings together a variety of themes:
the association of syphilis with women so that the disease is virtually personified as female; the motif of poison; and the connection between sex and
contagion that is by implication moral as well as physical:

Alexander Benedictus, a Veronese physician, was the first to admit, as a contagious
principle, *a venereal taint produced in the sexual organs of women by the alteration of
humors which they exhale;* this was admitted by Fernel, and received the name of *lues
venerea,* poison, venereal virus, &c., and since that time most writers on syphilis have
acknowledged the existence of a specific cause, of a peculiar deleterious principle.[30]

The ambiguous placement of "they" makes it unclear whether it is the
women or their sexual organs that exhale the poison, but the dual possibility
links the two sides of Hawthorne's analogy between the poison damsel with
whom, according to tradition, sexual union will prove deadly, and Beatrice
Rappaccini, who supposedly need only breathe on a plant or insect in order
to kill it.

There are other connections between Ricord and Hawthorne worth
noting. Not only is the French physician an advocate of medical experimentation, but he also locates the scientific work on venereal diseases within a
problematic context supplied by theology. For example, he refers to the
earlier experiments of one Luna Calderon, which were badly received
during the scientist's age because "the search for a preservative against
diseases sent by Heaven to punish libertinism, was perhaps still regarded as
a sacrilege."[31] Ricord congratulates his own time because "the foolish
prohibitions of false morality no longer compel [him] to regard venereal
disease as a punishment" for immoral living. Ricord thus effectively draws
lines to separate sex, sin, and medical studies, differentiating what Giovanni
tends to merge, sometimes indiscriminately. For Ricord, "the truly wise,
virtuous, and philanthropic moralist will say . . . that he must be considered
as the true benefactor and preserver of his race, who should discover the
true secret of preserving us from the most terrible contagion which ever
threatened mankind."[32]

Giovanni may have been predisposed to view Beatrice as a poison damsel
because he too is infected by syphilis and may be inclined to think of himself

as already poisoned by some woman—to invoke, that is, any number of the myths of feminine evil available to men seemingly forever. Naples was, according to one prevalent theory, the place from which syphilis spread through Europe, and at one point in the story Giovanni is asked by Baglioni what "disease of body or heart" has him "so inquisitive about physicians?" (99). Such a question might implicitly be extended: one might ask if he had come to Padua, a seat of medical learning and new cures, only for study. Dr. Rappaccini, whose medicines are supposed to have effected near-miraculous cures, is said at one point to have been "heard of as far as Naples" (94). And as already noted, Hawthorne may have drawn from Keats's poem the image of a feverish knight for his portrayal of Giovanni, whose frequently alluded to feverish state infers a physical problem, a disquieted state of mind, or both. Or, as Bensick points out, there may be a literal meaning to Beatrice's dying words that there was more (physical) poison in Giovanni than the (moral) poison he attributed to her. As with other details in the story, the situation is ambiguous: in Bensick's words, Giovanni

may have been a healthy youth who became infected by contact with Beatrice or, in his own right, an unwitting carrier of Neapolitan syphilis. In the latter case, he could have been marked as a carrier by the professional eye of Rappaccini, who therefore chooses him to be his daughter's appropriate bridegroom. . . . Giovanni's statement, "She is the only being whom my breath may not slay," may well translate poetically as, "she is the only one whom sexual intercourse with me would not infect."[33]

Once the argument is made for the presence of syphilis as a submerged theme in "Rappaccini's Daughter," what can be done with it to resolve the differing interpretations of "Rappaccini's Daughter"? Bensick herself admits that in her study of how Hawthorne drew on the "famous sixteenth-century pandemic of syphilis" to create an allegory of New England debates over theology, it is not absolutely necessary to her thesis that anyone in the story actually have syphilis, although the pandemic is sufficient to account for one of the most puzzling aspects of Giovanni's behavior, his "automatic conflation of poison with sex and sin."[34] The specific disease rather than a vaguely conceived of poison has further significance, however, and while simplistic arguments for the "relevance" of a past literary work to the concerns of the contemporary world probably involve an insult to both, Hawthorne's story is particularly telling, not only for the past but also for today. For "Rappaccini's Daughter" addresses one of the major, extraphysical afflictions suffered by one who has a contagious disease, especially if it is associated with sexual transmission. Whatever Hawthorne's specific intentions, Beatrice Rappaccini becomes a case study of the crisis experienced by one struggling to free herself of an identity that *equals* her illness, of the assumption by others that her physical condition automatically reveals her character.[35]

In Chaucer's "Physician's Tale," it will be remembered, nature formed a beautiful but still mutable Virginia, whose soul no natural power could supply, and Pygmalion the artificial but soulless Galatea. So do Rappaccini, Baglioni, and Giovanni forever create and recreate Beatrice. The process is best illustrated when Baglioni begins by admitting that he knows "little of the Signora Beatrice" and urging Giovanni to ignore "absurd rumors" (101), and ends not only by planting the idea of the poison damsel in the young man's consciousness but also by supplying the supposed antidote. What Dr. Rappaccini's intentions were with regard to his daughter are never clear because the reader never hears from Rappaccini himself about them; but Beatrice, who would "fain rid [herself] of even that small knowledge" (111) that her father has taught her about his science of plants, believes he has tampered with her very being. Dying, she reproves him with, "I am going, father, where the evil, which thou hast striven to mingle with my being, will pass away like a dream" (127). Her confidence in herself as a secure subject had apparently survived her transformation by others into an object for study; as Bensick argues, "Beatrice evidently has an absolutely assured sense of an essential 'I' independent of the earthly accident of mortal matter, of which poisonousness is finally only a parody."[36]

But Beatrice has nonetheless failed to communicate that about which she has remained secure. Unable to present a coherent self to Giovanni, she asks him first to ignore others and "believe nothing" of her save what he sees with his own eyes (111), and then realizes that the "outward senses" of her lover cannot grasp her true "essence" (112). Taken alone, her body is as ambiguous as the garden in which she walks, its essence seemingly confused and hence unknowable. But she assures Giovanni that "the *words* of Beatrice Rappaccini's lips are true from the depths of the heart outward [and] those you may believe!" (112; emphasis added). And when Giovanni's own "terrible words" (124), his accusations of a poisoned *being* as well as a poisoned body, turn into a rejection of her own claims for a language faithful to truth, she herself points out his error by drawing the distinction between her body and whatever beyond the corporeal constitutes her self:

"I dreamed only to love thee and be with thee a little time, and so to let thee pass away, leaving but thine image in mine heart. For, Giovanni—believe it—though my body be nourished with poison, my spirit is God's creature, and craves love as its daily food." (125)

In differentiating between Beatrice's body and the essence that is her *self,* Hawthorne raises issues that are not only philosophical and psychological but also sociological. For if syphilis is the poison to which Beatrice refers, then Hawthorne is also effectively writing about the venereal infection of what Fournier called a virtuous woman. It is also worth an ironic note that given the acknowledged influence of Keats on Hawthorne, of "Lamia" on "Rappaccini's Daughter," Keats's reference in a letter to taking mercury as well as his angry words directed at women in general has provoked specu-lation that the English poet was being treated for syphilis. Keats's life explains his obvious ambivalence towards women: his belief that they would not find him attractive, and his uneasy feelings about a mother who, after his father died, had lovers until she married again, and who died young of tuberculosis; his wish to marry Fanny Brawne, whom, however, he would have to support, perhaps at the cost of abandoning poetry. Keats's biogra-phy, that is, can be invoked to interpret the *belles dames sans merci* of his poems. But Keats was also aware that traditionally the muse was a woman, vulnerable to attacks by science, in need of the artist's protection.

The romantic poet asks in "Lamia" whether all charms do not "fly / At the mere touch of cold philosophy?" Science is blamed by Keats for clipping an angel's wings and unweaving the rainbow. In Rappaccini's garden con-verge the elements of science and art. Within the rivalry between them can be located the problem of Lamia's and Beatrice's identity. Keats asks whether his serpent woman is the demon's self or a penanced lady elf. Giovanni similarly queries himself about Beatrice: "What is this being?—beautiful, shall I call her?—or inexpressibly terrible?" (103), later express-ing his ambivalence by deciding, temporarily, that it "mattered not whether she were angel or demon" (109). Is Beatrice, "maiden of a lonely island" (112), Shakespeare's Miranda[37] or Porter's Miranda—the latter another possible poison damsel, perhaps infecting Adam with the influenza from which he died and she recovered? If Hawthorne's Miranda, does Beatrice await her "Ferdinand" only to be betrayed by Giovanni as she already had been by the false Prospero, her father? Or does Beatrice Rappaccini inhabit less a lonely island than a bower of bliss far more complex than any Spenser could have imagined, an Acrasia not necessarily because she *is* a dangerous temptress but because Giovanni reads the signs that he thinks say she is and ignores those that argue that she is not? Or, to put this another way, Giovanni cannot separate Beatrice's identity from that of the garden she inhabits.

Of all the gardens and pseudoparadises in plague literature, Hawthorne's in "Rappaccini's Daughter" is the least susceptible to coherent interpretation. The varying literary sources from which Hawthorne drew depictions of the earthly paradise, and the different meanings he could derive from them, suggest in themselves the expulsion from Eden, from a centrality of vision to a diversity that resists patterning. These other literary gardens exist in Hawthorne's tale almost as separate languages, the scattering of meaning suggesting the Tower of Babel[38]—another story of a fall. Hawthorne himself can be invoked to confirm such a reading of his tale. In a story written about a year earlier, "The New Adam and Eve," he depicts an uninhabited, corrupt world that remains intact and a newly created man and woman who are born into it and who instinctively react positively to the few remaining signs of nature and recoil from the cultural signs they encounter. One of the buildings they chance upon is a library, but the story's narrator reacts against a supposedly new literature in the future that will be merely a reworking of the old: "And his literature, when the progress of centuries shall create it, will be no interminably repeated echo of our own poetry, and reproduction of the images that were moulded by our great fathers of song and fiction, but a melody never yet heard on earth" (266).

"The New Adam and Eve" also creates another context for Rappaccini's garden, beginning with the claim that "Art has become a second and stronger Nature; she is a step-mother, whose crafty tenderness has taught us to despise the bountiful and wholesome ministrations of our true parent." Therefore, it is not to be "adequately know[n] how little in our present state and circumstances is natural, and how much is merely the interpolation of the perverted mind and heart of man" (247). It is this puzzle that informs Dr. Rappaccini's strangely landscaped domain, with its admixture of the natural, the exotic, the beautifully crafted, and the decadently artificial.

By now, the appearance of the false paradise in the midst of pestilence will be an easily recognized theme in plague literature. On one side Rappaccini's domain is likened in the story to Eden, but because it is the place of Rappaccini's experiments, it is also the origin of poison rather than a realm free of it—at least according to Baglioni, who says of his rival that Rappaccini "cultivates" his poisonous plants "with his own hands, and is said even to have produced new varieties of poison, more horribly deleterious than Nature, without the assistance of this learned person, would ever have *plagued* the world withal" (100; italics added). Giovanni's landlady similarly points out that the "garden is cultivated by the own hands of Giacomo Rappaccini," a doctor whose fame is widespread (94). By her and Baglioni's description, Rappaccini rules over his garden as a private kingdom. In this he is comparable to Poe's landscape gardener, who seeks to create a new paradise through the art of horticulture, although Rappaccini, who remains aloof from his own blooms, holds an uneasy position between art and science. Beatrice herself refers to the "flowers of Eden" when she dies, and she distinguishes them from her father's "poisonous flowers" (127), seeming to believe she had dwelt in a ruined paradise. And whereas Poe's landscaper looks back to a world before the fall and epidemics, Rappaccini brings pestilence *into* his garden in order to conquer plagues.

Early on, Beatrice had told Giovanni not that Rappaccini cultivated his garden but that he "created" (123) the mysterious shrub from which, or so Giovanni believes, Beatrice derives her poison. But when she says her father created the plant, she uttered her words "with simplicity," as if unaware of the tension between her meaning and the word she employs to convey it (123). For if Rappaccini creates these blooms rather than cultivates them, then his work is *outside* of nature, which would sustain Giovanni's "instinct" concerning the garden's "appearance of artificialness," indicating an "adultery of various vegetable species," a "production" that is "no longer of God's making," but rather "an evil mockery of beauty" (110). Rappaccini's science is thus akin to artifice, medicine itself reduced to a deceptive artfulness that would seem to bear out Baglioni's contention that the miraculous cures attributed to Rappaccini came about merely by chance.

Thus the shrub that figures as an important image and symbol in the tale would be accurately described in terms of the false and artificial blooms characteristic of Spenser's garden in book 2 of *The Faerie Queene*. The gorgeous plant seems to Giovanni to hang its "gem-like flowers over the fountain" (102). Giovanni is displeased with them; they later seem to him "fierce, passionate, even unnatural" (110). Like Sir Guyon, Giovanni is prepared to destroy the bower of bliss. More to the point, under Baglioni's influence, he is equally ready to destroy Rappaccini's garden-laboratory. But there is a special irony in Giovanni's confusion concerning artifice and science, and he is symbolically, if not literally, employing Rappaccini's method when he carries Baglioni's antidote into the supposedly false garden in order to bring Beatrice, "this miserable child within the limits of ordinary nature" (119). For the antidote itself is contained in the "little silver vase" artfully "wrought" by Cellini (119).

That artifice and poisonous medicines coexist in the garden is not a view confined to Giovanni, however. The narrator describes the plants and herbs whose "individual virtues" were "known to the scientific mind that fostered them" (95). Some of these were placed in "common garden-pots" (95), others in "urns, rich with old carving" (95). The gorgeous but fatal shrub with which Giovanni identifies Beatrice and with which she identifies her-self is "set in a marble vase in the midst of a pool" (95), the flower as much a work of art as its container, but also a product of esoteric knowledge nurtured by pure elements. This commingling of opposites is also reflected when Rappaccini views his daughter and Giovanni together in the garden, apparently satisfied by what he looks at:

As he drew near, the pale man of science seemed to gaze with a triumphant expression at the beautiful youth and maiden, as might an artist who should spend his life in achieving a picture or a group of statuary, and finally be satisfied with his success. (126)

The use of "as might" reduces the metaphor to a simile, sustaining a distance between "man of science" and "artist," between the garden of medicinal herbs and the palace of art. Moreover, time and mutability have resulted in images that work against any positive identification of doctor with creative artist. In Rappaccini's garden "there was the ruin of a marble fountain, in the centre, sculptured with rare art, but so wofully shattered that it was impossible to trace the original design from the chaos of remain-ing fragments" (94). But Giovanni has not yet decided that Rappaccini's is a false garden, an inverted Eden of poisonous medicinal plants, and he feels "as if the fountain were an immortal spirit that sung its song unceasingly, and without heeding the vicissitudes around it; while one century embodied it in marble, and another scattered the perishable garniture on the soil" (94–95). Again, the "as if" reveals that Giovanni has not yet decided how to read the garden.

Giovanni is an allegorizor—if an unreliable one. He had come from Naples to Padua to study medicine, but is "not unstudied in the great poem of his country" (93). In his acquired knowledge, he represents the antithesis of Hawthorne's newly created Adam, and there is in Giovanni's reading of Rappaccini's garden and, ultimately, of Beatrice, the potential cacophony in the "interminably repeated echo" of past masters that Hawthorne alludes to in "The New Adam and Eve." Moreover, as Deborah Jones has argued, the genre of the *Divine Comedy,* allegory, presuppose a "fall," a descent from transcendent unity to chaos.[39] It is such chaos that is figured by the ruin of Rappaccini's garden, where science and art are in conflict. But the allusion to Dante's work also evokes the disadvantage Hawthorne would have to have experienced, for the great Italian poet could adhere to a moral centrality significantly weakened by the nineteenth century. Dante, not Hawthorne, could defend himself against old and traditional accusations that art was a veritable poison damsel. By Hawthorne's time, the artist had experienced another "fall," which is why Jones is probably correct to argue that Hawthorne's story is in part about the "conditions of its own unreadability."[40] To take that argument a step further, Beatrice's death is paradoxically, then, a relatively coherent symbol of that incoherence, of the seeming impossibility of writing meaningfully about plague.

SEVEN

Medicine and Humanism in Albert Camus's *The Plague*

The characters in Albert Camus's novel *The Plague* are not attempting to decipher pestilence, to read transcendent meaning into it—with the exception of Father Paneloux, a Catholic priest. And even he abandons theodicy, the search to explain an all-good and all-powerful God in the face of the devastating plague with which the small Algerian city of Oran is embattled, and against which it is essentially helpless until the disease recedes in a temporary, almost cosmic remission. Paneloux affirms his faith in God because the only choice as he sees it is to affirm everything or deny everything. And from his point of view, who would dare deny everything? Among the many, closely intertwined themes in *The Plague,* most can be attached to the implicit question of whether indeed this is the choice.

From the point of view of Camus's narrator, the physician Bernard Rieux, the plague is a fact and insofar as it exists, it must be fought and lives must if possible be saved, although not many are. This much is simple, as is the "common decency" (l'honnêteté) (150) that serves Rieux as an ethic.[1] But the simplicity is deceptive: Rieux's is an ethic probably harder to live by and certainly harder—probably impossible—to argue for than the priority of the soul over the body, or the so-called natural law of self-preservation. Like civic duty, detached from any historical or philosophical mooring, and understood in *The Plague* as the uncomplicated necessity for people to do what they have to in order to fight the plague and face together that which concerns them all, human decency becomes the manifestation not of human nature (for that would imply the possibility of definition) but of Camus's contention, which his novel can demonstrate but not prove, that "there are more things to admire in men than to despise" (270), that the evils in the world help people to "rise above themselves" (115)—although one would have to be mad to pretend that the plagues that test human virtue are therefore in some way desirable.

The Plague is often read as an allegory, either of World War II and the French resistance to the Nazis, or of the struggle against arbitrary evil in a philosophically meaningless world.[2] The novel's literal level, its powerful depiction of a city under a siege of bubonic and pneumonic plague, tends therefore to be slighted, although it is also a powerfully dramatic depiction of the fight against pestilence, almost despite the narrator's professed intention to write only an objective chronicle of events. When Camus wrote *The Plague*, medical science had not advanced far against the bubonic plague since the times of Boccaccio and Defoe, and Camus's account is as horrific as theirs, with the significant addition that his focus is on a detailed account of the plague's psychological assault, the wearing down of the citizens' spirit until even the courageous fight against the pestilence becomes monotonous and mechanical. At first Rieux feels dazed when he thinks about the plague; finally he realizes that he is afraid. When a curfew is imposed on the town in order to keep order, darkness "silenced every voice," but had little effect on the "darkness also in men's hearts" (156). It becomes virtually impossible for people to communicate what they feel. For even though Oran's citizens recognize the commonality of their predicament, in the realm of feelings they are individuated. Language is inadequate to express this difference in likeness. How then can a narrative about plague hope to articulate what they could not be other than silent about?

That is, a problem thematically central to Camus's novel is, *how does one write about plague?* If not as vexing a question as how to cure it, this query reveals the writer's predicament to be parallel to the doctor's. In a ruse so transparent that it is difficult to believe any reader would be fooled by it, Rieux reveals himself only at the end to be the narrator to whom he has been referring throughout the account of Oran's siege, as if hiding behind anonymity. Camus, that is, has resolved the distinction and potential tension between physician and artist with an authorial sleight of hand, by making them one and the same person. At the same time, Camus calls attention to the vulnerability of his solution when one of his least sympathetic characters, Cottard, proclaims his envy of the authorial role and its power, "because an author has more rights [droits] than ordinary people, as everybody knows. People will stand much more from him" (52). It is consistent, as will be seen, that Cottard's own ethic (or lack of one) allows him to define the word "droits" as "rights" while ignoring its other meaning, "duty." In the word's ambiguity as well as in the way that Cottard reduces its meaning for his own ends when defining the privilege of the writer, Camus has posed his own challenge to any author who treats the subject of plague.

Any attempt to summarize *The Plague* must depend on constructing a cast of its characters. Rieux is, again, both the book's narrator and a physician who comes close to realizing the ambition of his friend Tarrou, which is to be a saint in a world without God. Rieux's ethic is, again, that of common decency, and if he adheres to any ideal, it is that of human love. For him, a "loveless world is a dead world" (237). Committed to fighting the plague, he nonetheless resists any associations the fight might have with adherence to an ideal, and argues that for "nothing in the world is it worth turning one's back on what one loves" (188–89). When his own wife dies of the White Plague, tuberculosis, at the very time that the pestilence recedes in Oran, Rieux might seem to have been punished for not having given love enough importance in his own life, a failure he admits. But such a reading would not only be too simplistic but would also imply a logical universe. Rather, Rieux's aloneness is a sign that although the plague must be fought determinedly, it must be fought without any assurance of personal reward.

Tarrou is Rieux's fellow combatant against the plague, a self-exile in Oran whose life had been transformed when he witnessed his father in his role as prosecutor, calling for the condemnation of a criminal, that is, for his life. Since then, Tarrou has been obsessed with a symbolically plague-ridden world, and is an introverted picaresque-type character dedicated to fighting against pestilence wherever he finds it. Tarrou keeps a diary in which he records that which interests him in the plague, and Rieux draws on this notebook for his narrative, Tarrou himself having died just when, ironically, the plague was abating. A third person, the journalist Rambert, who finds himself trapped when Oran is cordoned off from the outside world as a quarantine measure, completes a triangle with Rieux and Tarrou. At first Rambert works with the other two against the plague only until he can arrange an illegal exit from the city to rejoin the woman he loves in Paris. Then, about to achieve his ends, Rambert reverses himself. Giving up his position as significantly alien in the city of Oran, he understands that the struggle belongs to everybody; moreover, his shame, if he left, would affect his relationship to the woman he loved. Two other significant characters are the novel's implied villain and its both ironically and sincerely designated hero. The first, Cottard, is a criminal first encountered in the book when he attempts suicide, and last seen when he is forcefully carried away by the police. The other is Grand, a municipal clerk whose wife had left him because he could neither find the words to convince the municipality to deliver on its promise to promote him to higher rank and higher pay, nor to dissuade his wife from going away. Almost as compensation, he spends his free time writing a piece of fiction whose first sentence he revises over and over in what appears almost a parody of literary formalism.[3] Insofar as *The Plague* has a hero, it is, according to Rieux, Grand—for reasons to be discussed below.

It is in the treatment of Cottard that *The Plague* rejects an ethic of self-preservation. But the novel also reveals the difficulty of mounting arguments against such an ethic in a secular world. Perhaps this is why so much attention is given to Father Paneloux and the problem of theodicy; the priest's beliefs supply a backdrop for Cottard's obsession with saving his own life. Paneloux must sustain his trust in an all-good and all-powerful God despite the plague, despite—in particular—the agonized death of a child, a traditional symbol of the destruction of innocence by incomprehensible evil. Deciding he must stand by his faith or deny God, Paneloux carries his decision to what is paradoxically less a point of faith than the logical conclusion of a theological argument, and he refuses medical care when stricken himself with plague.

It is Paneloux who brings to this contemporary novel the world of Boccaccio's *Decameron*. There is, in fact, a link between Boccaccio and Camus supplied by what is either a coincidence or variants of a legend that had grown up about the Black Death. In condemning Boccaccio's storytellers for their flight from Florence, Bernardo argues that Boccaccio was almost certainly acquainted with a letter written by Petrarch to his brother, the monk Gerardo, who during the plague had "determined to remain firm in the place assigned to him by Christ, [and] had refused to obey his Prior's order to abandon the monastery." The Prior died, as did the thirty-four monks who stayed with Gerardo, but the latter survived, to, as Petrarch wrote to Gerardo, "found a second time your venerable monastery made barren by death and guarded and defended by your faith and your wise chastity." In the second of two sermons, Paneloux recounts a similar event recorded in the "chronicles of the Black Death at Marseille" in which only "four of the eighty-one monks in the Mercy Monastery survived the epidemic," three of these having run away.[4]

Father Paneloux had found his thoughts fixed on that monk who stayed on by himself. . . . And, bringing down his fist on the edge of the pulpit, Father Paneloux cried in a ringing voice: "My brothers, each one of us must be the one who stays." (204–5)

To negate self-preservation in a world *without* God is, however, quite another matter. It is another way to ask how it is possible to be a saint in one, to define oneself in terms of sainthood. Problems of self-definition pervade Camus's novel.

Through Cottard and his overwhelmingly obvious drive for self-preservation, Camus reveals that preoccupation with the self results from too little
rather than too much self-love. To invoke Camus's designation of Grand as
the hero of a book that essentially disclaims heroism, it is possible to claim
that Cottard is *The Plague*'s pitiable villain, one, however, who lacks even
the dynamism of an active evil. A criminal who tries to take his own life
rather than face prosecution, Cottard finds in the plague a reprieve, because
the officials' attention is by necessity turned away from his, relatively speaking, insignificant offenses. He knows, however, that when the quarantine is
over, "they'll drop [him] like a live coal!" (249). As one of society's condemned, Cottard fascinates Tarrou, who provides both stories about Cottard and interpretations of them. It is Tarrou who notes that Cottard was
alone among the city's people in not being hopeful during the "days when
the plague seemed to be retreating, slinking back to the obscure lair from
which it had stealthily emerged" (247)—that is, describing the plague in
such a way as to create an analogy between the pestilence and Cottard
himself. Instead, Cottard viewed "this retreat with consternation" (247).
During the siege, he was "blossoming out," actually "expanding in geniality
and good humor" (174). Moreover, he is convinced of an immunity to the
disease, having the idea "that a man suffering from a dangerous ailment or
grave anxiety is allergic to other ailments and anxieties" (175).

Cottard's ethics are reflected in his pronouncement on economic issues,
which are extended to his general view that life is a struggle for survival:
"Big fish eat little fish " (les gros mangent toujours les petits) (51).[5] He not
only thrives psychologically during the plague but profits from it as well,
selling cigarettes and liquor at increasingly high prices, amassing a personal
fortune for himself. It is Cottard who supplies Tarrou with anecdotes about
people's response to the plague, and one of these may have been borrowed
by Camus from Defoe's *Journal*,[6] in which, it will be remembered, H. F.
was so horrified at the idea that infected people deliberately and with malice
infected others that he preferred to believe that they were maddened by the
disease. In Camus's novel, an ambiguously constructed version of such an
incident is intended mainly to reveal Cottard's disregard for others. His
story

was about a man with all the symptoms and running a high fever who dashed out
into the street, flung himself on the first woman he met, and embraced her, yelling
that he'd "got it."

"Good for him!" was Cottard's comment. (74)

Feeling helpless and already imprisoned, Cottard experiences during the plague a negative communality: gratified by the quarantining of the city, he was getting "quite fond of these people shut up [emprisonnés] under their little patch of sky within their city walls" (177). According to Tarrou, Cottard's view of things allows Cottard a special understanding of how fear of contagion operates during a plague, of how it exaggerates the problematic relationship that already exists between self and other. Cottard's insight into the human condition is derived from his own status as among the condemned, who "have an instinctive craving for human contacts" (178) but resist significant relations with others because of an essential mistrust.

Cottard is a case history in Tarrou's obsession with society's condemned. It is Rieux, however, not Tarrou who grasps the significance of Tarrou's record of Cottard's expressed disregard for how the plague had wrought changes in people's hearts: "Indeed, they were the last thing he bothered about" (251). Participating in the community only as a fellow-prisoner, Cottard from the outset defeats his own ambition to make a new start if the Oran government would wipe his former slate clean. His intention in effect to recreate himself is futile, for he never understands that there is no self in isolation. It is Rieux, not Tarrou, who describes how Cottard's last scene is played out, his being dragged away kicking and screaming after trying to hold off the authorities with a machine gun. In a gesture whose meaning is ambiguous, Rieux turns his face away as they pass.

Tarrou, who eschews self-preservation as a principle by which to live, but who understands that the condemned have only one drive and that is to survive, is perhaps the most complex character in *The Plague,* and his personal complexity vies with the supposed simplicity with which he, like Rieux, approaches the problem of the plague. For Tarrou the plague is both a real event and a symbolic disease that each person carries within himself — Tarrou coming closer than any other character in the book to enunciating a doctrine of original sin, however secularized. He contends that although it "may sound simple to the point of childishness," on "this earth there are pestilences and there are victims, and it's up to us, so far as possible, not to join forces with the pestilences" (229). To see it any other way is according to him the result of "our failure to use plain, clean-cut language" (230). And yet the symbolic language with which he begins his personal narrative, the story of his past, belies his argument for absolute straightforwardness:

Let me begin by saying I had plague already, long before I came to this town and encountered it here. Which is tantamount to saying I'm like everybody else. Only there are some people who don't know it, or feel at ease in that condition; others know and want to get out of it. Personally, I've always wanted to get out of it. (222)

That Tarrou perceives himself to be both like and different from others is part of a life that Rieux comes to understand as being "riddled with contradictions" (le déchirement et la contradiction), (263).

Ever since the day that he realized his father was asking that a person pay for a crime with his life, Tarrou had renounced the family life associated with his quite ordinary background. For him the prisoner was a "living human being" whom the officials of the justice system "were set on killing." In an "uprush of some elemental instinct," Tarrou sided with the man, and continued thereafter to obsess over the processes by which the law could demand a life (224). But that living human being is for Tarrou almost as much an abstraction as he was for the state. Like Lord Jim, whom Joseph Conrad depicts as realizing himself by leaving a flesh-and-blood woman for a shadowy ideal, Tarrou leaves home and his broken-hearted parents to conduct what Rieux calls his "quest for peace by service in the cause of others" (263).

When Tarrou confesses to Rieux his aspirations to be a saint, Rieux responds that he himself is only interested in "being a man." Ironically, Tarrou seems to understand the difference even better than Rieux: "Yes, we're both after the same thing, but I'm less ambitious." Rieux "supposed Tarrou was jesting" (231), but Tarrou knows that it is easier to live by an ideal than by common decency. The dialectic between human being and saint is dramatized in a verbal confrontation between Tarrou and Rambert. When Rambert renounces his intention to escape the city, Tarrou is almost indifferent to his altered decision. For Tarrou there had never been any other choice besides battling the plague. Rambert, who had had to work through the conflict between personal happiness and shame, asks,

"Tell me, Tarrou, are you capable of dying for love?"

"I couldn't say, but I hardly think so—as I am now."

"You see. But you're capable of dying for an idea; one can see that right away. Well, personally, I've seen enough of people who die for an idea. I don't believe in heroism; I know it's easy and I've learned it can be murderous. What interests me is living and dying for what one loves." (149)

To this exchange Rieux pays keen attention, but his response is ambiguous —"Man isn't an idea, Rambert" (149)—rejecting at the same time the self-sufficiency of both personal happiness and the abstract ideal of humanity.

For Rieux, Tarrou is a fellow fighter, a recorder of the plague through whose diary Rieux himself is described for the reader, and he is also a friend. But the portrait Rieux draws of Tarrou after he dies is in part a negative one, focused less on virtue than on deficiency. It is because of Tarrou that Rieux fully realizes how "sterile" is a "life without illusions."

How hard it must be to live only with what one knows and what one remembers, cut off from what one hopes for! It was thus, most probably, that Tarrou had lived. . . . There can be no peace without hope, and Tarrou, denying as he did the right to condemn anyone whomsoever—though he knew well that no one can help condemning and it befalls even the victim sometimes to turn executioner—Tarrou had never known hope's solace. (262–63)

Fascinated with Cottard, who in some way constitutes his alter ego, Tarrou would seem at first totally unlike one whose life was lived by the principle of big fish eating little fish. In the end, however, they both prove incomplete.

If for Rieux illusions are necessary in the ambition to be a man, he nonetheless has no illusion that he can say just what that would be. As a creative thinker, he understands that "what's needed is imagination" to fight the plague (58). But as a doctor, Rieux must equate the person with the body. When Paneloux tells him they both work for "man's salvation," Rieux demurs: salvation, he replies, is not what he is after. "I'm concerned with man's health, and for me his health comes first" (197). When one of his patients dies, Rieux feels responsible, as if the death were his personal failure. So long as people need curing, he will attempt to cure; the bigger, philosophical questions will have to then be postponed. Significantly, it is during what he knows is a futile effort to save Tarrou's life by innoculating him with serum that he tries to imagine what it is that makes Tarrou himself struggle to live and acknowledges that the person is more than his body:

In this struggle Tarrou's robust shoulders and chest were not his greatest assets; rather, the blood that had spurted under Rieux's needle and, in this blood, that something more vital than the soul, which no human skill can bring to light [ce qui était plus interieur que l'âme]. (256)

Rieux has no ambition of his own to join the ranks of Tarrou's "true healers," but knows that to fight plague, he cannot be *only* a physician.

Nor does the plague itself allow him to be, for it is impervious to medicine. Unable to save lives, Rieux orders the evacuation of the infected and provides instructions and information to devastated families and sanitary workers. No Dr. Rappaccini, Rieux cannot harden himself to suffering and knows at one point that his "sensibility is getting out of hand" (172). Not equipped with any magic bullet, he is worn down by the expectations others have of him.

Before the plague he was welcomed as a savior. He was going to make them right with a couple of pills or an injection, and people took him by the arm on his way to the sickroom. Flattering, but dangerous. Now, on the contrary, he came accompanied with soldiers, and they had to hammer on the door with rifle-butts before the family would open it. (173)

And while the book never makes clear what can be expected of the imagination, it is this—again—that the doctor insists is the key to fighting the plague. Imagination, however, maintains only a problematic relation to science, and as Rieux gropes in his memory for what he had been taught as a student about plague, the word itself "conjured" up visions that have little to do with his professional training:

The doctor was still looking out of the window. Beyond it lay the tranquil radiance of a cool spring sky; inside the room a word was echoing still, the word "plague." A word that conjured up in the doctor's mind not only what science chose to put into it, but a whole series of fantastic possibilities utterly out of keeping with that gray and yellow town under his eyes. (36–37)

This transformation of the pestilence into a word is extremely important. As doctor, Rieux must distrust language, because it could conceivably make two plus two equal five rather than four. His colleagues turn physical symptoms into jargon, for example "syndrome," whereas he knows only what he sees, "buboes, and high fever accompanied by delirium, ending fatally within forty-eight hours" (47). It doesn't matter how it is phrased, he tells the city's other doctors, "whether you call it plague or some rare kind of fever. The important thing is to prevent its killing off half the population of this town" (46).

It is the word "plague" that Rieux's fellow physicians resist, especially Dr. Richard, who, like Dr. Ricord in Brieux's play, downplays the contagiousness of what he insists has not yet been positively identified as plague. And when Rambert fails to secure a health certificate that he hopes will allow him to return to Paris, and accuses Rieux of "using the language of reason," of living in a "world of abstractions," Rieux refuses to let words about words manipulate him: "He did not know if he was using the language of reason," but "he knew he was using the language of the facts as everybody could see them—which wasn't necessarily the same thing" (79–80).

Given the tenuous link between language and reality, the reality of the facts as everybody could see them and the reality of feelings that resist generalizations, genre becomes particularly important in contemplating how to write about plague. Rieux rejects a subjective narrative although he understands that whatever he writes will be transformed into one by the reader:

A narrator cannot take account of ... differences of outlook. His business is only to say: "This is what happened," when he knows that it actually did happen, that it closely affected the life of a whole populace, and that there are thousands of eyewitnesses who can appraise in their hearts the truth of what he writes. (6)

This distinction between the authorial self and the other who is reader is both affirmed and denied. On the one hand, the quasi-anonymous narrator refers to himself in the third person:

He has deliberately taken the victims' side and tried to share with his fellow citizens the only certitudes they had in common—love, exile, and suffering. (272)

But, on the other hand, like Defoe's H. F., he admits to a private realm of feeling he will not make public:

Regarding his personal troubles and his long suspense, his duty was to hold his peace. (272)

In making the question of how to write about plague explicit in his novel, Camus creates a text that is about other texts,[7] a narrative that is in part about narration, because, again, plague itself resists the ordinary relationships of form to content, subject to audience.

The Plague makes very clear what kind of a narrative it is *not*. It is not a sermon, although it allows Father Paneloux two long ones. It is not a journalist's account because as Rambert admits, he will not be allowed in the course of his work to tell the whole truth; in this regard, Rambert can be placed in the company of Ibsen's Hovstad and Brieux's Dumont. But journalism is eschewed primarily because the media, even when sincere, expresses its concerns and sympathies "in the conventional language" with which men try to express what unites them with mankind in general; this is a "vocabulary quite unsuited" to the "small daily effort" made by ordinarily unheroic persons against the plague (127). And these ordinary people were on the whole silent, unable even to write letters. For while the shut-up town is desperate for communication with the outside, they were frustrated by the distance between what they were writing about and what they actually said,

with the result that after a certain time the living words, into which we had as it were transfused our hearts' blood, were drained of any meaning. Thereafter we went on copying them mechanically, trying, through the dead phrases, to convey some notion of our ordeal. And in the long run, to these sterile, reiterated monologues, these futile colloquies with a blank wall, even the banal formulas of a telegram came to seem preferable. (63)

In these thwarted efforts is a figurative account of the comparable difficulty of writing literature about plague.

Although *The Plague* is replete with characters, it also refuses to be a "stage-play," because it is a "narrative made with good feelings—that is to say, feelings that are neither demonstrably bad nor overcharged with emotion" (126). For implicitly similar reasons, the narrator purports to take on the "part of a historian" (7) rather than write a possibly falsifying fiction that would, for example, attribute heroism to those who act out of common decency. Nonetheless, the narrator of *The Plague* "will continue being the chronicler of the troubled, rebellious hearts of our townspeople under the impact of the plague" (121). If this description evokes Defoe's *Journal*, it does so in part to repudiate Defoe's solution, the journal that constantly threatens to become a private diary.

The chronicler uses sources, even such a diary, as Rieux uses Tarrou's (and Camus uses H. F.'s), and by writing history instead of personal reminiscence, maintains community. If the plague poses a common threat, then the private diary subverts the common interest. The tension between the individual and community is persistent throughout *The Plague,* and a retreat into the self is an ever-present danger:

From now on, it can be said that plague was the concern of all of us. Hitherto, surprised as he may have been by the strange things happening around him, each individual citizen had gone about his business as usual, so far as this was possible. And no doubt he would have continued doing so. But once the town gates were shut, every one of us realized that all, the narrator included, were, so to speak, in the same boat, and each of us would have to adapt himself to the new conditions of life. Thus, for example, a feeling normally as individual as the ache of separation from those one loves suddenly became a feeling in which all shared alike— and—together with fear—the greatest affliction of the long period of exile that lay ahead. (61)

The pestilence attacked the "solidarity of a beleaguered town," for obvious reasons launching "its most virulent attacks on those who lived, by choice or by necessity, in groups." It disrupted "long-established communities and sent men out to live, as individuals, in relative isolation" (154).

In eschewing the personal narrative, Rieux also avoids the solipsism that threatens to isolate the individual as effectively as Oran is isolated from the outside world. In the "extremity of solitude" brought on by the plague, no one could "count on any help from his neighbor," nor could anyone "unburden himself" or "say something about his feelings." He would be hurt by the response until he would realize that he and the other person "weren't talking about the same thing."

For while he himself spoke from the depths of long days of brooding upon his personal distress . . . this meant nothing to the man to whom he was speaking, who pictured a conventional emotion, a grief that is traded on the market-place, mass-produced. Whether friendly or hostile, the reply always missed fire, and the attempt to communicate had to be given up. This was true of those at least for whom silence was unbearable, and since the others could not find the truly expressive word, they resigned themselves to using the current coin of language, the commonplaces of plain narrative. (69)

Rieux's everyday language (langue des marches), like the ordinary conversations with which people had to make do, sustains communication, whereas the personal diary in which the writer talks to himself threatens to subvert it.

Rieux evokes one of the romantic images of the writer, as described by Wordsworth for example, as a man speaking to other men. Rieux is portrayed as attractive but by no means an artistic type, with his broad shoulders, tight-set lips, tanned skin with "black down on his hands and arms." That "he reminds one of a Sicilian peasant" (27) is consistent with an ethic of common decency, the French "paysan" suggesting not only a peasant but also a countryman bound to others by common bonds. But Camus is also supplying another example of difference within similarity. The ethic of *The Plague* concerns a notion that Rieux understands may mean different things to others, but that for him consists of "doing [his] job" (150). As chronicler of the plague rather than one who talks to himself about it, he is also as a writer doing a job, with "little claim to competence for [such a] task, had not chance put him in the way of gathering much information, and had he not been, by the force of things, closely involved in all that he proposes to narrate" (7).

But the novel also asks, perhaps only implicitly, the question of whether a chronicle can make a claim to being thought of as art? Is *The Plague* as a novel repudiating itself at each moment that it is being written? It is in asking such questions that it is possible to discover in Camus's work the theme of the earthly paradise, which has for centuries reflected the antithetical motifs of reality versus artifice. David Richter is correct in arguing that in Camus's world, there is no Eden to which the individual can return to evade human predicaments: "The absurdity of the universe inheres in its nature and in that of man."[8] That being the case, Camus can still avail himself of the symbolism of myths, including those of an imagined paradise in which plagues do not exist. It is even possible to glimpse in *The Plague* the palest shadow of the femme fatale, the cousin of the poison damsel. It is by means of these traditional figures from the realm of art that Camus is able to bring into sharp relief the problems inherent in attempting to create artistic beauty out of plague.

One way to look at the quarantined Oran is as Defoe's shut-up house writ large. In this regard, Rambert's efforts to escape form a paradigm for the entire town. And the difficulty of the citizens adequately to communicate their feelings of isolation is a complex inversion of the plight of those residents of London who, if they could, hid the symptoms of their disease in order to prevent their neighbors' refusing to converse with them. But there is a difference between a single shut-up house (or even a collection of them) and a quarantined town. In Defoe's *Journal* those who were able fled London, as did those who were unable but nonetheless sufficiently desperate to make the attempt. The countryside beyond the city is hardly the earthly paradise: for one thing, it is not totally free of the pestilence. But insofar as it promises relief from the severity of plague in London, the exodus takes on the semblance of a collective return to Eden. The city prefigures the world after the fall, the countryside the illusion of a prelapsarian refuge.

Like Defoe, Camus makes what in *The Plague* is a rare differentiation between the classes imprisoned in the city. Like H. F., Rieux notes that the combination of deaths and the deterioration of business during the plague made people available for necessary "rough work" (160), such as the carrying away and burying of bodies. He does not say that without such employment and the wages that went with it, the city's poor would have risen up in rebellion, but he does describe how in black-market conditions, "poor families were in great straits, while the rich were short of practically nothing" (214). Denied both escape from the city and whatever comforts were available in it, it is the seriously deprived who imagine an earthly paradise:

Poor people who were feeling the pinch thought still more nostalgically of towns and villages in the near-by countryside, where bread was cheap and life without restrictions. Indeed, they had a natural if illogical feeling that they should have been permitted to move out to these happier places. (214)

A paradigm for the transformation of paradise into a fallen world is that of Oran's sports stadium converted to a camp where individuals exposed to the disease are interred with, of course, the same dangers that Defoe pointed to when people without signs of the pestilence were nonetheless shut up with the ill if they happened to be living in or visiting the home of a sick person. Since Rieux admits that the plague naturally attacked those living in groups, the gathering of the exposed in a single place only increased the chances of the infected among them infecting those who might have otherwise escaped.

Ordinarily, the stadium is an arena for play, and as Mazzotta informs his reader in his discussion of plague and play in the *Decameron*, play itself was thought by some to provide a remedy against pestilence. And Chaucer's audience is reminded that however moral the aim of literature, one ought not always to make "ernest of game."[9] In Camus's *The Plague*, the stadium represents the place of sport that for the ordinary people of Oran in ordinary times had been comparable to the villas and gardens of pleasure to which Boccaccio's aristocratic brigada retreats from the Black Death. But in *The Plague*, the stadium's meaning has been inverted, the rules operative within it no longer those of a game but pertaining to the strict regulations mandated to control the disease, regulations that stifle the play instinct.[10] In Oran, the stadium comes to represent what is, second only to death, the most frightening aspect of plague: people's isolation from the healthful bonds of their community. But in his very inversion of this quasi-earthly paradise, Camus may be calling into question the role of play and, by extension, of art.

The scholar and sports commissioner A. Bartlett Giamatti, who understood very well the similarities between an earthly paradise and a sports stadium,[11] has described in detail the magic gardens of Renaissance epics, miracles of artifice, natural realms from which the defects of nature are eliminated (as, for example, in the landscaped garden of Poe's "The Domain of Arnheim"). The appeal of these horticultural palaces of art becomes for many Boccaccio critics the basis for a defense of the brigada's graceful society outside of Florence as providing an efficacious and justifiable respite from the evils of the city. Their innocent community, according to such arguments, stands for an ideal against which physically and morally diseased Florence can be measured. Art, in short, has supplanted both nature and social organization.

Oran, too, has such a place, the Municipal Opera House, which despite the plague offers one performance a week. The ritual of opera going by some citizens can be read as another parody of Boccaccio's brigada, with its miniature society based on decorum and good manners. Camus may also be rendering his own version of Poe's "Masque of the Red Death." Oran's opera plays to full houses, "filled to capacity with the cream of Oran society":

It was interesting to see how careful they were, as they went to their places, to make an elegant entrance. While the musicians were discreetly tuning up, men in evening dress could be seen moving from one row to another, bowing gracefully to friends under the flood of light bathing the proscenium. In the soft hum of well-mannered conversation they regained the confidence denied them when they walked the dark streets of the town; evening dress was a sure charm against plague. (179)

But in the last act of Gluck's *Orpheus*, when the leading performer sings his duet with Eurydice, "at the precise moment when Eurydice was slipping from her lover," this unreal world is transformed into what resembles Poe's grotesque version of such artful escapes from plague. Death enters the Oran opera house as Orpheus

chose this moment to stagger grotesquely to the footlights, his arms and legs splayed out under his robe, and fall down. . . . The audience rose and began to leave . . . slowly and silently at first, like worshippers leaving church when the service ends, or a death-chamber after a farewell visit to the dead . . . but gradually their movements quickened, whispers rose to exclamations, and finally the crowd stampeded toward the exits, wedged together in the bottlenecks, and pouring out into the street in a confused mass, with shrill cries of dismay. (180)

A recent essay has explored the Orpheus theme in *The Plague*, explaining —among other things—the absence of important women in the novel (even the female nurses reviled in Defoe's time). Rieux, Rambert, and Grand are all, in a sense, Orpheus. Rieux's wife has left the city for a tuberculosis sanitarium and while her husband battles the plague in Oran, she dies. Rambert had left the woman he loved in Paris, and when he obeys his conscience and remains in Oran, he must do so at the expense of being with her. Grand has lost his wife because he is helpless before the strains of their relationship. Each man has temporarily or permanently lost the woman he loves and is powerless to effect a reunion. Orpheus, however, was not only a bereaved husband but also a poet. According to the study of how Camus used the Orpheus myth, Camus found in it a metaphor for art and for "lost language." Grand's "personal hell is a descent into incommunicability; his return, a Sisyphean struggle to reconstruct at each rewriting [of the opening sentence of his fiction] a perfect facsimile of ineffable emotions."[12]

There is, however, another tradition surrounding Eurydice that provides an additional dimension to the metaphor for art.[13] In the Middle Ages, she was associated with the wicked Herodias, and Orpheus's descent into the underworld read as his pursuit of passion instead of reliance on reason.

This other view is that Eurydice's death from snakebite is a rationalization of an earlier myth in which she appears as the serpent goddess of the underworld to which human men were sacrificed. As such she is an ancestress of Beatrice Rappaccini, Lamia, and the poison damsels. Since Orpheus is renowned as a poet, Eurydice can be viewed as his ambiguous muse, at the same time inspiring and deadly. Orpheus's death in the Oran opera house at the moment when the mythical poet is about to lose his beloved suggests—once again—how plague challenges a variety of aesthetic theories. It transforms the medieval opposition between passion and reason to one between art for art's sake (a "charm" against plague) and an art that in some way can meaningfully contribute to the fight against pestilence.

The Plague does in fact invoke the old-fashioned aesthetic of an art that both pleases and instructs and achieves the latter by the creation of human models. When Rieux designates Grand the "hero" of Oran's fight against the pestilence, it is because in his self-effacing way, Grand exemplifies the ethic of common decency. The "true embodiment of the quiet courage that inspired the sanitary groups," he is as matter-of-fact as Rieux about his actions: "Plague is here and we've got to make a stand, that's obvious. Ah, I only wish everything were as simple" (123). But characteristic of *The Plague*, there is a counterpoint between the theoretical simplicity of the need to stand up to the pestilence and the *inspiration* necessary to move Oran's citizens to action. Rieux's desgnation of Grand as hero is contextually linked to a *theory* of literature:

Yes, if it is a fact that people like to have examples given them, men of the type they call heroic, and if it is absolutely necessary that this narrative should include a "hero," the narrator commends to his readers, with to his thinking, perfect justice, this insignificant and obscure hero. (126)

It is one of the paradoxes in *The Plague* that it should be Grand who nonetheless comes to represent art for art's sake. It is precisely after his pronouncement about the need to make a stand against the plague that "he went back to his phrase" (123), to the writing and rewriting of the opening sentence of the book that occupies his leisure time. Grand wants nothing more from life and work than that he be sufficiently free from want to pursue his project, to perfect his image of the young horsewoman riding in the Bois de Boulogne with which his fiction inexplicably begins. Such a depiction of his endeavor appears remote from the myth of the Sisyphean poet who descends into the otherworld in search of art and lost language.

Grand's literary endeavors are thus rendered both important and trivial. Instead of creating an ethical model for his reader, Grand is working on "the growth of a personality" (40), Camus's words, "l'essor d'une personnalité," suggesting something even transcendent. Grand's writing thus appears intended as an apotheosis of the self, something antithetical to the communality expressed in his daily work against plague. What Steven Kellman says about Rieux's refusal to be the traditional writer, that is, "the Orphic liar," is even more applicable to Grand: "Post-Renaissance conceptions of art as the mysterious gift of a singular ego clearly are impertinent during a plague."[14] Grand has actually made the impertinence of the individual his announced theme. In this contrast between art and action, his writing seems beside the point rather than addressed to it. Its formalism is turned back upon itself as a symbol of the kind of literature that will make no difference. It is therefore meaningful that the last version of Grand's forever-revised line is read by Rieux when Grand himself is infected by the plague:

One fine morning in May, a slim young horsewoman might have been seen riding a glossy sorrel mare along the avenues of the Bois, among the flowers. (238–39)

Oran has at this time reached that stage of the plague that brings to mind the desperation of Defoe's London when the pestilence seemed about to wipe out the entire population. At this point in the *Journal of the Plague Year*, Defoe's apocalyptic image is of death on a pale horse;[15] a similar image, of course, supplied title and theme to *Pale Horse, Pale Rider*, where at the beginning Miranda dreams about herself as a horsewoman in a race with death. The seemingly contrasting picture of Grand's young horsewoman among the flowers of a Paris garden is transformed by the author's impending demise into an aestheticized image of the plague. It is thus appropriate that Grand demands that his manuscript be burned, for the aestheticization of plague and death may be perverse.

Grand's young horsewoman is also a figure of death if she is Grand's substitute bride, an alternative to rather than imitation of life. Just before he is stricken with plague, a weeping Grand is met on the street by Rieux. In extreme anguish, Grand relates how he wishes "I could have time to write to her!" He would tell her that she might be "happy without remorse" (237), for Grand suspects that when she left him it was to be with another man. Again, so long as the erotic impulse has been entirely transposed to art, his Eurydice is as bride of Hades a seductress and his muse.

The division between art and life finds its analogue in *The Plague* in what has been described by Paul Friedrich as a paradigmatic split in Western thought between woman as erotic partner and woman as maternal nurturer. Lacking female lovers, Camus's novel is replete with mothers. One of the anecdotes probably borrowed from Defoe concerns a mother overcome with agony when she learns her daughter is infected with plague. It is his mother that Tarrou most pities when he leaves home, perceiving her to be the victim of her conventional marriage (once mother, she ceases to be erotic partner, and her husband is unfaithful): when his father dies, Tarrou takes her to live with him until her death. Tarrou is strongly drawn to Rieux's mother, who helps him through his last hours, and like Mary, the archetypal mother, intercedes for him when she convinces Rieux to let Tarrou be sick and perhaps die in their home rather than in the isolation ward of a hospital. And Rambert's initially obsessive attempt to escape Oran to be with his mistress is witnessed by the mother of the man Rambert hopes will arrange his exit. She asks Rambert if his wife is pretty and then if he believes in God. When he says yes to the former and no to the latter, she tells him that in that case, he must go to his wife, for nothing else would be left for him. In their exchange, the maternal and the erotic appear particularly split (183–84).

When Rieux's wife leaves for the tuberculosis sanitorium, his mother comes to take care of him, which he finds comforting. She is not only domestically competent but also quietly reassuring. Because of what Tarrou calls her self-effacement, Madame Rieux reminds him of his own mother, Tarrou repeating that what he "loved most in [his] Mother was her self-effacement [effacement],[16] her 'dimness,' as they say, and it's she [he'd] always wanted to get back to" (248). In *The Plague* it is on the diminution of self in mothers that man's selfhood may rest. It is perhaps in this dichotomy between female eroticism and mothering that an essential split in art is implicated. In the femininization of art, the beloved, the muse, represents the beauty of aesthetic form; the nurturing mother—like the healing physician—representing significant content. Rieux's wife and mother, while in no essential conflict with each other, would nonetheless represent a split in Rieux's self-definition. Without the illusions of art, Rieux is like Tarrou, incomplete, his life empty. Without the healing powers of medicine, Rieux is indeed an impotent Orpheus, who looks back at his bride of death to find nothing.

In a study of Camus's fiction significantly entitled *The Narcissistic Text*, a corrective is offered to the usual emphasis on themes in the writer's work. In focusing on Camus's form, Brian Fitch argues that when language draws "attention to itself and away from the fiction that provided its ostensible raison d'être," it "revealed a precoccupation with self, a certain narcissism."[17] His chapter on *The Plague* is called "The Autoreferential Text," it being argued that "the real subject of *La Peste* is none other than the text in all its various forms."[18] Fitch locates in the novel the paradox that "while the text insists that what really matters, the experience of the plague, 'n'est pas une affaire de vocabulaire,' its own status does tend to become reduced to a mere question of words and language."[19] His claim, that the way that the "text never ceases to refer to itself" actually undermines "all and every fiction,"[20] has been challenged by the above analysis of Camus, in which I have contended that the real question is how to write about plague, how to unite writer and doctor.

Fitch's argument nonetheless throws significant light on Camus's *themes*. The critical endeavor to correct the emphasis on theme with attention to form yields a great deal of insight into how *The Plague* is constructed around many kinds of texts, so that as in "Rappaccini's Daughter," virtually each piece of the narrative must be qualified according to a shifting point of view. In Fitch's discussion, however, plague and physician virtually disappear except in direct quotations from Camus. Thus, brilliant as it is, the analysis of Camus's form sustains Camus's theme, Fitch revealing what, emptied of its content, the novel would conceivably be like if it *were* only its form. The analysis, that is, is in itself an ironic replication of Camus's own concern for art's narcissism. But, in fact, *The Plague* is not a narcissistic text, for whatever its formal devices, it never ceases to remind the reader of what Mason cautioned about the staging of *As Is*: however artistic its presentation, and however pleasing to its audience, the play's subject is deadly.

The Plague is virtually guaranteed a place in the syllabus of any literature course taught to premedical and medical students.[21] And there is growing pressure for such courses to be taught. In November 1989 the science section of *The New York Times* featured a story headlined "Physicians Endorse More Humanities for Premed Students," arguing that "mounting evidence of the medical profession's estrangement from the public has led many leaders to blame much of the problem on the narrowness of a physician's training," which has not provided doctors "with enough skills in dealing with people."[22] Although Camus's Dr. Rieux contends that as a physician in a time of plague he must postpone contemplating the larger philosophical issues surrounding the disease and concentrate on healing the sick, as chronicler of the plague he makes it clear that at issue in the battle against pestilence are humanistic values. If the literal bubonic plague of Camus's novel is distinguished from any of its possible metaphoric meanings, then plague *is* in the latter case the diseased degeneration of such values. *The Plague* is thus not only an obvious choice to be read by medical students but also contributes to the very debate about whether seminars in the humanities are likely to have value and achieve their desired ends.[23] Rieux's periodic fatigue and discouragement during the plague might extend from the near impossibility of defeating the pestilence to pessimism about the value of writing about it.

As the science of medicine becomes more and more technological, with diagnosis and prognosis a function of highly specialized machines and computers, the psychological distance between a physician and patient is likely to increase, and the body more than ever is likely to be thought of as itself a machine. In asking questions about what *beside the body* is implicated in surviving plague, literature about pestilence encourages the understanding that survival has to be more than physical, although philosophers who study personal identity tend to agree that for the person to survive, the body has to: "What matters to us in our personal survival seems to involve, partly because in our experience it always has involved, the preservation of at least our bodily identity over time."[24] But if there were not more than that, no one could be declared brain dead. As Georges Rey remarks in the ongoing debate over what survives in survival, "our brains are more crucial to us than our hearts," which is why it is brain rather than heart transplants that "arouse philosophical worry."[25] Gerald Jay Sussman, professor at the Massachusetts Institute of Technology, is apparently not worried. Not in the soul but in the mind does he foresee personal immortality: "If you can make a machine that contains the contents of your mind, then that machine is you. The hell with the rest of your physical body, it's not really very interesting. Now, the machine can last forever."[26] His is a science fiction fantasy—or nightmare, as the case may be.

Would such a machine be a person? To use the question of David Lewis,

When it's all over, will I myself—the very same person now thinking these thoughts and writing these words—still exist? Will any one of those who do exist afterward be me? In other words, *what matters in survival is identity*—identity between the I who exists now and the surviving I who will, I hope, still exist then.[27]

Lewis answers his question by arguing that "*what matters in survival is mental continuity and connectedness.* . . . I find that what I mostly want in wanting survival is that my mental life should flow on. My present experiences, thoughts, beliefs, desires, and traits of character should have appropriate future successors."[28] But Lewis's choice of words negates the idea that the self could be preserved even in a machine advanced in artificial or even real intelligence, for what he describes—beliefs, desires, and traits of character —has to do with emotions, not only thoughts.

It is emotional rather than merely physical bonds that unite people, and in *The Plague* emotions thereby survive the death of an individual and, strangely enough, make sense of the fight against pestilence. When Tarrou dies and Rieux's frustration as an impotent doctor and grief as a friend are described, the very language is both of defeat and, in its very emotional intensity, of hope:

And now Rieux had before him only a masklike face, inert, from which the smile had gone forever. This human form, his friend's, lacerated by the spear-thrusts of the plague, consumed by searing, superhuman fires, buffeted by all the raging winds of heavens, was foundering under his eyes in the dark flood of pestilence, and he could do nothing to avert the wreck. (260)

This is a passage not only about Tarrou's death but also, symbolically, about his life, which had been dedicated to the fight against plague wherever he found it—about Tarrou's passionate struggle for not only his own but also others' survival. And it is therefore appropriate that at this point in his so-called chronicle, Rieux invokes the imagistic language of art. As Raphael Stern has said about the self, that subject that unites medical doctors with psychologists, philosophers, and artists, "if we are to understand the self," then we need to employ the "languages of aesthetics and ethics, and to wed these to more technical languages."[29] In this argument can be found the humanistic basis for a literature about plague.

Notes

1. Introduction

1. Duffy viii.
2. In his introduction to the new Oxford edition of the *Journal*, David Roberts mentions Boccaccio and quotes from an historian of the Black Death that in plague literature "the same phrases are used to describe the appearance of the disease, the same exaggerated estimates of mortality appear, the same passions are aroused, the same economic and social consequences ensue," adding himself that plague literature, "in other words, exhibits striking rhetorical consistency in describing strikingly consistent events" (vii). That may in fact be why writers on plague borrow from each other. For my discussion of Boccaccio and Defoe, and Chaucer and Defoe, see chapter 2. See Steel for a general essay on plague writing.
3. Bernardo. See chapter 3, n. 23 below.
4. I have written on this theme elsewhere. See my chapter on *The Magic Mountain* in Fass [Leavy], *La Belle Dame sans Merci.*
5. For a romantic treatment of tuberculosis, which links it to genius, see Moorman.
6. Jacobsen has referred me to a recent book that uses leprosy as a literal and politically symbolic theme: Amin Maalouf, *Leo Africanus.*
7. Marks and Beatty xi.
8. After writing this chapter, I read Foege, who also deals with questions of definition. He, too, uses the example of lung cancer.
9. Sontag 6.
10. Robinson 11. The word *plague* appears to be commonly associated with AIDS. A review in *The New Yorker* of the film *Longtime Companion* is subtitled "Plague." In the play *The Lisbon Traviata,* one of the characters refers to AIDS as the gay community's own bubonic plague. Also see Holleran's introduction to *The Normal Heart;* and Brandt's essay on "AIDS and Metaphor."
11. *Letters* 177.
12. Zinsser 88. Those interested in researching the Black Death might start with Morrison's review of Gottfried's *The Black Death;* Swenson's essay is a useful popular introduction to the plague theme from bubonic plague to AIDS.
13. Lerner 533.
14. Mazzotta, *The World:* 30.
15. Thody 47.
16. Rosebury xvi-xvii.
17. R. Porter, "Ever since Eve": 597; also see chapter 6 for discussion of this female stereotype. Fine writes on the emergent folklore of the female spreader

of AIDS; and in the concluding chapter of her book, Baruch supports the view
that the popular film *Fatal Attraction* can be understood as a visual allegory of
AIDS and explores in a provocative discussion the implications of the AIDS
personifier being a seductress.

18. Zinsser 9.

19. See n. 30 below.

20. Stephanson, "Plague Narratives": 239.

21. Zimmerman, *Defoe and the Novel:* 126. Richetti exemplifies this treatment of
plague. He writes of Defoe's *Journal* that the "plague is an extended moment of
total uncertainty, an exaggerated, nearly metaphysical version provided by history of the random destructiveness of an environment. Perfectly, one can add,
that environment is both natural and social" (234). It is a conventional theological tenet—one that Defoe would not have lost sight of—that although the
universe may appear unreadable, events are not random. Human beings just
cannot presume to grasp God's design or intentions.

22. I am borrowing here from Lillian Feder's ideas of the self. See chapter 5, n. 38
below.

23. Walsh 85–86. See also chapter 5, n. 38 below.

24. Toulmin 315.

25. Collins 74.

26. Detrick 430.

27. Cohen and Abramowitz 171. Their study is a very comprehensive account of
the psychological disintegration of the AIDS patient and the reasons for it—an
account particularly applicable to literary analysis because, in general, the self
psychology perspective, its focus on self/selfobject relationships, bears on essential literary themes and character interactions.

28. Andreski 156.

29. Gilman 271.

30. McNeill 5–6.

31. Thompson 17.

32. Glen 208.

33. For significant analyses of Blake's "London," close readings of the text (which,
however, neglect the plague theme), see Ferber; Pagliaro; and Punter.

34. I discuss the *Journal* as if it were accurate history. The scholarship on Defoe is
replete with discussions of the gap between Defoe's account and reality, or of
how he drew on the sources of his time and their accuracy. Many such discussions refer to the work of Nicholson.

35. Dolores Greenberg reminds me in personal conversation that her contention is
based on wide reading of others. See her essay for valuable references to studies
of the earthly paradise. Given what my book takes to be the inherent connection
between literary treatments of a new Eden and disease, I find it noteworthy that
Dolores Greenberg has written on the quest for the earthly paradise and the
relationship of this quest to modern technology (e.g., Brandt's magic bullet),
while her husband, the late Robert A. Greenberg, wrote on medicine and
literature in the nineteenth century. See references.

36. Landa xxvii.

37. Welty 48.
38. B11.
39. Marshall W. Mason in Hoffman 59. See Edelman for the argument that given the terrible reality of AIDS, literary criticism about it is pretentious.

2. The Historical and Ethical Significance of Daniel Defoe's *A Journal of the Plague Year*

1. Landa xxxvi.
2. Roberts xii.
3. Willey 6. I have borrowed the image of Janus from the apt illustration on the 1953 Doubleday Anchor paperback edition of this book.
4. Curtis 4.
5. Bolt xii.
6. Backscheider 6. About the tension between religion and empiricism, Richter has pointed out that Defoe makes the point over and over in his bio-fictions that despite the desire to avoid trusting to providence, life is not really calculable, and success entails irrational faith as well as rational effort (private correspondence).
7. See nn. 32–34 below.
8. Landa xvi.
9. Burgess 17.
10. For background on Defoe and medical aspects of plague, see Roberts's "Medical Note" at the end of his edition of Defoe's *Journal*: 288–91.
11. Landa xxvi.
12. Curtis 71.
13. Cullerier 43; Fournier 18–19.
14. See review in *The Economist,* April 5, 1986, 104.
15. It is on the theme of isolation and alienation that Rocks compares Defoe and Camus.
16. Brandt 5.
17. Burgess 18.
18. Novak, *Realism:* 66.
19. Tawney 240.
20. Novak, *Defoe and the Nature of Man:* 15.
21. For a comprehensive and interesting essay on this subject, see Edgerton.
22. Backscheider 135.
23. Novak, *Defoe and the Nature of Man:* 11.
24. Ibid. 21.
25. For an excellent discussion of this trio as well as Defoe's treatment of individual and communal survival, see Birdsall.
26. Most of Novak's book on *Defoe and the Nature of Man* bears directly or indirectly on the social contract.
27. According to Landa, Defoe was "rebuked and ridiculed in 'no less than three different Companies' for disordering 'the People with Melancholy Notions of the Plague' " (xii).

28. Curtis 67.
29. Pocock 335. Also see Novak, *Defoe and the Nature of Man:* 14–15.
30. Andreski 204, 205.
31. Novak, *Defoe and the Nature of Man:* 19.
32. Landa xxxiv.
33. Zimmerman, *Defoe and the Novel:* 108.
34. Birdsall 102. Also see Zimmerman, *Defoe and the Novel:* 126. Roberts explains H. F.'s secrecy about his private meditations in terms of other Defoe works, "as if there were something indecent, given the subject of the book, about the solipsistic form of Defoe's other narratives" (xii).
35. The capitalization of *Self* in one instance but not in the other suggests the possibility that Defoe is allowing H. F. to conduct what Matthew Arnold would later call the dialogue of the mind with itself.
36. Stephanson, "'Tis a Speaking Sight": 690, 691. See also Landa xiv–xv.
37. Roberts says that the *Journal* suppresses "the assertive 'I' of Defoe's other works only to assert it yet more intensely" at the end (xiii).

3. The Diseased Soul in Chaucer, Boccaccio, and Poe

1. See Hutton translation: 1:21.
2. See Pocock's treatment of the subject of Fortune in fifteenth-century Florence. For the conflict between flesh and spirit implied in the dualism of the City of God and the City of Man, see Miller, *Chaucer: Sources:* 23. Also see the chapter on "Augustine, Boethius, and Chaucer" in Dahlberg, *Literature of Unlikeness.*
3. Most of the days of storytelling in the *Decameron* are addressed to an agreed-upon theme among the narrators, and several of these themes have to do with Fortune.
4. See, for example, Gottfried.
5. Wenzel 131–32.
6. Beidler 257. For interpretations of "The Pardoner's Tale," see the notes to the second and third editions of *The Riverside Chaucer;* Faulkner; Halverson; and Sedgewick.
7. For a study of the thematic links between the two tales and a more detailed theological context than I supply, see Trower. Despite the similarities in our approach, our discussions overlap surprisingly little. I appreciate the discussions I had with Gordon Whatley on the subject of fragment 6.
8. Those who taught me Chaucer always reminded me that a subject that might be repellent to a twentieth-century audience was not necessarily received in the same way by a medieval audience.
9. Robinson's edition of *Chaucer* 10.
10. Folklorists use the Aarne and Thompson classification of this story: Tale Type 763, The Treasure Seekers Who Find Death. See Robinson 729.
11. Robinson 11.
12. *Vindication* 12.
13. McNeill 237. For a study of Chaucer's physician that is essentially a defense, see Ussery.

14. See Beidler for a discussion of the economics of plague in "The Pardoner's Tale."
15. Miller, "Chaucer's Pardoner": 180–81. Also see Trower.
16. McNeill 236.
17. Bernardo and Mazzotta differ markedly on the significance of the ending of the *Decameron*. Bernardo argues that the silence concerning the plague at the conclusion "dramatizes the extent to which the *brigata* was unconcerned about" its horrors, "except on the level of self-preservation" (58–59). Mazzotta claims that the "*brigata* dissolves at the end because no finality is possible for the pastoral interlude" (68).
18. *Boccaccio on Poetry* 39, 49, 51.
19. For a comprehensive survey of criticism concerning the didactic element in the *Decameron*, see Hastings.
20. "Marginality" is Mazzotta's term. His essay is also a chapter in his book (see references).
21. Mazzotta, "Marginality": 65.
22. This is the thrust of Almansi's study.
23. Bernardo 39.
24. Mazzotta, "Marginality": 64.
25. Because Mazzotta emphasizes the play theme in the *Decameron*, he believes he must account for Boccaccio's "moral vocabulary" (*World*: 241). See his chapter on ethics in *The World at Play*. My discussion below suggests that the play theme must *interact* in medieval literature with the more sober matters of human ethics.
26. Bernardo writes, "One can only conclude from Boccaccio's subtitle that his book, too, may be an instrument of death and destruction if not read with care" (40).
27. See Brucker.
28. Hastings 29.
29. Almansi 10.
30. Bernardo 59–60
31. Giamatti, The Earthly Paradise: 80.
32. Ibid. 85.
33. Ibid. 71.
34. Ibid. 83.
35. Dahlberg, "Macrobius": 579.
36. Hastings 29.
37. Kern 522.
38. Hastings 29.
39. Bernardo 52.
40. I am quoting from "Natural Law" in *The Encyclopedia of Philosophy*. This entry is particularly useful not only as a survey but also for pointing out the problems in the doctrine of natural law. Also see Mazzotta's chapter in *The World at Play* for the specific context of natural law for the *Decameron*. Mazzotta does not take into account the problem of natural law as an enigmatic reference point for human behavior.
41. *Encyclopedia of Philosophy* 452.

42. Bolt x.
43. For a discussion of these different kinds of love, see Dahlberg, *Literature of Unlikeness*: 74–76.
44. Doubrovsky 84.
45. What I call Poe's tales of pestilence are not ordinarily studied together. Levin is one of the few who looks at them as a group, but only in a very short discussion: 149–51.
46. Singleton 119.
47. Vanderbilt points to the neglect of the "Masque" as a story in which Poe's aesthetic ideas inform his themes. See his essay for a discussion different from mine, one stressing the element of taste in art.
48. The Notes to Poe's tales include a comparison: "Poe's setting for his tale recalls that of Boccaccio's *Decameron*" (669). There were translations that Poe could have known: see McWilliam's discussion of translations in his edition of the *Decameron*.
49. Reece 114. The most complete study of Poe's sources is the unpublished dissertation by Tritt.
50. Wilbur 372. There has been a great deal of scholarship on Poe since Wilbur's 1962 "Introduction," but it remains an excellent discussion, worth consulting.
51. DeFalco 643.
52. Dayan 128–29.
53. Wilbur 374.
54. Notes to Poe's tales 668. For a survey of interpretations of the "Masque," see Roppolo. Since his essay, there have been several studies that emphasize the theme of consciousness and the dangers of solipsism in Poe. See Godwin's and Michael's essays; and Dayan's book.
55. Zapf 214. Also see Godwin 23, 24.
56. See DeFalco.
57. Michael 8. For other discussion of Poe and language, see Davidson.
58. See Fleissner.
59. Notes to Poe's tales 255.
60. Because Poe's protagonist in the "Masque" is Prince Prospero, there are several comparisons of Poe and Shakespeare. See Cheney; Roppolo 61; Vanderbilt 379; Notes to Poe's tales 678.
61. This may be what Davidson is implying when he mentions "The Masque of the Red Death" as an example of Poe's stories whose aim is "to reduce man from his assumed humanity to his bestial counterpart" (152). The "Masque" is not a work that Davidson analyzes in his book on Poe. For important discussions of Caliban, see James; Langbaum; and Hankins.
62. For a discussion of the earthly paradise theme in Poe, see Jacobs.
63. Rainwater supplies an interesting overview of the garden motif in Poe. See also Zanger; and Dayan's chapter, "The Poet in the Garden."
64. Dayan 84.
65. Ibid. 86.
66. See Baskett for the influence of "Kubla Khan" on Poe, but in a discussion quite different from mine. Also see Hess 184; Godwin 23; Pitcher 246; Notes

to Poe's tales 646, 1284. Davidson studies the influence of Coleridge's theories on Poe; Dayan focuses, in contrast, on Shelley's.

67. In the Notes to Poe's tales, there is a disclaimer about any "kinship" between Poe and Defoe's *Journal* (239). I disagree. Poe's language also invites comparison with Blake's "London," although I am not arguing for the direct influence of Blake on Poe.

4. Ibsen's *Ghosts* and the Ghosts of Ibsen

1. Downs 164.
2. Williams 70.
3. Gray 68.
4. Rosebury 127.
5. Sprinchorn 366, n. 3
6. Meyer 488, n. 28.
7. Rosebury 127.
8. Gilman 256.
9. Meyer 488, n. 28.
10. Cullerier; see n. 14 below.
11. I browsed, at first randomly and then more systematically, in books on infectious disease and generalized histories of venereal disease (not textbooks). Many of them discussed congenital syphilis, but none of them the infectiousness of the newborn. I finally consulted a physician to learn that the newborn is highly contagious but that this infectiousness shortly subsides. "Undetected congenital syphilis," according to Rinear, "generally manifests itself early in life, but symptoms may not appear until 30 years of age or later" (175). If Oswald suffered from congenital syphilis, his case would therefore be unusual but not impossible.
12. Fournier iii.
13. See chapter 6 below.
14. Cullerier 70.
15. Cullerier 71.
16. Cullerier 74.
17. Cullerier 62.
18. Fournier 18–19.
19. Fournier 52–53.
20. Downs 164, n. 2. Downs writes that it is not clear whether Ibsen believed Oswald could communicate the disease.
21. Fournier 180–81.
22. Cullerier 74.
23. Williams 70.
24. Downs 163.
25. This represents Kapferer's approach to the nature-culture conflict in Sri Lanka, but it seems more generally applicable.
26. Corrigan 171.
27. Koht 328.

28. Meyer 488.
29. Brandt 5.
30. Kaufmann 236.
31. Gravier 152 (my translation).
32. Gravier 152 (my translation).
33. Gravier 152.
34. Leavy, *Ibsen's Forsaken Merman:* 17.
35. Sprinchorn 365.
36. Jacobsen 36–37.
37. Jacobsen 32–47.
38. Davis 383.
39. Northam 102.
40. Masterson 23.
41. Koht 331.
42. Sprinchorn 358.
43. Jorgenson 347.
44. Fergusson 112.
45. Ibsen's Norwegian (jeg er andelig nedbrutt, — odelagt) allows for a translation of "mind" or "spirit" (as Meyer translates it); this ambiguity in the Norwegian is not present in either English word. I appreciate Jacobsen's help with this passage.
46. Secord 254.
47. Collins 73–74.
48. Cavell 59.
49. Again, I am drawing on Secord.
50. Dervin 1010.
51. Goldberg, *A Fresh Look at Psychoanalysis:* 37.
52. For a comprehensive discussion of ideas about schizophrenia, see Gilman's essay "Constructing Schizophrenia as a Category of Mental Illness" in *Disease and Representation,* 202–30.
53. Kroll makes a passing reference to the tradition supplied by *Ghosts* but does not suggest more direct connections (87).
54. According to Kleinberg, Hoffman's and Kramer's plays raise but do not adequately address the issue of gay identity (30). I would certainly disagree, however, that the playwrights merely stumble onto the subject. As I will suggest in my discussion, the theme of identity is an important element in both dramas.
55. Green's unpublished lecture on theatrical treatments of AIDS. My colleague David Kleinbard informs me that the term is also a legal one, used in contracts to make clear that the buyer acknowledges awareness of purchasing damaged goods.
56. Jacobsen 35–36.
57. Nelson quotes from Hoffman: "This play is implicitly political, but I didn't set out to make a political statement as such. I was hoping to paint a portrait of a modern marriage under stress" (58). Reviewers who compare *As Is* and *The Normal Heart* tend to distinguish between the lack of polemics in one and its presence in the other.
58. The preface first appeared in *Vogue,* July 1985, 174–75.

59. In his review, Frank Rich refers to New York's "demimonde of sex bars" (C12); Edith Oliver surveys the specific places made thematically significant in *As Is* (118).
60. Jacobsen 71–72.
61. Jacobsen, in a conversation with me about Hoffman's play.
62. About a play in which the image of a bridge is significant, one might say that the subject of AIDS requires a bridge between the two poles of traditional aesthetic theory—teaching and entertaining. So pressing is that need that in his review, which is itself highly polemical in urging the importance of both Hoffman's and Kramer's plays, Thorpe writes as if such a bridge already exists: "When the theatre educates, it is at its best. When it has a purpose it is a tool and mirror of society. When it enlightens and informs, it is entertaining" (13). Mimi Kramer writes that *The Normal Heart* is the only play she had "ever seen that made [her] think that theatre as propaganda might have some value" (135).
63. Virchow 1:121.
64. Virchow 1:117.
65. According to Hill, this egotism is characteristic of what he calls "the new man of medicine in the nineteenth century" (179).
66. Lepke 60.
67. Brustein 71.
68. See Meyer's table of contents.
69. Berman 569.
70. The review in *The Economist* meaningfully entitled "Kramer vs. Cruising," for example, refers to the gay community's reaction against Kramer because of his attack on sexual freedom. Just how AIDS was spread was still uncertain in 1985: In 1991, no enlightened person takes a casual position towards sexual promiscuity.
71. Comparisons between the stridency and stubbornness of Ned Weeks and Thomas Stockmann are made by Berman (569); Smith reviews *The Normal Heart* as a play in the tradition of *An Enemy of the People* without making direct connections (44).
72. On Wednesday, November 14, 1990, the *New York Times* had a front page story about an announcement of AIDS therapy for pneumonia that was delayed until scientists could publish findings in the *New England Journal of Medicine*. A following piece on December 2, section 4, p. 4, and a letter to the editors printed December 12, A22, signed by representatives of the *New England Journal* and the National Institutes of Health, who deny that any treatment was significantly delayed, indicate the matter remains open to debate.
73. See n. 65 above.
74. Simon 91.
75. See n. 54 above.

5. Microparasites, Macroparasites, and the Spanish Influenza

1. Collier 303.
2. Crosby 311.
3. Ibid.

4. Collier 304.
5. Crosby 318.
6. Crosby 46.
7. See Hudson's essay.
8. *Recapitulation* 178. In *A Sense of Place* Stegner protests against the conversion of wilderness space to recreation areas. His eloquent argument can serve as a significant commentary on Chet's fate.
9. I have heard this perhaps apocryphal anecdote assigned to Maurice Chevalier.
10. Ahearn 109.
11. Beach 20.
12. Stegner's North American West includes Saskatchewan, Utah, and Montana.
13. McNeill 69.
14. In my discussion of Porter I also speak of this "coincidence." Not everyone would agree that it is a coincidence: Virchow, for example, argued in the middle of the nineteenth century that "war, pestilence and starvation mutually engender one another" ("Diseases of the People": 122).
15. *Recapitulation* 116. *A Sense of Place* contains images of Eden and the fall.
16. This is a Catholic interpretation of Genesis 3.15, the enmity between the serpent and the woman. Marina Warner relates that in "the 'woman,' Christians had seen a prophecy of the Virgin Mary" and that "ever since the fourth century, the promised victory over the serpent had been used to develop the image of the second Eve who triumphs where the first Eve failed" (245). This Catholic tradition, however, had a wide cultural impact, the Eve-Mary dichotomy neatly fitting into a virtually age-old duality (existing in many cultures) supposed to be found in woman.
17. Crosby 319.
18. Youngblood 348.
19. *Letters* 177. Also see Givner 127.
20. DeMouy 5–6.
21. *Letters* 548–49.
22. See Fine; and my discussion of the poison damsel legend in chapters 6 and 7.
23. Richter, "Essay": 104.
24. Ibid. 101.
25. Yannella says that "Miranda is no less a 'soldier' in quest of survival" than are characters in war novels (638).
26. Warren 19.
27. Yannella 637–38.
28. Walsh 81.
29. Johnson 602–5.
30. Richter, "Essay": 110.
31. Rey 57.
32. Richter, "Essay": 102–3.
33. Detrick 432.
34. Warren 19.
35. Loe 86.
36. Richter, "Essay": 103.

37. Very little has been made of the name Miranda in Porter criticism. Warren treats the connection to Shakespeare in a few sentences, but not in any way helpful for a feminist approach to Porter's story (19–20). Interestingly, the many feminist studies of Shakespeare that have been appearing have little to say about Miranda.

38. Yanella admits that it is possible to locate faint optimism at the end, but argues that the novella is a "dismal assessment of modern selfhood" whose "gloom is pervasive" (642). Loe argues that at the end Miranda is "bereft of hope, cleansed of expectation," with "no story left" (93). DeMouy infers that there is growth in Miranda's "death as a lover and her resurrection as an independent loner" (157). And Cheatham contends that as compensation for the death of Adam, "Miranda gains another sort of love: the sacrificial love of Adam for her, which parallels that of Christ for mankind and which symbolically frames the story," and that underpinning that story "is the symbolic structure of the fall of mankind, mankind's consequent suffering and death, and mankind's subsequent redemption" (396). (It is curious that Cheatham, who draws heavily for his argument on Porter's choice of names, should have overlooked the emergence of Towney's real name, Mary, at the symbolic ending of the novella.) Hardy's view of Miranda's "consuming devotion to some idea of [herself]" suggests a narcissism she may have done well to abandon: "In the stories that have usually been considered Miss Porter's finest work, the central figures are people whose desperate preoccupation with themselves cuts them off from effective communication with all other human beings" (62). In contrast, Feder's concept of the self, while not being applied to Porter, elevates Miranda's striving to heroism: the self constitutes the "individual's biological and psychological resistance to his own adaptation to political and social constraints" (392–93).

6. Plague, Physician, Writer, and the Poison Damsel

1. Fournier 5.

2. Fournier 1–2.

3. There is a contradiction here that continues to plague contemporary physicians. How can a doctor warn others (e.g., wet nurses or the sexual partners of those with infectious diseases) about a danger to their health without betraying patient confidentiality? See Rosenkrantz for a discussion of the problem, which, despite her title, does not include an analysis of Brieux's play.

4. So far as I can determine, the criticism of *Damaged Goods* has been confined to theater reviews. For studies of Brieux, his other plays, and reviews of *Damaged Goods*, consult SantaVicca's bibliography. Rosebury briefly discusses Brieux's play, but the discussion is less analysis than summary added to historical background about the play's production and about advances in research on syphilis.

5. This is my translation, the dedication to Fournier not being included in the English edition of Brieux's plays. According to Rosebury, "Four prominent French syphilologists were godfathers to the play," but in his discussion, the other three remain anonymous (127). My argument is that Fournier warrants

the prominence Rosebury gives him because *Damaged Goods* is a dramatization of Fournier's book on marriage and syphilis.

6. McNeill 239.
7. This is my translation, my discussion being based on a disparity between the French original and English translation.
8. My translation. The English text is, "Loches. We ought to hound out these vile women who poison the very life of society" (249). This is slightly different from labeling the women poisoners, and thus the French text is closer to the poison damsel legend.
9. For a thorough survey of how "Rappaccini's Daughter" as a whole as well as individual motifs and characters have been interpreted, see Ayo.
10. See Swan and Hooper 21–22.
11. For discussions of Dr. Baglioni's role in the story, see Gale; and Scott.
12. Dreher 255.
13. Ibid. 256.
14. For Penzer's discussion of syphilis and related issues, see pp. 44–68 of his essay.
15. See Goodwin.
16. See Teit.
17. Jordan de Caro 64.
18. See Fass [Leavy], *La Belle Dame* 30, 276, n. 11. For further discussion of the lamia theme in Keats and Hawthorne, see Gallagher.
19. See the chapter on Keats's "Lamia" in Fass [Leavy], *La Belle Dame.*
20. Gross 141.
21. See essays by Gross and by Uroff.
22. These are the charges against the medical profession described by Uroff.
23. Uroff 141.
24. See essays by Jones and by Cuddy.
25. Uroff 64.
26. Ibid. 63–64.
27. Bensick 97.
28. Ibid. 110–11.
29. Professor Bensick gave me this valuable reference and I very much appreciate her helpfulness.
30. Ricord 7.
31. Ibid. 84.
32. Ibid. 216.
33. Bensick 112.
34. Ibid.
35. Gilman's essay on AIDS patients supplies a significant context for appreciating Beatrice Rappaccini's predicament.
36. Bensick 78–79.
37. Jones points out the connection to Shakespeare's Miranda (159).
38. I am borrowing this allusion from Jones 154.
39. Ibid.
40. Ibid. 155–56.

7. Medicine and Humanism in Albert Camus's *The Plague*

1. For a discussion of Camus's ethics, see Doubrovsky.

2. For the different ways of reading *The Plague,* see Thody; and Kellman's introduction to *Teaching Approaches.*

3. Grobe has written an important essay on Grand's sentence and the meaning of its variants, showing that Grand's form changes with his altered view of the world. Grobe begins with Grand's need to believe in the "existence of a rational order" and shows how he comes to accept that if "life is to present any positive values, they must be accrued within life itself, in the very substance of its horror, and [are] not to be sought in some posthumous utopia" (255, 259).

4. Bernardo 59; Crawfurd's account of the Bishop of Marseilles (204–6).

5. This is another image that Camus and Porter share: see chapter 5.

6. For comparisons of Defoe and Camus, see Stephanson, "The Plague Narratives"; Rocks; Tavor.

7. See Fitch for a very complete account of the narrative genres represented in *The Plague* (15–16).

8. Richter, *Fable's End:* 165.

9. See my discussion of Boccaccio and games in chapter 3.

10. For a discussion of the portrayal of Nazi concentration camps in *The Plague,* see Felman.

11. Richard McCoy has pointed out to me that Giamatti's book *Take Time for Paradise* makes this connection specific. Charles Dahlberg has suggested to me that a baseball field in particular is comparable to the earthly paradise, since the game is in effect timeless: if the score is tied, as many innings as necessary are played until one side or the other wins.

12. Finel-Honigman 216–17.

13. For discussion of this other tradition attached to Eurydice, see Leavy, "Faith's Incubus."

14. Kellman, "Singular": 505

15. See Goodman on the connection between Grand's description of his female rider and the Four Horseman of the Apocalypse (85).

16. The original French lacks the immediate reflexiveness of the English *self-effacement,* but the verb "s'effacer" is consistent with the translation. I want to thank Elaine Hoffman Baruch for consultations on translating from French to English.

17. Fitch xvi.

18. Ibid. 15.

19. Ibid. 18.

20. Ibid. 33.

21. See Kellman, "Introduction" to *Teaching Approaches;* and, particularly, Goodman's essay.

22. Tuesday, November 14, 1989, C3.

23. Subjectively, I would contend that if any book reached medical students or physicians, Camus's would. But I have already expressed in a book review my suspicion that such courses achieve their ends only when preaching to the

already converted. See Leavy, review of *Healing Arts.* Yet I would welcome a chance to attempt to promote humanistic values by teaching a literature course to medical students; some of my best English majors have gone on to be doctors. My own ambivalence doubtless resulted in a special sensitivity to the ambivalence of writers who treat the subject of plague.

24. Rey 41.
25. Ibid. 58–59.
26. Professor Sussman's statement was downloaded from a computer bulletin board on November 11, 1990, via ExecNet Transatlantic Conference from Big Blue Exec Network BBS, apparently echoed from Channel 1 BBS, Cambridge, Massachusetts.
27. Lewis 18.
28. Ibid. 17.
29. Stern x.

References

Primary Sources

Boccaccio, Giovanni. *The Decameron.* Translated by G. H. McWilliam. Harmondsworth, England: Penguin, 1972.

———. *The Decameron.* Translated by Edward Hutton [1620]. 2 vols. 1909. Reprint. New York: AMS Press, 1967.

———. *Boccaccio on Poetry* [*The Genealogy of the Gentile Gods*]. New York: Liberal Arts Press, 1956.

Brieux, Eugene. *Théâtre Complèt de Brieux.* 9 vols. [*Les Avariés,* Vol. 6.] Paris: Librairie Stock, 1923.

———. *Three Plays by Brieux.* With Preface by Bernard Shaw. (*Damaged Goods,* translated by John Pollock). New York: Brentano's, 1911.

Camus, Albert. *The Plague.* Translated by Stuart Gilbert. New York: Alfred A. Knopf, 1962.

Chaucer, Geoffrey. *The Riverside Chaucer.* 3d ed. Edited by Larry D. Benson. Boston: Houghton Mifflin, 1987.

———. *The Riverside Chaucer.* 2d ed. Edited by F. N. Robinson. Boston: Houghton Mifflin, 1957.

Defoe, Daniel. *A Journal of the Plague Year.* Oxford: Oxford University Press, 1990.

———. *A Vindication of the Press; or, An Essay on the Usefulness of Writing, of Criticism, and the Qualifications of Authors.* 1718. Reprint. New York: Garland, 1972.

Hawthorne, Nathaniel. *Mosses from an Old Manse.* Columbus, Ohio: Ohio State University Press, 1974.

Hoffman, William M. *As Is.* New York: Dramatists Play Service, 1990.

Ibsen, Henrik. *The Oxford Ibsen.* Edited by James W. McFarlane. Translated by McFarlane et al. 8 vols. Oxford: Oxford University Press. 1970–77. [*Ghosts,* Vol. 5; *An Enemy of the People,* Vol. 6.]

Kramer, Larry. *The Normal Heart.* New York: New American Library, 1985.

Poe, Edgar Allan. *Essays and Reviews.* New York: Library of America, 1984.

———. *Collected Works.* [*Tales and Sketches,* 1831–1842, Vol. 2; 1843–1849, Vol. 3.] Edited by Thomas Olive Mabbott. Cambridge, Mass.: Belknap Press, 1978.

Porter, Katherine Anne. *The Collected Stories.* New York: Harcourt, Brace and World, 1965.

———. *Letters of Katherine Anne Porter.* Edited by Isabel Bayley. New York: Atlantic Monthly Press, 1990.

Stegner, Wallace. *Collected Stories.* New York: Random House, 1990.

———. *Recapitulation.* Garden City, N.Y.: Doubleday and Co., 1979.

NOTE: Citations have been made only to the literary works that are the focus of analysis. Wherever it seemed warranted to supply a word, phrase, or brief passage in the original language, it has been provided, but without citations to specific editions. Only in the case of Brieux's play did my analysis sometimes rest on disparities between the original French and the English translation. For this reason, both French and English editions are cited.

Secondary Sources

Ahearn, Kerry. "The Big Rock Candy Mountain and the Angle of Repose: Trial and Culmination." In Arthur. 109–23.

Allen, N. J. "The Category of the Person: a Reading of Mauss's Last Essay." In Carrithers. 26–45.

Almansi, Guido. *The Writer as Liar: Narrative Technique in the Decameron.* London: Routledge and Kegan Paul, 1975.

Andreski, Stanislav. *Syphilis, Puritanism, and Witch Hunts: Historical Explanations in the Light of Medicine and Psychoanalysis, with a Forecast about AIDS.* London: Macmillan, 1989.

Arthur, Anthony, ed. *Critical Essays on Wallace Stegner.* Boston: G. K. Hall, 1982.

Ayo, Nicholas. "The Labyrinthine Ways of 'Rappaccini's Daughter.'" *Research Studies* 42 (1974): 56–69.

Backscheider, Paula R. *Daniel Defoe: Ambition and Innovation.* Lexington: University Press of Kentucky, 1986.

Barnes, Clive. Review of *As Is. New York Post,* March 12, 1985, 50.

———. Review of *The Normal Heart. New York Post,* May 4, 1985, 12.

Baruch, Elaine Hoffman. *Women, Love, and Power: Literary and Psychoanalytic Perspectives.* New York: New York University Press, 1991.

Baskett, Sam. "A Damsel with a Dulcimer: An Interpretation of Poe's 'Eleanora.'" *Modern Language Notes* 73 (1958): 332–37.

Bastian, Frank E. "Defoe's *A Journal of the Plague Year* Reconsidered." *Review of English Studies* 16 (1965): 151–73.

Bayley, Isabel, ed. *Letters of Katherine Anne Porter.* New York: Atlantic Monthly Press, 1990.

Beach, Joseph Warren. "Life-Size Stegner." In Arthur. 19–20.

Beidler, Peter G. "The Plague and Chaucer's Pardoner." *Chaucer Review* 16 (1982): 257–69.

Bensick, Carol Marie. *La Nouvelle Beatrice: Renaissance and Romance in "Rappaccini's Daughter".* New Brunswick, N.J.: Rutgers University Press, 1985.

Berman, Paul. Review of *As Is. Nation,* May 11, 1985, 569–70.

Bernardo, Aldo S. "The Plague as Key to Meaning in Boccaccio's *Decameron.*" In Williman. 39–64.

Birdsall, Virginia Ogden. *Defoe's Perpetual Seekers: A Study of the Major Fiction.* Lewisburg, Pa.: Bucknell University Press, 1985.

Blaire, Walter. "Poe's Conception of Incident and Tone in the Tale." *Modern Philology* 41 (1944): 118–40.

Bloom, Harold, ed. *Katherine Anne Porter: Modern Critical Views.* New York: Chelsea House, 1986.

Bolt, Robert. *A Man for All Seasons.* New York: Vintage, 1962.

Brandt, Allan M. "AIDS and Metaphor: Toward the Social Meaning of Epidemic Disease." In Mack, 91–110.

———. *No Magic Bullet: A Social History of Venereal Disease in the United States since 1880.* New York: Oxford University Press, 1985.

Brody, Saul Nathaniel. *The Disease of the Soul: Leprosy in Medieval Literature.* Ithaca: Cornell University Press, 1974.

Brucker, Gene A. "Florence and the Black Death." In *Boccaccio: Secoli di vita,* ed. Marga Cottino-Jones and Edward F. Tuttle. Ravenna: Longo, 1977. 22–30.

Brustein, Robert. *The Theater of Revolt.* Boston: Little, Brown, 1962.

Bulger, Roger J. *In Search of the Modern Hippocrates.* Iowa City: University of Iowa Press, 1987.

Burgess, Anthony. "Introduction." *A Journal of the Plague Year.* Harmondsworth, England: Penguin, 1966.

Burr, Suzanne. "Ghosts in Modern Drama: Ibsen, Strindberg, O'Neill, and Their Legacy." Ph.D. diss., University of Michigan, 1987.

Carrithers, Michael, et al., eds. *The Category of the Person: Anthropology, Philosophy, History.* Cambridge, England: Cambridge University Press, 1985.

Cavell, Marcia. "A Response to Otto Kernberg's 'The Dynamic Unconscious and the Self.'" In Stern. 58–63.

Cheatham, George. "Fall and Redemption in *Pale Horse, Pale Rider.*" *Renascence* 39 (1987): 396–405.

Cheney, Patrick. "Poe's Use of *The Tempest* and the Bible in 'The Masque of the Red Death.'" *English Language Notes* 20 (1983): 31–39.

Cohen, Jeffrey, and Sharone Abramowitz. "AIDS Attacks the Self: A Self-Psychological Exploration of the Psychodynamic Consequences of AIDS." In Goldberg, *Realities.* 157–72.

Collier, Richard. *The Plague of the Spanish Lady: The Influenza Pandemic of 1918–1919.* New York: Atheneum, 1974.

Collins, Steven. "Categories, Concepts, or Predicaments? Remarks on Mauss's Use of Philosophical Terminology." In Carrithers. 46–82.

Corrigan, Robert W. "The Sun Always Rises: Ibsen's *Ghosts* as Tragedy." *Educational Theatre Journal* 11 (1959): 171–80.

Crawfurd, Raymond. *Plague and Pestilence in Literature and Art.* London: Oxford University Press, 1914.

Crosby, Alfred W., Jr. *Epidemic and Peace, 1918.* Westport, Conn.: Greenwood Press, 1976.

Cuddy, Lois. "The Purgatorial Gardens of Hawthorne and Dante." *Modern Language Studies* 17 (1987): 39–53.

Cullerier, Adrien. *Atlas of Venereal Diseases.* Translated by Freeman J. Bumstead. Philadelphia, 1868.

Curtis, Laura. *The Elusive Daniel Defoe.* London and New York: Vision and Barnes and Noble, 1984.

Dahlberg, Charles. *The Literature of Unlikeness.* Hanover, N.H.: University Press of New England, 1988.

———. "Macrobius and the Unity of the *Roman de la Rose.*" *Studies in Philology* 58 (1961): 573–82.

Davidson, Edward H. *Poe: A Critical Study.* Cambridge, Mass.: Belknap Press, 1964.

Davis, Derek Russell. "A Re-Appraisal of Ibsen's Ghosts." In McFarlane. 369–83.

Dayan, Joan. *Fables of Mind: An Inquiry into Poe's Fiction*. New York: Oxford University Press, 1987.

DeFalco, Joseph M. "The Source of Terror in Poe's 'Shadow—A Parable.' " *Studies in Short Fiction* 6 (1969): 643–49.

DeMouy, Jane Krause. *Katherine Anne Porter's Women*. Austin: University of Texas Press, 1979.

Dennie, Charles C. *A History of Syphilis*. Springfield, Ill.: Charles C. Thomas, 1962.

Dervin, Daniel. "Psychoanalysis of the Self." In *Dictionary of Literary Themes and Motifs*, ed. Jean-Charles Seigneuret. 2 vols. New York: Greenwood Press, 1988. 2:1009–19.

Detrick, Douglas W. "Self Psychology, Psychoanalysis, and the Analytic Enterprise." In *Self Psychology: Comparisons and Contrasts*, ed. Douglas W. Detrick and Susan P. Detrick. Hillsdale, N.J.: Analytic Press, 1989. 429–63.

Doubrovsky, Serge. "The Ethics of Albert Camus." In *Camus: A Collection of Critical Essays*, ed. Germaine Bree. Englewood Cliffs, N.J.: Prentice Hall, 1962. 71–84.

Downs, Brian W. *Ibsen: The Intellectual Background*. Cambridge, England: Cambridge University Press, 1948.

Dreher, Diane Elizabeth. "Hawthorne and Melancholy: A New Source for 'Rappaccini's Daughter.' " *American Transcendental Quarterly* 52 (1981): 255–58.

Dubos, Rene J. *The White Plague: Tuberculosis, Man, and Society*. Boston: Little, Brown, 1952.

Duffy, John. *Sword of Pestilence: The New Orleans Yellow Fever Epidemic of 1853*. Baton Rouge: Louisiana State University Press, 1966.

Edelman, Lee. "The Plague of Discourse: Politics, Literary Theory, and AIDS." *South Atlantic Quarterly* 88 (1989): 301–17.

Edgerton, Robert B. "Anthropology, Psychiatry, and Man's Nature." In *Interface between Psychiatry and Anthropology*, ed. Iago Goldstein. New York: Brunner/Mazel, 1971. 28–54.

Encyclopedia of Philosophy. Edited by Paul Edwards. New York: Macmillan, 1972. 8 volumes in 4.

Evans, Oliver. "Allegory and Incest in 'Rappaccini's Daughter.' " *Nineteenth-Century Fiction* 19 (1964): 185–95.

Fass, Barbara. See Leavy.

Faulkner, Dewey R. *Twentieth-Century Interpretations of "The Pardoner's Tale"*. Englewood Cliffs, N.J.: Prentice Hall, 1973.

Feder, Lillian. "Selfhood, Language, and Reality: George Orwell's *Nineteen Eighty Four*. " *Georgia Review* 37 (1983): 392–409.

Felman, Shoshana. "Narrative as Testimony: Camus's *The Plague*. " In *Reading Narrative: Form, Ethics, Ideology*, ed. James Phelan. Columbus: Ohio University Press, 1989. 250–71.

Ferber, Michael. " 'London' and Its Politics." *ELH: Journal of English Language History* 48 (1981): 310–38.

Fergusson, Francis. "Ghosts: The Tragic Rhythm in a Small Figure." In *Ibsen: A Collection of Critical Essays*, ed. Rolf Fjelde. Englewood Cliffs, N.J.: Prentice Hall, 1965. 109–19.

Ferrante, Joan M. "The Frame Characters of the *Decameron*: A Progression of Virtues." *Romance Philology* 19 (1965): 212–26.

Fine, Gary Alan. "Welcome to the World of AIDS: Fantasies of Female Revenge." *Western Folklore* 46 (1987): 192–97.

Finel-Honigman, Irene. "The Orpheus and Eurydice Myth in Camus's *The Plague.*" *Classical and Modern Literature* 1 (1981): 207–18.

Fitch, Brian T. *The Narcissistic Text: A Reading of Camus' Fiction.* Toronto: University of Toronto Press, 1982.

Fleissner, Robert F. "Caliban Converted: or *The Tempest* as the Tempering of the Pest." *Shakespeare Newsletter* 37 (1987): 56.

Foege, William H. "Plagues: Perceptions of Risk and Social Responses." In Mack. 9–20.

Fournier, Jean Alfred. *Syphilis and Marriage.* Translated by P. Albert Morrow. New York, 1881.

Friedrich, Paul. *The Meaning of Aphrodite.* Chicago: University of Chicago Press, 1979.

Gagnon, John H. "Disease and Desire" [on AIDS]. *Daedalus* 118 (1989): 47–77.

Gale, Robert L. "Rappaccini's Baglioni." *Studi Americani* (Rome) 9 (1963): 83–87.

Gallagher, Kathleen. "The Art of Snake Handling: *Lamia, Elsie Venner,* and 'Rappaccini's Daughter.' " *Studies in American Fiction* 3 (1975): 51–64.

Giamatti, A. Bartlett. *Take Time for Paradise: Americans and Their Games.* New York: Summit Books, 1990.

———. *The Earthly Paradise and the Renaissance Epic.* Princeton, N.J.: Princeton University Press, 1966.

Gilman, Sander L. "Seeing the AIDS Patient." *Disease and Representation: Images of Illness from Madness to AIDS.* Ithaca, N.Y.: Cornell University Press, 1988. 245–72.

Givner, Joan. *Katherine Anne Porter.* New York: Simon and Schuster, 1982.

Glen, Heather. *Vision and Disenchantment: Blake's "Songs" and Wordsworth's "Lyrical Ballads."* Cambridge, England: Cambridge University Press, 1983.

Godwin, Sarah Webster. "Poe's 'Masque of the Red Death' and the Dance of Death." In *Medievalism in American Culture: Special Studies,* ed. Bernard Rosenthal and Paul E. Szarmach. Binghamton, N.Y.: Center for Medieval and Early Renaissance Studies, 1987. 17–28.

Goldberg, Arnold. *A Fresh Look at Psychoanalysis: The View from Self Psychology.* Hillsdale, N.J.: Analytic Press, 1988.

———, ed. *The Realities of Transference.* Vol. 6 in *Progress in Self Psychology.* Hillsdale, N.J.: Analytic Press, 1990.

Goodman, Aileen S. "The Surgical Masque: Representations of Medicine in Literature." In Kellman. 78–89.

Goodwin, Grenville. "Vulva Woman." In *Myths and Tales of the White Mountain Apache.* New York: American Folk-Lore Society, 1939. 38–39.

Gottfried, Robert S. *The Black Death: Natural and Human Disaster in Medieval Europe.* New York: Free Press, 1983.

Gravier, Maurice. "Le drame d'Ibsen." *Ibsenårbok* (1970–71): 140–60.

Gray, Ronald. *Ibsen—A Dissenting View.* Cambridge, England: Cambridge University Press, 1977.

Green, William. "Some Theatrical Treatments of the AIDS Disease." Unpublished Lecture delivered at the World Congress of the International Federation for Theatre Research, Stockholm, May 1989.

Greenberg, Dolores. "Energy, Power, and Perceptions of Social Change in the Early Nineteenth Century." *American Historical Review* 95 (1990): 693–714.

Greenberg, Robert A. "Plexus and Ganglia: Scientific Allusion in *Middlemarch.*" *Nineteenth-Century Fiction* 30 (1975): 33–52.

Grobe, Edwin P. "Camus and the Parable of the Perfect Sentence." *Symposium* 24 (1970): 254–61.

Gross, Seymour L. "Rappaccini's Daughter and the Nineteenth-Century Physician." In *Ruined Eden of the Present: Hawthorne, Melville, Poe,* ed. G. R. Thompson et al. West Lafayette, Ind.: Purdue University Press, 1981. 129–41.

Halverson, John. "Chaucer's Pardoner and the Progress of Criticism." *Chaucer Review* 4 (1970): 184–202.

Hankins, J. E. "Caliban, the Bestial Man." *PMLA: Publications of the Modern Language Association of America* 62 (1947): 793–801.

Hanning, Robert. *The Individual in Twelfth-Century Romance.* New Haven, Conn.: Yale University Press, 1977.

Hardy, John Edward. *Katherine Anne Porter.* New York: Frederick Ungar, 1973.

Hastings, R. "To Teach or Not To Teach: The Moral Dimension of the *Decameron* Reconsidered." *Italian Studies* 44 (1989): 19–40.

Hess, Jeffrey A. "Sources and Aesthetics of Poe's Landscape Fiction." *American Quarterly* 22 (1970): 177–89.

Hill, James Norman. "The New Man of Medicine in Nineteenth-Century British Fiction." Ph.D. diss., University of Iowa, 1984.

Holleran, Andrew. Introduction to *The Normal Heart,* by Larry Kramer. New York: New American Library, 1985. 23–28.

Hudson, Lois Phillips. "The Big Rock Candy Mountain: No Roots—and No Frontier." In Arthur. 137–45.

Jacobs, Robert D. "Poe's Earthly Paradise." *American Quarterly* 12 (1960): 404–13.

Jacobsen, Per Schelde. See Leavy with Jacobsen.

James, D. G. *The Dream of Prospero.* Oxford: Clarendon Press, 1967.

Johnson, James William. "Another Look at Katherine Anne Porter." *Virginia Quarterly Review* 36 (1960): 598–613.

Jones, Deborah L. "Hawthorne's Post-Platonic Paradise: The Inversion of Allegory in 'Rappaccini's Daughter.' " *Journal of Narrative Technique* 18 (1988): 153–69.

Jordan de Caro, Rosan. "A Note about Folklore and Literature: (The Bosom Serpent Revisited)." *Journal of American Folklore* 86 (1973): 62–65.

Jorgenson, Theodore. *Henrik Ibsen: A Study in Art and Personality.* 1945. Reprint. Westport, Conn.: Greenwood Press, 1978.

Kapferer, Bruce. *A Celebration of Demons.* Bloomington: Indiana University Press, 1983.

Kaufmann, F. W. "Ibsen's Search for the Authentic Self." *Monatshefte* 45 (1953): 232–39.

Kellman, Steven. "Singular Third Person" [Camus]. *Kentucky Romance Quarterly* 25 (1978): 499–507.

——, ed. *Approaches to Teaching Camus' "The Plague".* New York. Modern Language Association of America, 1985.

Kern, Edith. "The Gardens in the Decameron Cornice." *PMLA: Publications of the Modern Language Association of America* 66 (1951): 505–23.

Kirkpatrick, Robin. "The Wake of the *Commedia*: Chaucer's *Canterbury Tales* and Boccaccio's *Decameron."* In *Chaucer and the Italian Trecento,* ed. Piero Boitani. Cambridge, England: Cambridge University Press, 1983.

Kleinberg, Seymour. Review of *The Normal Heart. New Republic,* August 11–18, 1986, 30–33.

Koht, Halvdan. *Life of Ibsen.* New York: Benjamin Blom, 1971.

Kramer, Mimi. Review of *Just Say No. New Yorker,* November 7, 1988, 134–35.

"Kramer vs. Cruising: *The Normal Heart."* *The Economist,* April 5, 1986, 104.

Kroll, Jack. Review of *As Is. Newsweek,* May 13, 1985, 87.

Kuhns, Richard. "Governing of the Self." In Stern. 48–58.

La Fontaine, J. S. "Person and Individual: Some Anthropological Reflections." In Carrithers. 123–40.

Landa, Louis, ed. Introduction to *A Journal of the Plague Year.* London: Oxford University Press, 1969.

Langbaum, Robert, ed. "Introduction." *The Tempest.* New York: New American Library, 1964.

Leavy, Barbara Fass. "Faith's Incubus: The Influence of Sir Walter Scott on Hawthorne's 'Young Goodman Brown.' " *Dickens Studies Annual* 18 (1990): 277–308.

——. Review of *Healing Arts in Dialogue: Medicine and Literature,* ed. Joanne Trautmann. *Journal of the History of the Behavioral Sciences* 21 (1985): 86–88.

——. *La Belle Dame sans Merci and the Aesthetics of Romanticism.* Detroit: Wayne State University Press, 1974.

Leavy, Barbara Fass, with Per Schelde Jacobsen. *Ibsen's Forsaken Merman: Folklore in the Late Plays.* New York: New York University Press, 1988.

Lepke, Arno K. "Who Is Doctor Stockmann?" *Scandinavian Studies* (32) 1960: 57–75.

Lerner, Robert E. "The Black Death and Western European Eschatological Mentalities." *American Historical Review* 86 (1981): 533–52.

Levin, Harry. *The Power of Blackness.* 1958. Reprint. New York: Alfred A. Knopf, 1970.

Lewis, David. "Survival and Identity." In Rorty. 17–40.

Lipari, Angelo. "Meaning and Real Significance of the *Decameron."* In *Essays in Honor of Albert Feuillerate,* ed. H. M. Peyre. *Yale Romantic Studies* 22 (1943): 43–83.

Loe, Thomas. "Plot and Anti-Plot in Katherine Anne Porter's *Pale Horse, Pale Rider."* *Mid-Hudson Language Studies* 9 (1986): 85–93.

McFarlane, James. *Henrik Ibsen: A Critical Anthology.* Harmondsworth, England: Penguin, 1970.

McNeil, David. "*A Journal of the Plague Year*: Defoe and Claustrophobia." *Southern Review* 16 (1983): 374–85.

McNeill, William H. *Plagues and Peoples*. Garden City, N.Y.: Anchor Press/Doubleday, 1976.

Maalouf, Amin. *Leo Africanus*. Translated by Peter Sluglett. New York: Norton, 1989.

Mack, Arien, ed. *In Time of Plague: The History and Social Consequences of Lethal Epidemic Disease*. New York: New York University Press, 1991.

Marks, Geoffrey, and William K. Beatty. *Epidemics*. New York: Charles Scribner's Sons, 1976.

Masterson, James F. *Treatment of the Borderline Adolescent: A Developmental Approach*. New York: Wiley-Interscience, 1972.

Mauss, Marcel. "The Category of the Person." In Carrithers. 1–25.

Mazzotta, Giuseppe. *The World at Play in Boccaccio's "Decameron"*. Princeton, N.J.: Princeton University Press, 1986.

———. "The *Decameron*: The Marginality of Literature." *University of Toronto Quarterly* 42 (1972): 64–81.

Meyer, Michael. *Ibsen: A Biography*. Garden City, N.Y.: Doubleday, 1971.

Michael, John. "Narration and Reflection: The Search for Grounds in Poe's 'The Power of Words' and 'The Domain of Arnheim.' " *Arizona Quarterly* 45 (1989): 1–22.

Miller, Robert P. *Chaucer: Sources and Backgrounds*. New York: Oxford University Press, 1977.

———. "Chaucer's Pardoner, the Scriptural Eunuch, and 'The Pardoner's Tale.' " *Speculum* 30 (1955): 180–99.

Mischel, Theodore, ed. *The Self: Psychological and Philosophical Issues*. Totowa, N.J.: Rowman and Littlefield, 1977.

Moorman, Lewis J. *Tuberculosis and Genius*. Chicago: University of Chicago Press, 1940.

Morris, Colin. *The Discovery of the Individual: 1050–1200*. New York: Harper and Row, 1972.

Morrison, Alan. "Review of *The Black Death*: A Biological Appraisal." *Journal of Modern History* 59 (1987): 809–11.

Morton, R. S. *Sexual Freedom and Venereal Disease*. London: Peter Owen, 1971.

Nance, William L. *Katherine Anne Porter and the Art of Rejection*. Chapel Hill: University of North Carolina Press, 1963.

Nelson, Anne. Review of *As Is. Maclean's*. June 24, 1985, 58.

"News of AIDS Therapy Gain Delayed Five Months by Agency." *New York Times*, November 14, 1990, A1.

Newtown, George. "Sex, Death, and the Drama of AIDS." *Antioch Review* 47 (1989): 209–22.

Nicholson, Watson. *The Historical Sources of Defoe's Journal of the Plague Year*. Boston: Stratford Co., 1919.

Northam, John. *Ibsen: A Critical Study*. Cambridge, England: Cambridge University Press, 1973.

Novak, Maximillian E. *Realism, Myth, and History in Defoe's Fiction*. Lincoln: University of Nebraska Press, 1983.

————. "The Disordered City." *PMLA: Publications of the Modern Language Association of America* 92 (1977): 241–52.

————. *Defoe and the Nature of Man.* London: Oxford University Press, 1963.

Oliver, Edith. Review of *As Is. New Yorker,* March 25, 1985, 118.

Pagliaro, Harold. *Selfhood and Redemption in Blake's Songs.* University Park: Pennsylvania University Press, 1987.

Penzer, N. M. *Poison Damsels and Other Essays in Folklore and Anthropology.* London: Charles J. Sawyer, 1952.

Phillips, Michael, ed. *Interpreting Blake: Essays.* Cambridge, England: Cambridge University Press, 1978.

"Physicians Endorse More Humanities for Premed Students." *New York Times,* November 14, 1989, C3.

Pitcher, Edward W. R. "Beyond 'Gothic Flummery': A Cosmoramic View of Poe's Symbolism and Ideas." *Sphinx: A Magazine of Literature and Society* 4 (1985): 241–49.

Pocock, J. G. A. *The Machiavellian Moment: Florentine Political Thought and the Atlantic Republican Tradition.* Princeton, N.J.: Princeton University Press, 1975.

Porter, Roy. "Ever since Eve: The Fear of Contagion." *Times Literary Supplement,* May 27–June 2, 1988, 582.

Punter, David. "Blake and the Shapes of London." *Criticism: A Quarterly for Literature and the Arts* 23 (1981): 1–23.

Quen, Jacques M., ed. *Split Minds/Split Brains.* New York: New York University Press, 1984.

"Rain or Shine, More Texas Flooding Is on the Way." *New York Times,* May 17, 1990, A1.

Rainwater, Catherine. "Poe's Landscape Tales and the 'Picturesque' Tradition." *Southern Literary Journal* 16 (1984): 30–43.

Rambuss, Richard M. " 'A Complicated Distress': Narrativizing the Plague in Defoe's *A Journal of the Plague Year." Prose Studies* 12 (1989): 115–31.

Reece, James B. "New Light on Poe's 'The Masque of the Red Death.' " *Modern Language Notes* 68 (1953): 114–15.

Review of *Longtime Companion. New Yorker,* May 21, 1990, 71–72. [Subtitled "The Plague."]

Rey, Georges. "Survival." In Rorty. 41–66.

Rich, Frank. Review of *As Is. New York Times,* March 11, 1985, C12.

————. Review of *The Normal Heart. New York Times,* April 22, 1985, C17.

Richards, David A. "Human Rights, Public Health, and the Idea of Moral Plague." In Mack. 169–206.

Richetti, John J. *Defoe's Narratives: Situations and Structures.* Oxford: Clarendon Press, 1975.

Richter, David H. "Essay" on *Pale Horse, Pale Rider.* In *Forms of the Novella: Ten Short Novels.* Teacher's ed. New York: Alfred A. Knopf, 1981. 100–10.

————. *Fable's End: Completeness and Closure in Rhetorical Fiction.* Chicago: University of Chicago Press, 1974.

Ricord, Philippe. *A Practical Treatise on Venereal Diseases; or, Critical and Experimental Researches on Inoculation, Applied to the Study of These Affections.* New York, 1842.

Rinear, Charles E. *The Sexually Transmitted Diseases*. Jefferson, N.C.: McFarland, 1986.

Roberts, David. Introduction and Medical Note to *A Journal of the Plague Year*, by Daniel Defoe. Oxford: Oxford University Press, 1990. vii-xxii; 288–291.

Robinson, Paul. Review of *Aids and Its Metaphors*, by Susan Sontag. *New York Times Book Review*, January 22, 1989, 11.

Rocks, J. E. "Camus Reads Defoe: *A Journal of the Plague Year* as a Source of *The Plague*." *Tulane Studies in English* 15 (1967): 81–87.

Roppolo, Joseph Patrick. "Meaning and 'The Masque of the Red Death.'" *Tulane Studies in English* 13 (1963) 59–69.

Rorty, Amelie Oksenberg, ed. "Introduction." *The Identities of Persons*. Berkeley: University of California Press, 1976.

———. "A Literary Postscript: Characters, Persons, Selves, Individuals." In Rorty. 301–23.

Rosebury, Theodor. *Microbes and Morals: The Strange Story of Venereal Disease*. New York: Viking Press, 1971.

Rosenkrantz, Barbara Gutmann. "*Damaged Goods*: The Dilemmas of Responsibility for Risk." *Milbank Memorial Fund Quarterly* 57 (1979): 1–37.

Ruddick, Nicholas. "The Hoax of the Red Death: Poe as Allegorist." *Sphinx: A Magazine of Literature and Society* 4 (1985): 268–76.

SantaVicca, Edmund F. *Four French Dramatists: A Bibliography of Criticism of the Works of Eugene Brieux, Francois de Curel, Emile Fabre, Paul Hervieu*. Metuchen, N.J.: Scarecrow Press, 1974.

Schwartz, Edward G. "The Fictions of Memory" [Katherine Anne Porter]. *Southwest Review* 45 (1960): 204–15.

Scott, Arthur L. "The Case of the Fatal Antidote: Rappaccini's Daughter Reexamined—with Apologies to Edgar Allan Poe." *Arizona Quarterly* 11 (1955): 38–43.

Secord, Paul F. "Making Oneself Behave." In Mischel. 250–73.

Sedgewick, G. G. "The Progress of Chaucer's Pardoner: 1880–1940." *Modern Language Quarterly* 1 (1940): 431–58.

Shatzky, Joel. "Heredity as Metaphor in Ibsen's Plays." *Edda* 74 (1974): 227–34.

Shinagel, Michael. *Daniel Defoe and Middle-Class Gentility*. Cambridge, Mass.: Harvard University Press, 1968.

Simon, John. Review of *The Normal Heart*. *New York Magazine*, May 6, 1985, 91–92.

Singleton, Charles. "On Meaning in the *Decameron*." *Italica* 21 (1944): 117–24.

Smith, Dinitia. "The Cry of the Normal Heart" [Review]. *New York Magazine*, June 3, 1985, 42–46.

Sontag, Susan. *AIDS and Its Metaphors*. New York: Farrar, Straus, Giroux, 1989.

Sprinchorn, Evert. "Science and Poetry in Ghosts: A Study in Ibsen's Craftsmanship." *Scandinavian Studies* 51 (1979): 354–67.

Steel, David. "Plague Writing: From Boccaccio to Camus." *Journal of European Studies* 11 (1981): 88–110.

Stephanson, Raymond. "The Plague Narratives of Defoe and Camus: Illness as Metaphor." *Modern Language Quarterly* 48 (1987): 224–41.

———. "'Tis a Speaking Sight': Imagery as Narrative in Defoe's *A Journal of the Plague Year*." *Dalhousie Review* 62 (1982–83): 680–92.

Stern, Raphael, ed. *Theories of the Unconscious and Theories of the Self.* Hillsdale, N.J.: Analytic Press, 1987.

Swan, Charles, and Wynnard Hooper, trans. "Of the Poison of Sin" [Poison Damsel]. In *Gesta Romanorum.* London, 1877. 21–22.

Swenson, Robert M. "Plagues, History, and AIDS." *American Scholar* 57 (1988): 183–200.

Tavor, Eve. "Fictional Facts and Science in Defoe and Camus' Plague Year." *Orbis litterarum* 40 (1985): 159–70.

Tawney, R. H. *Religion and the Rise of Capitalism: A Historical Study.* 1926. Reprint. Gloucester, Mass.: Peter Smith, 1962.

Taylor, Stephen M. "Portraits of Pestilence: The Plague in the Work of Machaut and Boccaccio." *Allegorica* 5 (1980): 105–18.

Teit, James. "Rattlesnake-Woman." In "Mythology of the Thompson Indians." *Memoirs of the American Museum of Natural History* 8 (1912): 339.

Thody, Philip. *Albert Camus.* New York: St. Martin's Press, 1989.

Thompson, E. P. "London" [Blake]. In Phillips. 5–31.

Thorpe, John C. Reviews of *The Normal Heart* and *As Is. Crisis,* October 1985, 13.

Toulmin, Stephen E. "Self-Knowledge and Knowledge of the Self." In Mischel. 291–317.

Tritt, Michael Lambert. "Plotting Influence: Indebtedness and Innovation in 'The Pit and the Pendulum' and 'The Masque of the Red Death.' " Ph.D. diss., Columbia University, 1987.

Trower, Katherine B. "Spiritual Sickness in the Physician's and Pardoner's Tales: Thematic Unity in Fragment VI of *The Canterbury Tales." American Benedictine Review* 29 (1978): 67–86.

Unrue, Darlene Harbour. *Truth and Vision in Katherine Anne Porter's Fiction.* Athens: University of Georgia Press, 1985.

Uroff, M. D. "The Doctors in 'Rappaccini's Daughter.' " *Nineteenth-Century Fiction* 27 (1972): 61–70.

Ussery, Huling E. *Chaucer's Physician: Medicine and Literature in Fourteenth-Century England. Tulane Studies in English,* Vol. 19. New Orleans, La.: Tulane Department of English, 1971.

Valency, Maurice. *The Flower and the Castle: An Introduction to Modern Drama.* New York: Macmillan, 1963.

Vanderbilt, Kermit. "Art and Nature in 'The Masque of the Red Death.' " *Nineteenth-Century Fiction* 22 (1968): 379–90.

Virchow, Rudolf. *Collected Essays on Public Health and Epidemiology.* 2 vols. Edited by L. J. Rather. [Canton, Mass.]: Science History Publications, 1985.

Walsh, Thomas F. "The Dreams Self in *Pale Horse, Pale Rider."* In Bloom. 81–96.

Warner, Marina. *Alone of All Her Sex: The Myth and the Cult of the Virgin Mary.* New York: Alfred A. Knopf, 1976.

Warren, Robert Penn. "Irony with a Center" [Katherine Anne Porter]. In Bloom. 7–22.

Welty, Eudora. "The Eye of the Storm" [Katherine Anne Porter]. In Bloom. 43–52.

Wenzel, Siegfried. "Pestilence and Middle English Literature: Friar John Grimestone's Poems on Death." In Williman. 131–59.

Wilbur, Richard. "Introduction: Edgar Allan Poe." In *Major Writers of America*, ed. Perry Miller. 2 vols. New York: Harcourt, Brace & World, 1962. 1:369–82.

Willey, Basil. *The Seventeenth-Century Background: Studies in the Thought of the Age in Relation to Poetry and Religion.* New York: Columbia University Press, 1967.

Williams, Raymond. *Drama from Ibsen to Eliot.* London: Chatto and Windus, 1954.

Williman, Daniel, ed. *The Black Death: The Impact of the Fourteenth-Century Plague.* Binghamton, N.Y.: Center for Medieval and Early Renaissance Studies, 1982.

Winslow, Charles-Edward Amory. *The Conquest of Epidemic Disease: A Chapter in the History of Ideas.* Princeton, N.J.: Princeton University Press, 1944.

Wolf, Ernest S. " 'Irrationality' in a Psychoanalytic Psychology of the Self." In Mischel. 303–23.

———. "Recent Advances in the Psychology of the Self: An Outline of Basic Concepts." *Comprehensive Psychiatry* 17 (1976): 37–46.

Yannella, Philip R. "The Problems of Dislocation in *Pale Horse, Pale Rider.*" *Studies in Short Fiction* 6 (1969): 637–42.

Youngblood, Sarah. "Structure and Imagery in Katherine Anne Porter's *Pale Horse, Pale Rider.*" *Modern Fiction Studies* 5 (1959): 344–52.

Zanger, Jules. "Poe's American Garden: 'The Domain of Arnheim.' " *American Transcendental Quarterly* 50 (1981): 93–103.

Zapf, Hubert. "Entropic Imagination in Poe's 'The Masque of the Red Death.' " *College Literature* 16 (1989): 211–18.

Ziegler, Philip. *The Black Death.* London: Collins, 1969.

Zimmerman, Everett. *Defoe and the Novel.* Berkeley: University of California Press, 1974.

———. "H. F.'s Meditations: *A Journal of the Plague Year.*" *PMLA: Publications of the Modern Language Association of America* 87 (1972): 417–23.

Zinsser, Hans. *Rats, Lice, and History.* 1934. Reprint. Boston: Atlantic Monthly Press, 1963.

Index